To Assaf,
my husband and my love,
my steadfast source of joy, laughter, patience, coffee, and tech support.
Let's do about 40 more years, yeah?

TABLE OF CONTENTS

FASHION SCHOOL
IN A BOOK

ZOË HONG

DESIGN AND
ILLUSTRATION
FOR THE
BEGINNER
AND THE
BRAND

Fashion School in a Book

Design and Illustration for the Beginner and the Brand

Zoë Hong
Zoehong.com

Project editor: Maggie Yates
Project manager: Lisa Brazieal
Marketing coordinator: Koryn Olage
Copyeditor: Maggie Yates
Layout: Kim Scott, Bumpy Design
Cover and interior design: Frances Baca

ISBN: 979-8-88814-233-2
1st Edition (1st printing, January 2025)
© 2025 Zoë Hong
All images © Zoë Hong

Rocky Nook Inc.
1010 B Street, Suite 350
San Rafael, CA 94901
USA

www.rockynook.com

Distributed in the UK and Europe by Publishers Group UK
Distributed in the U.S. and all other territories by Publishers Group West

Library of Congress Control Number: 2024935888

Printed in China

INTRODUCTION

Hey hey, party people!

If you watch my videos online, you know I hate a long intro. But I do want to address a few points.

One

People think fashion design is sketching out a bunch of ideas rolling around in your head, but nope! It's much cooler and involved and harder and funner than that.

Art is often a question thrown out into the universe, but design should always be an answer. Design should answer all kinds of questions, from the practical to the poetic. What should I wear? What will make me feel confident in myself? What will keep me warm? What will help me express myself? What will make my butt look good?

Two

This book is for anyone who wants to learn fashion design or illustration, but we can't be thinking about fashion in the future without thinking about sustainability. All companies across all industries need to be thinking about becoming more ethical and sustainable. I cringe a bit because I know by the time some of you read this, the technological advances I discuss might be old news. The point is to prompt you into your own research, to discover what materials and processes will work best for you and your brand.

This book isn't titled "How to Design a Fashion Collection Sustainably" because sustainability should be a foregone conclusion. There is no separate chapter on sustainability because the sustainability aspect should be considered along every step of the design process.

Three

The first time you do anything it will take forever, because everything is new and awkward and you're reading the instructions while you're doing it all. As you practice, you will get faster each time. I often say, "If your first one sucks, you're right on track." If you complete one project, even if it's awful, you're still a head above the others who sit around and talk the talk but never walk the walk. Take the plunge and embrace the mistakes you'll inevitably make.

Does it seem hard? Well, it's not easy and whoever said creative jobs were last-resort careers for unintelligent people needs to be ~~dropkicked~~ told nicely to be quiet.

With that, let's go!

BRAND

INSPIRATION

COLOR

PRINTS

FABRIC & TEXTURES

SHAPES & SILHOUETTES

DESIGN DETAILS

EDIT

1

FASHION DESIGN PROCESS OVERVIEW

The Steps

This book is written in sequential order of processes commonly seen in the fashion industry, or as streamlined as I can make it, as all fashion companies do things a little differently. This is also the order in which the process runs efficiently and makes sense creatively. However, in the real world, things rarely work in such an organized manner. Design and development in the industry sometimes looks more like a zigzag-meets-parabolic curve that doubles back on itself. Sometimes someone on the team will come up with a dress everyone loves, and it moves into patternmaking before everything else gets addressed. Sometimes you have a vision of the perfect print, and you sketch it out and decide everything is going to center around that print. This book is written in this order to guide you with a timeline that makes sense—not dictate a set of hard and fast rules.

I view the design process as a big, inverted triangle (**Figure 1.1**). We start with big, abstract ideas and ambiguous inspiration, and we start narrowing things down to a specific aesthetic direction. We then make decisions for the whole of the collection, like the color story and fabrics. Then we start getting into individual garments, designing silhouettes, interior shapes, fabric manipulations, and embellishments.

5

FIGURE 1.2. RIGHT Design
process flowchart for
businesses

The specifics for a portfolio project are a little bit different than for a business. We start with guidelines for the brand. A brand should always be aware of their customer's lifestyle: how they want to dress, how they shop, and how much they'll spend. When you are speaking about your project at a job interview, you should be able to articulate your muse and ideal shopper so the recruiter can determine if you did a good job designing for that customer.

We move on to collection direction. When you work for a larger company, things like inspiration images, colors, and fabrics will typically be determined by the leadership, usually the brand's creative director, and possibly the design directors of each department.

Fashion merchandisers give reports on what sold last season in terms of colors, fabrics, and cuts. "Oh, you want to do lilac again? It is historically our poorest selling color. And our customers don't buy capris." Merchandisers can also supply trend forecasting reports for the company. Contrary to popular belief, fashion merchandisers do not exist to burst the bubble on a designer's good time, but to make sure the design team is making clothes that customers will buy.

> If I had a dollar for every time I said, "Fashion sits at the intersection of art and commerce," I'd be writing this book warding off the cold in a Valentino couture coat.

The leadership of a fashion design company creates the collection's direction, which includes inspiration images, colors, and fabrics. Designers and associate designers design individual garments, prints, and embellishments, using the leadership's direction and information from merchandisers (**Figure 1.2**).

Do keep in mind that if you've been in business for more than a couple of seasons, while you are designing this current collection, you will also be dealing with sales from the previous season, and production of the season before that. The bigger the company, the more removed you will be from these other departments. If you have 2-3 employees, you will be very hands on with sales and production. If you have a business partner who tells you they will handle the production side, you should still have a hand in the production. If you're doing everything yourself, you will be doing all these things along with the designing.

Even if you are working by yourself, whether for a school project or your new brand, it's important to get organized, create a distinct visual direction, and keep to it so you can create a cohesive fashion collection suited

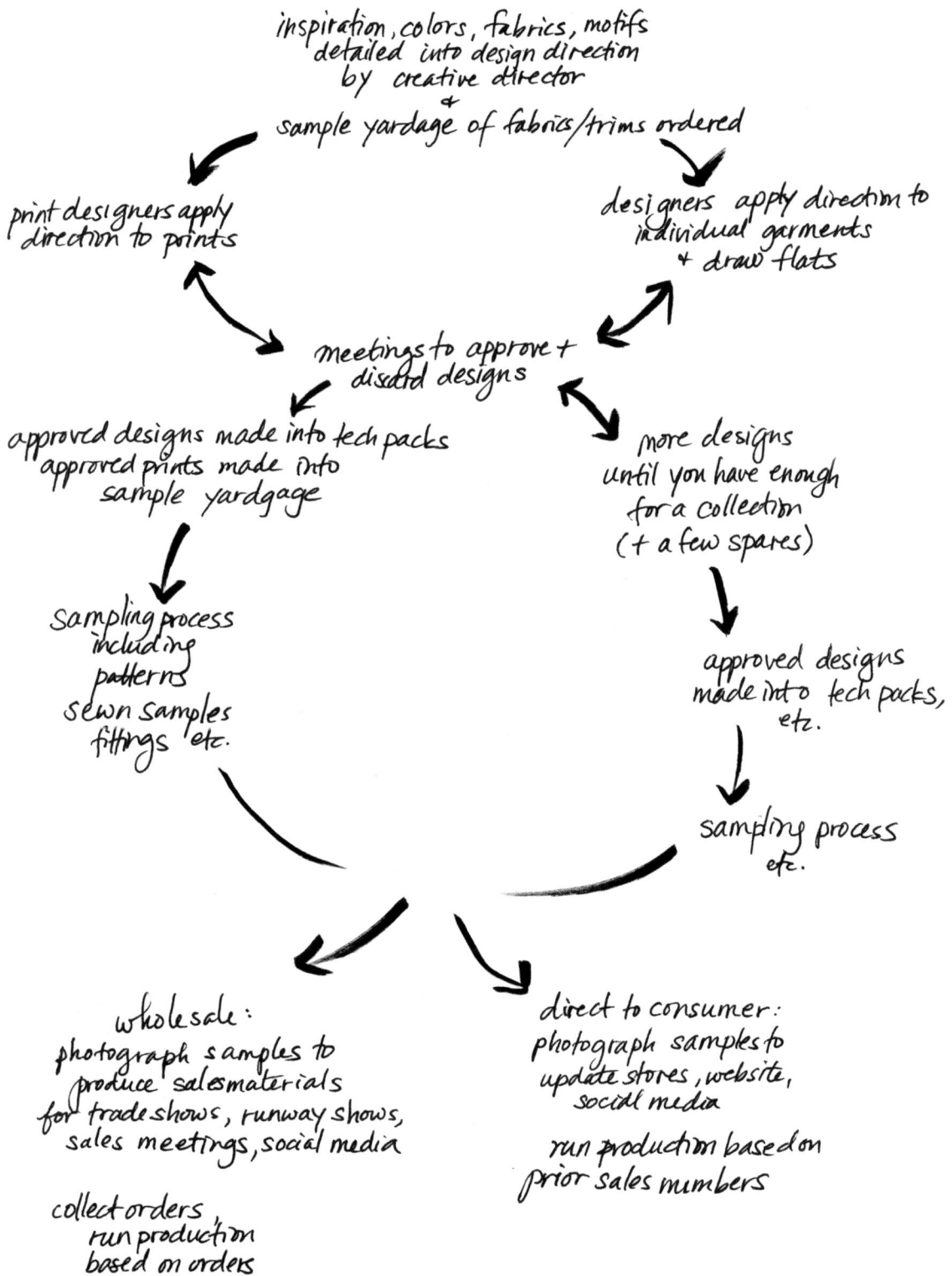

inspiration, colors, fabrics, motifs
detailed into design direction
by creative director
&
sample yardage of fabrics/trims ordered

print designers apply
direction to prints

designers apply direction to
individual garments
+ draw flats

meetings to approve +
discard designs

approved designs made into tech packs
approved prints made into
sample yardgage

more designs
until you have enough
for a collection
(+ a few spares)

sampling process
including
patterns
sewn samples
fittings etc.

approved designs
made into tech packs,
etc.

sampling process
etc.

wholesale:
photograph samples to
produce sales materials
for trade shows, runway shows,
sales meetings, social media

collect orders,
run production
based on orders

direct to consumer:
photograph samples to
update stores, website,
social media

run production based on
prior sales numbers

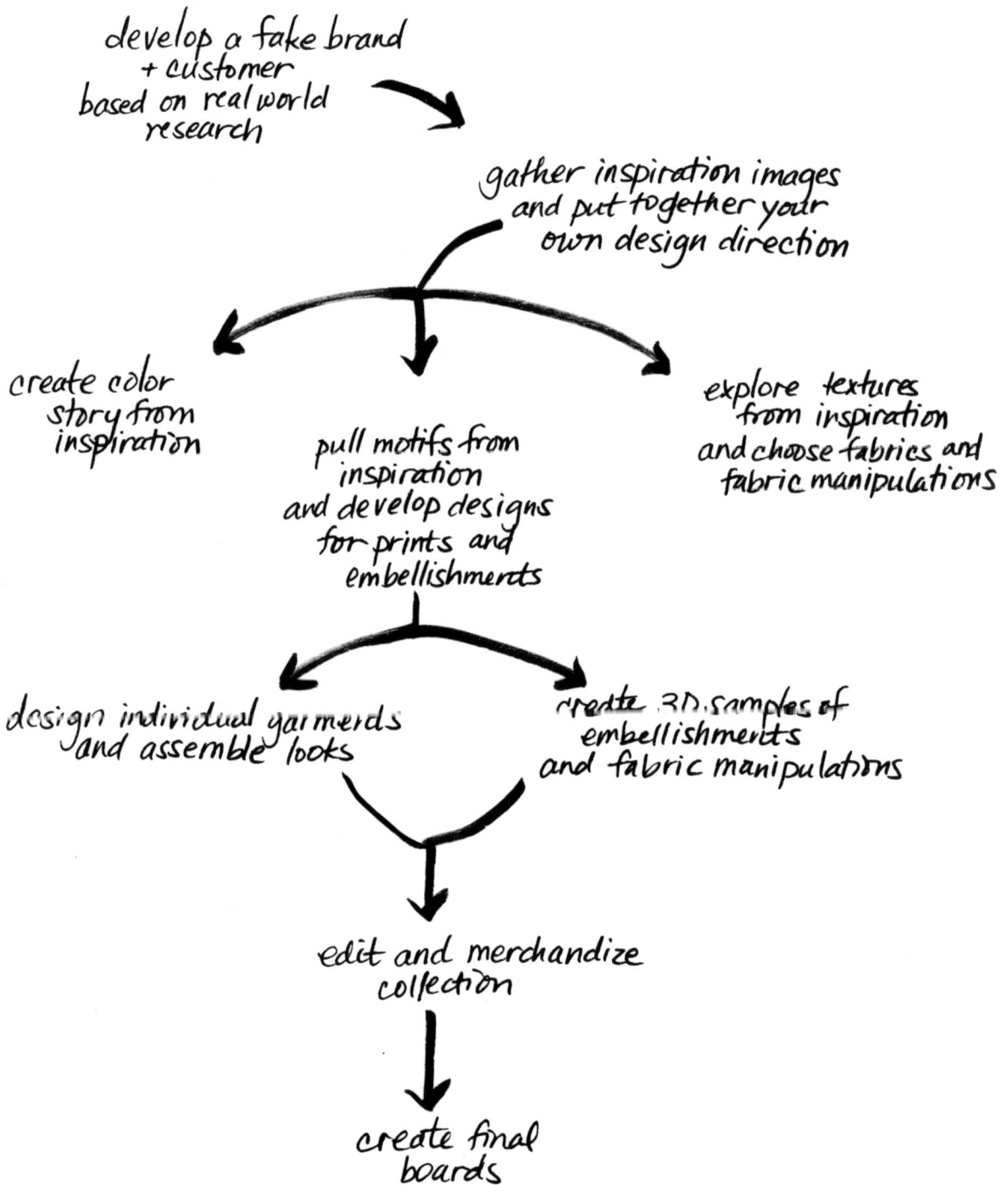

develop a fake brand + customer based on real world research

gather inspiration images and put together your own design direction

create color story from inspiration

pull motifs from inspiration and develop designs for prints and embellishments

explore textures from inspiration and choose fabrics and fabric manipulations

design individual garments and assemble looks

create 3D samples of embellishments and fabric manipulations

edit and merchandize collection

create final boards

FIGURE 1.3. LEFT Design
process flowchart for
portfolio makers

to your customer and muse and not a chaotic collage of underdeveloped 3 a.m. ideas. Gather images and materials that inspire you, create a color story from those materials, translate appealing textures from those images to select fabrics, and pull motifs from your mood board that you can turn into shapes, prints, and embellishments (**Figure 1.3**).

When you have a massive pile of sketches and a couple of papercuts, it's time to edit!

Editing is a process particularly important for portfolio projects and small, new brands. It's key that every garment creates impact and shows your flair for design. No basic tees, no basic jeans—unless there's something about the fabric or process that is new and groundbreaking.

Next for brands is product development: tech packs, patterns, sewn samples, and fittings.

Next for portfolios is final presentation boards, website, and resume.

And that's it! That's the fashion design process. So easy, right? Don't cry, I'm here for you. This book is full of exercises to teach you how to do every step. You should keep practicing these steps until they become second nature to you. I have created a design journal that will get you organized and give you a leg up on practicing process, but all the information you need is here.

Don't Start Sketching Right Away

BUT ZOE, why can't I just start sketching? That's the fun part! And I have so many ideas in my head right now!

The inefficiency of picking fabrics to suit each sketch will be detailed in the fabrics chapter. Or perhaps I can write you a book called *How to Go Bankrupt Starting a Fashion Brand*.

BUT ZOE, I remember your football-inspired collection; you told us you sketched out the whole thing on a plane without doing any planning!

Yes, there will be times when an idea strikes you so hard you revolve an entire collection around this idea, such as seeing an athlete with a huge equipment bag in the lobby of an airport, causing you to scribble furiously hunched over your miniscule airplane seatback tray in some sort of post-funeral fever dream (**Figures 1.4a–c, next pages**).

But that is not a sustainable process. You can't build a brand around waiting for inspiration to strike. You have to develop a process that not only pushes you creatively but a process that can be repeated regularly.

Anyone can design one killer dress; designers create collection after cohesive collection full of beautiful clothes (**Figure 1.5, following pages**).

Many people have asked me if they can make a career out of only selling design sketches and not do any of the rest. Yes, those people are called fashion illustrators. All joking aside, you can do that only if you've already built a career and reputation for designing gorgeous collections that sell well. Ghost designers exist, but they, too, have built up their careers and networks first. But usually, design is considered the fun part and people would rather pay someone to do things like accounts payable and sourcing. And no matter what you're hired to do, good design is never a stack of random drawings of unresearched dresses with no knowledge of customer, fabric, or construction.

FIGURES 1.4A, 1.4B, 1.4C. ABOVE AND RIGHT Original sketches of the football uniform-inspired collection. Pretend there was a lot of turbulence on the plane.

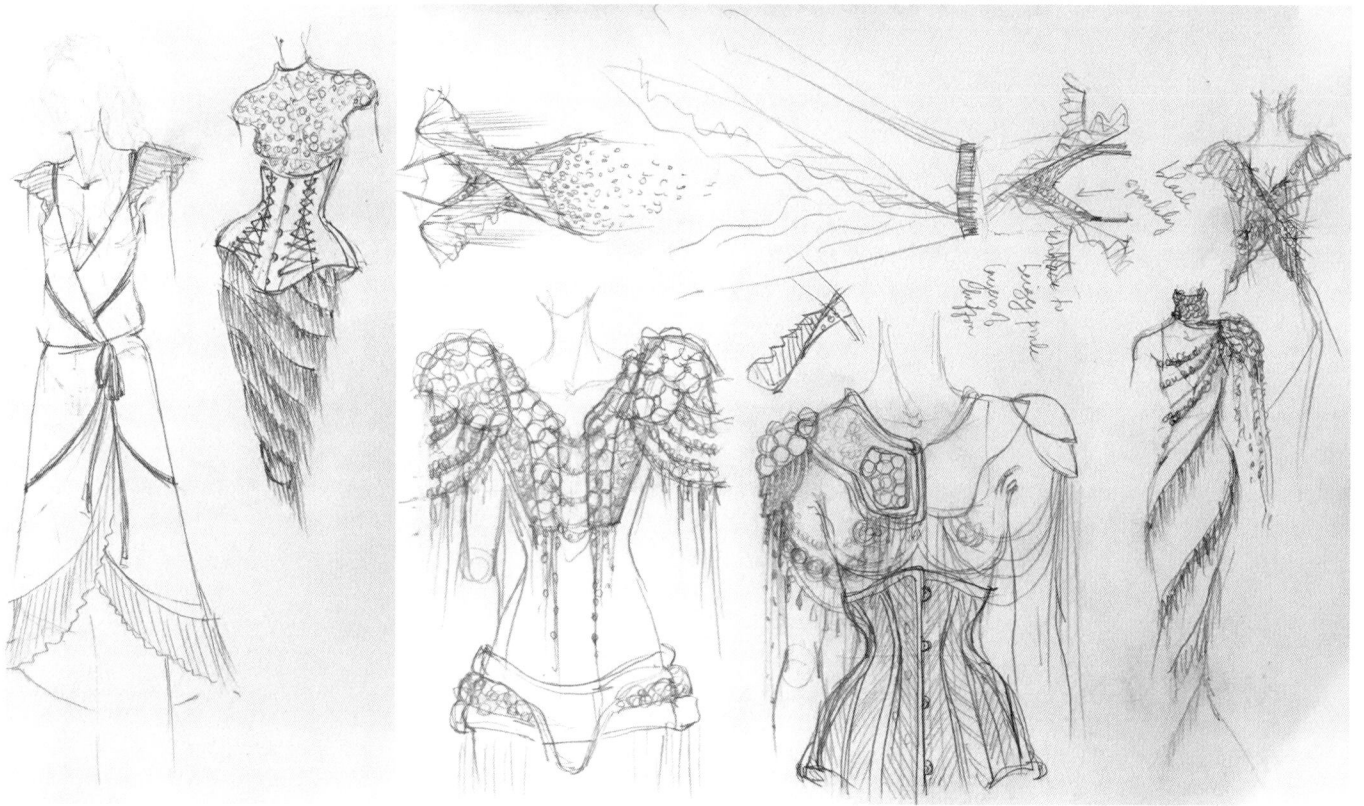

The Timeline for Portfolio Projects

If you're trying to mimic a fashion school education for yourself, here's a timeline for many fashion design schools' 4-year programs, on average:

Each class is a semester long.

Each semester is about 15 weeks long.

Most 4-year programs average 5-6 design classes to graduate.

In the beginner classes, each student will complete 2 design projects in a semester (7-8 weeks per project.)

More advanced students will complete 3 projects in a semester (5 weeks per project).

Please keep in mind that fashion school students are also taking classes like figure drawing, color theory, and garment construction at the same time.

FIGURE 1.5 Final illustration of the football uniform-inspired collection.

In a quarter system, as opposed to a semester system, each class is about 10 weeks long, with breaks spread out more evenly throughout the year. The semester system uses one long fall semester, one long spring semester, with an optional shortened summer term during the long break.

Each design project should include at minimum a mood board, a color/fabrics board, design illustrations on figures, and flats, preferably drawn in a vector-drawing program such as Adobe Illustrator. You can also include a board with sewn samples, like a small example of the ruffling/beading detail you added to the designs. These samples help people visualize your final designs better, even if you're a strong illustrator.

People often ask if I can recommend cheaper programs than Adobe products (or even something free), but since Adobe Illustrator is the industry standard, I don't recommend other programs. No, Adobe didn't pay me to say that.

A frequently asked question is about how to deal with works in progress. People only care to see works in progress if they see the final product as well. No one cares about your dozen toiles unless it leads to photos of your finished garment. No one cares about a hundred rough sketches unless we see which ones you chose for your final illustrations. You can make a "croquis book"—a small book of all your messy roughs that were the process sketches of a collection—but only if you have the rest of the project complete.

Finished garments are not necessary in a fashion designer's book, especially in the beginning of their career, but if you have them, make sure the photos are cleanly formatted and professional.

Including a tech pack shows you understand construction but is only necessary if you're applying for a tech designer's job.

We will go over each of these components more thoroughly later in the book.

This is when many of my online students freak out about creating 12+ projects, but remember that's over the course of several years. You know what's always bugged me? That saying, "Doing something over and over again expecting a different outcome is the definition of insanity." No, that's the definition of practice (**Figure 1.6a–b**). What do you think those Juilliard students are doing when they play the same song over and over again? Keep practicing and your process will become faster as you learn to put together color stories and develop ideas more quickly.

The Timeline for Business

FIGURE 1.7. RIGHT General calendar for a designer price point brand based in New York.

I wish I could give you a magic number of how long it should take you to design a collection, but your timeline will depend on your business structure. If your business is wholesale, and you hire an experienced salesperson or sales showroom, they can guide you on how often to show and how many pieces to show according to wholesale buying calendars for your price point/market category (**Figure 1.7**). If you're a direct-to-consumer brand, you can do whatever makes the most business sense to you.

It might seem like those brands who show in New York Fashion Week only design two collections a year, Spring/Summer and Fall/Winter, but those brands typically also design collections for Resort/Cruise and Pre-Fall, even if they don't produce runway shows for those seasons.

Pre-Fall is a fancy word for later in the summer than Spring/Summer. Hey, I don't make these things up.

Resort/Cruise was originally invented to give rich people options to wear on their tropical vacations during the dead of winter. Since travel has become more accessible to more people, more people have been seeking out bathing suits and shorts in the middle of winter and more brands are developing resort collections to cater to them (**Figure 1.8, following page**).

Some brands also do a Holiday collection or mini-collection consisting of pieces ready for the December holiday parties.

Consider that not everything designed in one collection is sold at the same time. Most brands will show a Spring/Summer collection and divide the garments up to a January delivery and a February delivery on their line-sheet. Who's buying spring clothes in January? All those people sick of the cold and looking forward to shedding parkas soon. Shopping is often a form of escapism.

Direct-to-consumer brands often design mini-collections every month so that their shops are always giving people a reason to revisit their website and social media. This is true for brands that try to chase every microtrend. I think we all know about the fast fashion two-week turnover—and we all know how I feel about fast fashion. Spoiler alert: I don't love it.

I've seen brands design one bigger collection a year and only show/sell part of that collection every season. This works better for brands that are less trend-driven.

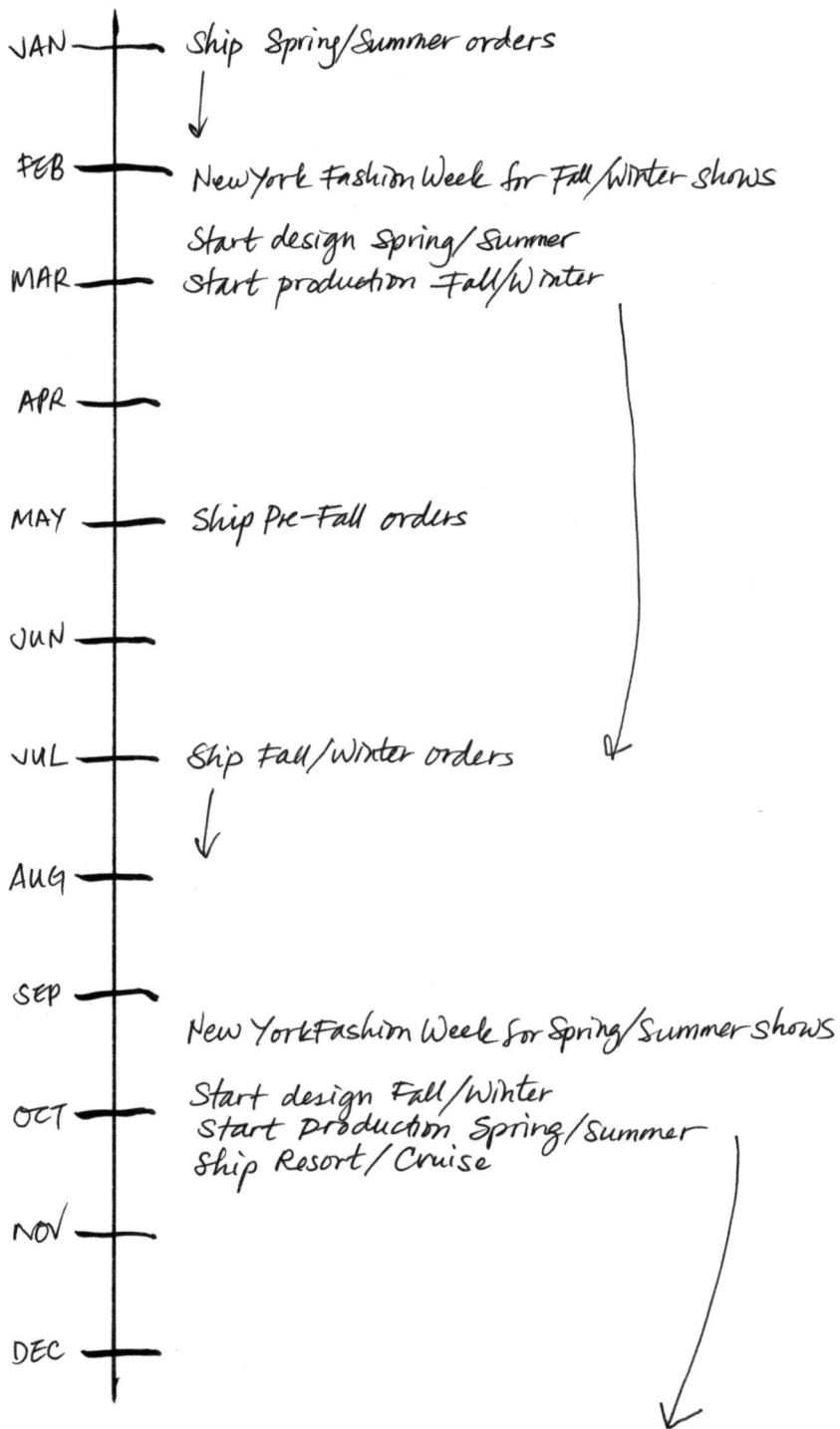

JAN — Ship Spring/Summer orders

FEB — New York Fashion Week for Fall/Winter shows

Start design Spring/Summer
MAR — Start production Fall/Winter

APR —

MAY — Ship Pre-Fall orders

JUN —

JUL — Ship Fall/Winter orders

AUG —

SEP —

New York Fashion Week for Spring/Summer shows

Start design Fall/Winter
OCT — Start Production Spring/Summer
Ship Resort/Cruise

NOV —

DEC —

FIGURE 1.8 I have a friend who owns a swimwear line, and she swears her busiest month is January.

I've seen brands sell the same exact bodies every season, just have new colors and prints every month, maybe introducing a new body every six months or so. This process is popular in many categories but especially lingerie and swim.

You need to think carefully about what kind of business you want to create and what your sales plan is and develop your timelines around that. You want the right kind of business to support your creativity and flow.

This is my top piece of advice for new brands: You'll never have as much time to design as you will before you officially launch your brand. Take this time to do more research not only on your customer's shopping habits, but also to research vendors for fabrics and processes like sampling, dyeing, and screen printing—anything you could potentially need. Develop patterns and perfect fits for your blocks. Research labeling, care instructions, and all the legalities of running your business, because once you launch, you will wish for that time back.

This is not to say I recommend procrastinating under the guise of research. Get to work.

BRAND DNA

STORY & PHILOSOPHY: WHY WE DO WHAT WE DO

BRAND VALUES: HOW WE DO IT

AESTHETICS: WHAT WE MAKE

2

BRAND DIRECTION

FIGURE 2.1. LEFT Elements of a brand's DNA

Before we begin designing, let's talk about all the moving parts that come together to define your brand, aesthetically and logistically (**Figure 2.1**).

Brand Aesthetic

What overall look do you want for your brand? This is not just about the clothes, but about the website, the styling, the shows and shoots—the whole aesthetic vibe of your brand. Think about whether you prefer neutrals over colors, whether you lean minimalist or maximalist, whether your style is loud or quiet. What's the effect you're trying to create? You can also think about it in terms of "Brand ABC but more colorful and for short people," or "if Brand XYZ and Brand LMN had a baby."

> *But Zoe, I am a custom clothier. I can make anything.*
> *Yes, but you should still put together a sampling of your abilities via a small collection.*

It's a good exercise to try to put your ideas into words. Write up a short description of your brand aesthetic, 2-3 sentences tops. It will help you sound professional and passionate when people ask you about your brand. This is not the description of a particular collection but for your whole brand. Here are some examples:

"Minimalism can still pack a punch. Clean lines, gorgeous colors, not just camel and white. Made for utility without looking like cargo pants."

"The fun of kids' clothes but in adult sizes."

"Suits cut for trans men, dapper, with adjustable details for changing bodies."

My brand aesthetic for the example project in this book is, "For older women who don't give any f's about what other people think: simple, unfussy shapes with fun details and embellishments."

What are House Codes?

House codes are visual elements that a brand repeats in every collection, something that the founding designer found appealing or connected to on a deep level. Repeated often enough, these elements become embedded in the brand's DNA.

Christian Dior (the man) considered lilies of the valley lucky, and Christian Dior (the brand) continues to use lilies of the valley as prints on clothes and dishes and as the base for one of their perfumes.

Jeanne Lanvin made dresses for her daughter and started her business when women wanted adult-sized versions of those dresses. Daisies were her daughter's favorite flower. Jeanne Lanvin (the woman) used daisies as a motif and Lanvin (the brand) still uses them often in designs.

Guccio Gucci, the founder of Gucci, was originally inspired by the rich equestrian set in London, and horse bits continue to be used today, as buckles, as trim, as prints, and as monograms.

Yves Saint Laurent loved his hearts, and what's a Cavalli collection without animal prints?

Do you need to choose your house codes now? No. Don't force it. They should be significant to you, something you naturally gravitate toward in your design work.

If I started a brand now, I would probably incorporate a lot of pompoms (**Figure 2.2**). I love clusters of pompoms and doodads that look even remotely like pompoms, like big pearls, buttons, especially round shank buttons, rhinestones, and fat, round quilting using interesting materials (**Figure 2.3**). I like them in odd, organically shaped clusters. Relatedly, I also love clusters of flat round things like scales, sequins, and paillettes. I also love clusters of irregular shapes.

FIGURE 2.2. RIGHT I like to sew pompoms to my clothes when I get bored.

FIGURE 2.3. BELOW Sketches from a project I did with my Patreon students.

FIGURE 2.4. NEXT PAGE The original hand drawing of the fairy print.

It has only occurred to me while writing this book that I can trace my love of clusters of round shapes to a print I designed back in 2003 (**Figure 2.4, next page**).

I love a lot of black. I love leather, I'm obsessed with proper pockets, and I think metallics are neutrals. I'm obsessed with uniforms: military uniforms, sports uniforms, and work uniforms (**Figure 2.5, next page**). I love chains. I love clusters and chains together. And these are long-term loves, things I love year after year (**Figures 2.6–2.9, following pages**).

Is this why I like Venn diagrams so much???

FIGURE 2.6. My work from 2007

FIGURE 2.7. My work from 2009

FIGURE 2.5. 0.00003% of my library

FIGURE 2.8. My work from 2011

FIGURE 2.9. A sketch from 2013, from a collection inspired by different work uniforms.

I have not loved all these things from the beginning of my design career but have fallen in love with different elements over time. House codes are meant to be meaningful. As the designer, you can evolve your house codes organically as your style changes.

Brand Values

What are your brand values? What do you stand for? What values resonate for your customer? Brand values are not about aesthetics but about your business priorities. They are the soul of your company.

Brand values can include, but are not limited to, the following:

- Body diversity: plus size, petites, talls, plus-size petites, specific body shape emphasis. Miniskirts for big bottoms, maternity, eveningwear for sizes 0-30 (**Figure 2.10**).

- Dressing a specific age bracket: clothes for older people that aren't frumpy; cute club clothes that aren't too revealing.

- Adaptive apparel, addressing one or more specific categories of disability: people who use wheelchairs; people with less hand agility (**Figure 2.11**).

- Gender inclusion: nonbinary specific, unisex, transgender needs.

- Using a specific workforce: Train unhoused women in X country to help them to economic independence.

- Clothing that is chic, yet modest, whether for personal or religious reasons.

- Highlighting the skills of a specific culture while working with people of that culture.

- Donating a percentage of proceeds to a specific charity that aligns with your values.

Sustainability starts here. Sustainability isn't about using recycled polyester to continue the same wasteful business practices as before. You have to change your mindset and start your business with sustainability woven into your brand values.

Don't freak out, you don't have to start out being the most perfect sustainable brand that ever existed. Think about where you can start and what you can incorporate next season and the season after that. Start making thoughtfully designed, well-made products that people will want to wear,

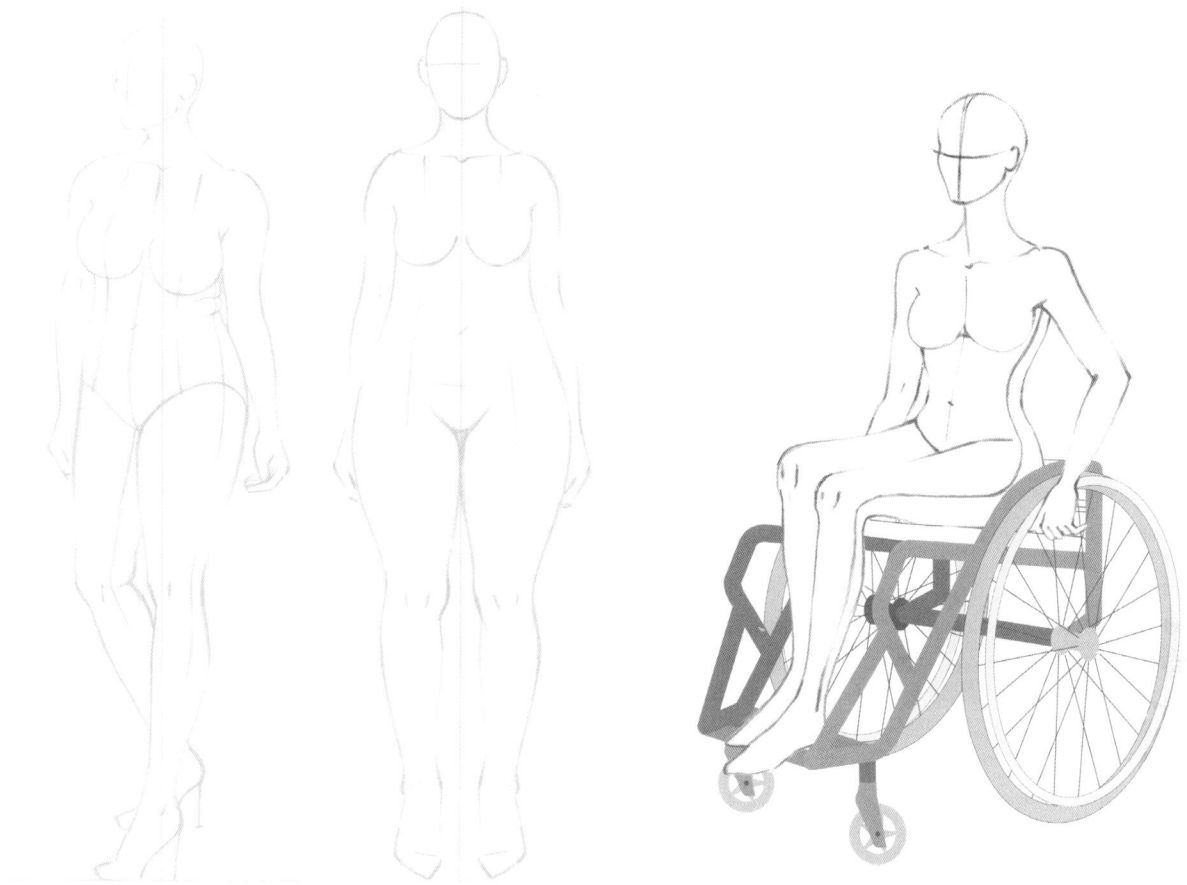

FIGURE 2.10. ABOVE
Fashion figure templates
of women of different sizes

FIGURE 2.11. ABOVE RIGHT
Fashion figure template for
wheelchair users

re-wear, keep, take care of, and wear again. Gorgeous pieces kids will steal from their parents, wear, take care of, and pass on to their own kids. Future heirlooms.

Sustainability Vocabulary

Let's take a moment to define some of these fancy-pants terms people throw around so you can make the right choices for your company.

Slow fashion: Slow fashion is a careful, thoughtful approach to fashion. Slow fashion thinks about the resources and processes used to make clothing, and about how to reduce the impact of these materials and processes on the planet by creating more timeless or versatile designs of high quality. The goal is to keep clothes out of landfills. It's called slow fashion because it's the opposite of chasing every microtrend by pumping out disposable trendy plastics as quickly as possible.

In a **linear fashion economy**, you use fresh, never-been-used raw materials to design and produce new clothes. People wear these clothes until they throw them away and these clothes end up in a landfill. In a **circular fashion economy**, the goal is to keep materials and finished garments out of landfills for as long as possible. Renewable materials are used, such as recycled polyester and biodegradable cotton. Clothes are designed and made to last many wears. In the aftermath, clothes are mended and re-worn, resold, rented to someone else to enjoy, upcycled, downcycled, or recycled.

> *Cotton denim jeans that are more than 5% stretch are no longer considered biodegradable!*

Upcycling recuts and resews old clothes to create a new design. This can also include making new non-garment soft goods like quilts and toys.

> *The term "soft goods" refers to anything made of fabric: clothes, toys, bedding, napkins. Not couches—they're made of hard materials and only covered in fabric.*

Downcycling takes apart clothes for other purposes like housing insulation, doll stuffing, and rags.

Ethical manufacturing pays employees and contractors fair, livable wages for their geographical region, and uses factories that pay their employees fair, livable wages and create a healthy, safe working environment for those workers. Ethical manufacturers produce high-quality goods using sustainable materials and processes.

Other ideas you might include in your vision for your brand's sustainable practices include:

◆ Secondhand programs: Some brands run programs to allow customers to return gently used goods for discounts on their next order. The brand then sells the secondhand goods to other customers.

◆ Educating customers on sustainability: Some brands have blogs on their website; some brands post infographics on social media; some brands have email newsletters.

◆ Charitable donations to sustainability focused nonprofits.

◆ Designs that incorporate aspects that allow for garment longevity (adjustable fits for childrenswear) or smarter materials usage (zero-waste cutting, upcycling scrap).

Think about the values you can incorporate into your brand DNA, and prioritize the ones most important to you. I know the impulse is to tell me all your brand values are the most important. But listen, if everything is the most important, nothing is the most important (**Figure 2.12**).

When you first start your brand, focus on the most important things and start incorporating others, one at a time. Here are the brand values for my project (**Figure 2.13, next page**).

BRAND VALUES

	1	2	3	4
_____	1	2	3	4
_____	1	2	3	4
_____	1	2	3	4
_____	1	2	3	4
_____	1	2	3	4
_____	1	2	3	4
_____	1	2	3	4
_____	1	2	3	4
_____	1	2	3	4
_____	1	2	3	4
_____	1	2	3	4
_____	1	2	3	4

1 = not essential but would be nice to include
2 = important, moderate priority
3 = high priority
4 = absolutely essential to my brand

BRAND VALUES

Sustainable materials + processes	1	2	3	④
Slow fashion	1	2	③	4
Size inclusivity	1	②	3	4
menopausal (+ peri) bodies	1	2	③	4
give older women more fun choices	1	2	3	④
BDE / IDGAF attitude	①	2	3	4
investment pieces that aren't classics	①	2	3	4
break stereotypes on how older women should live	1	2	3	④
ethical manufacturing	1	2	3	④
	1	2	3	4
	1	2	3	4

1 = not essential but would be nice to include
2 = important, moderate priority
3 = high priority
4 = absolutely essential to my brand

FIGURE 2.13. LEFT My brand values are not your values and that's okay.

FIGURE 2.14. RIGHT The era of the fashion designer as fashion dictator is over. Fashion should be conversation with your muses and customers.

FIGURE 2.15. BOTTOM RIGHT My customer

Customer Profile

I grew up watching fashion shows like Fashion File and FashionTelevision. The camera crews would go backstage to interview designers like Gianni Versace and Karl Lagerfeld talking about dressing the Versace woman, the Chanel woman. You, in turn, need to focus on who you're dressing. I've created a questionnaire to help you create your customer profile. Who is your customer and what kind of clothes do they need from you? These questions are designed to make you think about your customer's lifestyle, needs, and desires (**Figure 2.14**).

If you like to draw, illustrate your muse and customer. What does their body look like? Put that body in a pose that shows off your muse's attitude. Visually defining your muse through illustration can help inspire and focus your designs (**Figure 2.15**).

Another option is to make a collage of photos of people you would love to dress with your brand, people you think represent your customer well. These people do not have to be famous. Cruise some street style blogs and photos on sites like Pinterest. Maybe your muse is someone you know, like a stylish friend or your mom.

CUSTOMER PROFILE

1. Who is your muse and why/how do they inspire you?

2. What is the age and gender(s) of your customer?

3. What is your average customer income? How do they spend their money?

4. What is your product price point?

5. What is your customer's body type and size range?

6. What is your customer's lifestyle? Where do they live? Jobs? Everyday activities? What are they doing when wearing your clothes or accessories?

7. Do you have products, such as hiking boots or nursing bras, that help your customer engage in specific activities? Explain specific product performance and materials needs.

8. What is your customer's attitude toward your product category? If your product is a backpack, what is your customer's attitude towards backpacks? When and how often does your customer use your type of backpack? What do they need from a backpack?

9. How does your customer make their shopping decisions? Is price the most important? Shopping convenience? Exclusive products? Does your customer shop for trends or classic investment pieces? Do they trust peer reviews, or do they trust big fashion journalism outlets like magazines?

10. Where does your customer shop? What kinds of stores and what websites?

11. Who or what is your competition, at the same price point? What would make your product better than theirs?

12. What else is your customer wearing? Let's say you're making party shoes. If your customer's going out on a date and wearing your shoes, what brands, what kinds of clothes are they wearing? What jewelry is she wearing? Imagine your muse in the whole look.

13. What media does your customer consume? What TV and radio stations, which social media platforms, what podcasts, etc., do they use that can influence their lifestyles and shopping decisions?

Is AI Going to Take Our Jobs?

If you're having a panic attack about AI stealing your job, slow your roll. Technology is always coming to shake up the fashion industry, replacing the need for certain jobs, but also creating new ones. A lot of the fear is coming from a place of not understanding AI's capabilities, so let's talk about it.

What can AI do now? For our conversation, let's focus solely within the realm of fashion design. AI is great at making 2D art. How it works now is you input a description (and there's an art to writing these prompts) and the website generates an image based on your prompt. It can also generate 3-D models, but do not confuse these software models with actual 3-D clothes. AI has the possibility to help you explore ideas and can be especially helpful for people who aren't strong at sketching quickly.

Here are all the things, again within a design and product development context, AI can't do. AI can't actually make anything. And, at the end of the day, our end product is a tangible garment. A famous denim brand did this pretty cool video project using AI to generate some ideas, but ultimately, the video mostly showed their team, their human team, drafting, cutting, and sewing these AI-generated designs themselves.

Robots do not sew. Human hands can guide amazing machines running complex operations, but the human element is still needed.

AI is a cool tool to explore ideas and help teams visualize their thoughts by generating images, but AI can't come up with these ideas by itself. First of all, AI can't do anything unless you put in the prompts. You can't just tell it, "Hey, I'm stuck, come up with something," like you could possibly say (more nicely) to a coworker or employee. You have to write a direct description. AI doesn't make up things, it scrapes the internet of everything it thinks relates to your prompt to jigsaw mishmash something for you.

And most importantly: AI has no vision. It has no dreams for a better future for fashion, no fantastical creative purpose, and no desire to constantly build better product. But you have the potential for that. You sought out this book because you wanted to improve your creative process and learn how to be a better designer. Create a true vision for your brand, learn how to view AI as a tool instead of competition, and put energy into fit and craftsmanship.

What is Trend Forecasting?

Listen, you can google "trend forecasting," but to me, trend forecasters are like meteorologists. Meteorologists study weather patterns, both historical and in the recent past, to predict how the weather will behave in the future. They make educated guesses backed by science. And they're wrong some of the time because no one can predict the future perfectly. The weather is going to do what it wants. But they're right a lot, too.

Humans are a lot like the weather. Predictable in their unpredictable-ness.

Have you ever heard that saying, "Everything in fashion comes back around every 20 years"? Have you ever heard of the lipstick index? It's a term used to describe increased sales of cosmetics during economic recessions. You can't afford a new outfit to celebrate your birthday? Maybe you can treat yourself to a new lippie instead.

There are lot of events, patterns, and trends like these that the average consumer or fashion design teacher doesn't know about that help trend forecasters make their predictions.

It's harder than ever to forecast trends, thanks to the internet. Back in the day, and yes, you can picture me waving a cane at you, trend forecasters would travel to the runway shows, take notes, and compile presentations and books on what patterns they saw at the shows, and what they thought would be successful in the market next season. They would sell these books or give presentations to lower price-point fashion brands (contemporary to juniors).

Some would call this a bit of a self-fulfilling prophecy type situation. Big Forecasting Company said they saw a lot of jungle prints on the runways so you too should do jungle prints to stay on trend and Big Forecasting Company says this to enough people and lo and behold, a lot of brands are featuring jungle prints!

Now we get pictures of runway looks within hours of the show itself, if we're not watching the livestream. Anyone could click through the shows and start identifying patterns themselves (and post TikToks about them). The internet has also made the lifespans of trends shorter and shorter.

Not only that, but we don't all wear similar clothes like we used to. The internet has long been a platform for people to meet others and make connections. We have split into more and more subcultures because we try less to fit in with the crowd and try more to find our people. And many of these subcultures have a specific way of dressing that is unique. This diversification of fashion has had a major role in fashion designers no longer being heralded as trend dictators. Designers now have to truly give thought to what their customers want because there are so many options. On the flip side, there is space in the world for so many aesthetics. It's OK if you're not the next Lagerfeld, you can be the first You.

Do I Need to Hire a Trend Forecaster?

Ask yourself if your brand is about setting trends or following trends. I think we all think we want to be trendsetters but please be honest with yourself. Is your brand avant-garde? Are you brave enough to present ideas that will have to stand on their own, with no one else agreeing with you? Or do you want to offer something that's already out there, but with a twist? Are you a "strike while the iron's hot" person? Are you too young to have ever heard that saying?

> If you tell me your line is "elevated basics" but can't tell me specifically what's so elevated about it, I will flunk you.

What kind of clothes are you offering your customer? Is your brand about offering classic investment pieces? Sturdy utilitarian pieces designed around function? Maybe trends are not what your customer wants from you. Maybe your aesthetic doesn't follow trends but aren't "boring" classics, either.

Timing is everything in fashion. You can be too late to hop on a trend, but you can also be too early. You can say you thought of something first, but if you don't strike when the public is ready for it, it won't matter. If hitting a trend while it's hot is important to you, you may want to try out a service.

> This is also why so many new brands opt for the DTC route. When you're doing everything yourself, and you don't answer to stores, you have the agility to pivot quickly to hit trends at their peak.

As your company grows, you can hire a fashion merchandiser who does many things, including trend forecasting specific to your brand.

Business Structure:
Wholesale or Direct to Consumer

A wholesale business creates products to sell in bulk to a different business. In fashion, that means you create clothes and accessories and sell them to stores. Wholesale buyers are the representatives of their stores who will place the orders. These buyers can be (but are not always) the store owner. The stores, whether brick and mortar or online, sell your clothes to individual customers one at a time.

A direct to consumer, or direct to customer, business creates products to sell to individual customers one at a time. People see this as "cutting out the middleman" but there are pros and cons to both types of business. Let's review some of the biggest concerns.

Let's start with wholesale.

Pros:

◆ Less garbage. You gather orders and produce according to your orders. This reduces the guessing game of how much to order and the chances of overproducing excess inventory you can't offload.

◆ The business advantage of a marketing partner. People will know established boutiques and department stores before they hear about your fledgling brand and you can use that to your advantage.

◆ Legitimacy. It gives your brand legitimacy when you get the backing of a well-known buyer or store.

Cons:

◆ The money! When a store places an order with a designer, they do not pay upfront. They will typically demand "net 30" terms, which means they have to pay 30 days after they receive your goods. That means you need to foot the bill for that season's production on your own. Can you demand payment upfront? You can try, but sadly this is the norm of the industry, so don't be surprised if the store decides to not order from you unless you accept their terms.

◆ Chargebacks! Whenever a store places an order, they will give instructions on how the clothes are to be shipped. Some stores are stricter and more particular than others, especially department stores. These instructions can include where (which side of the garment and how many inches down from the armscye) to punch hangtags and how the garment is packaged. Department stores can and will charge you for each infraction, and these are called chargebacks. And yes, each chargeback can be hundreds of dollars. Read the fine print!

Department stores are a special beast, and some brands choose to not sell to them until they can get a solid handle on their production processes. I have heard horror stories of a department store who issued so many chargebacks that that bill cost more than the total invoice for the clothes!

Remember when that department store went out of business and there were all those stories about the massive amounts of money they allegedly still owed those prominent designer brands? Good times.

At this point, you may be firmly in Camp DTC, but let's discuss.

Pros:

◆ You get your money a lot faster.

◆ You can have a lot more control over your images and prices.

◆ You have the agility to follow trends and try out new designs.

Cons:

◆ You still have to foot the bill for production on your own, as no one's ordered anything yet. This excludes any crowdfunding situation.

◆ You're on your own for marketing and advertising. You have to set up your own ads, collabs, social media, and whatever marketing strategy you've planned. You would be doing this anyway, but now you don't get the extra boost (or foot traffic) of working with a bigger brand.

◆ Some of y'all are not self-motivated. Don't get mad at me, but it's true. Some of you need the external motivation of deadlines set by schools and other companies to get your butts in gear. Do some soul searching. Are you able to set your own deadlines and stick to them?

Wholesale:

cost to make garment
+
your markup
=
price to the store

---

price to the store
+
store's markup
=
price customers see

Direct to Consumer:

cost to make garment
+
cost to sell garment
+
your markup
=
price customers see

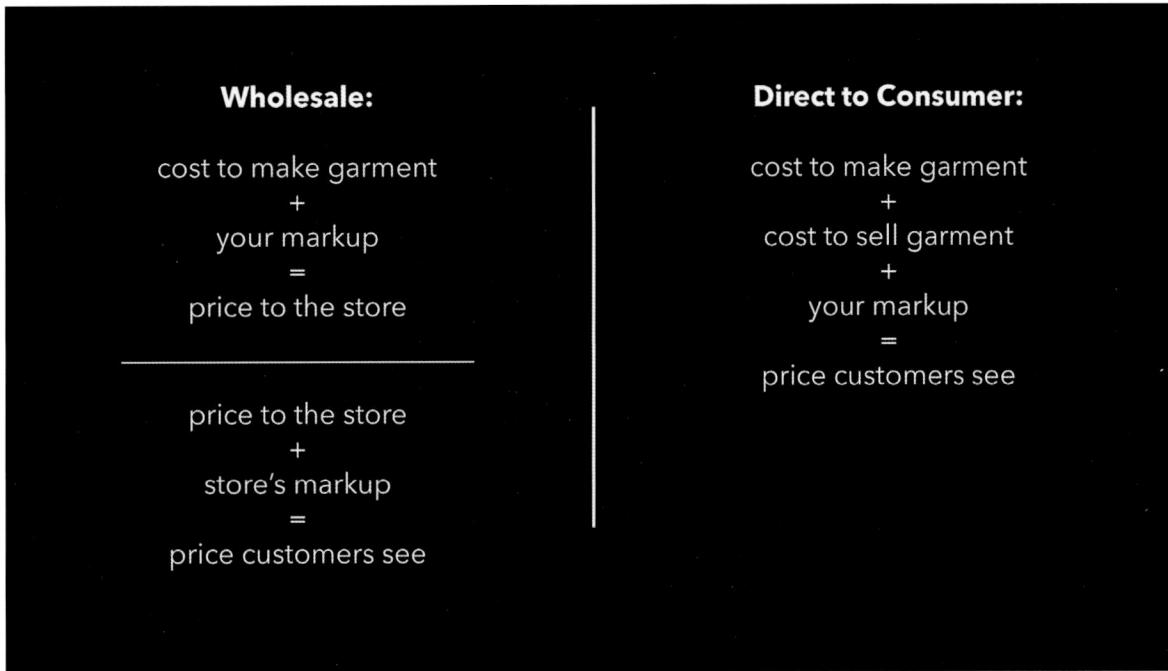

FIGURE 2.16 Basic formulas for pricing

Let's talk a little more about that "control over prices" thing. You don't get to slash your prices in half just because you're DTC (**Figure 2.16**).

Stores don't just markup the price and sit on it. They maintain a beautiful store, they market, they do social media, they provide customer service. When you're DTC, you have to pay money to people to do things like update and maintain your website, run your social media, and answer all the ~~annoying~~ emails from customers. Your cost to make the garment needs to accommodate these expenditures.

Made to Order

A subcategory of DTC is made to order. Made to order is exactly as it sounds: the garment isn't cut and sewn until there is an order for it. This category offers one-off pieces to individual customers in varying levels of customization. Bespoke and couture (made to measure) fit the customer's body precisely, and makes a pattern specifically for that customer, often including minute asymmetries that mass produced clothing does not.

You also have many brands on shopping platforms like Etsy that cut made to order but don't offer any changes. They are small businesses who either can't or don't want to produce in bulk in advance.

And you have everything in between, from offering minor tailoring services, like custom inseams, to picking a completely different fabric than shown and adding embellishments.

The biggest difference between a made-to-order business and a freelance dressmaker/tailor is a business offers ready-made styles (via photos or samples) that a client can customize, and a freelancer will make a fresh new design from scratch. Of course, a made-to-order business can incorporate this kind of dressmaking into their business as well.

This single design from scratch dressmaking/tailoring can be very time-consuming and expensive, with small margins, and hard to scale. Building a library of customizable ready-made samples can help both you and your clients.

Push versus Pull Manufacturing

You may have heard these terms before in regards to business structures and sustainability. Succinctly, pull manufacturing is cutting according to orders already placed, pulling numbers from your orders; push manufacturing is pushing into the market what you think the market will bear (**Figure 2.17**).

Pull manufacturing is considered more sustainable because you are less likely to have excess inventory. Push manufacturing relies heavily on previous sales information to form an educated guess on what will sell, which a new brand won't have. If you're going the DTC route, start small!

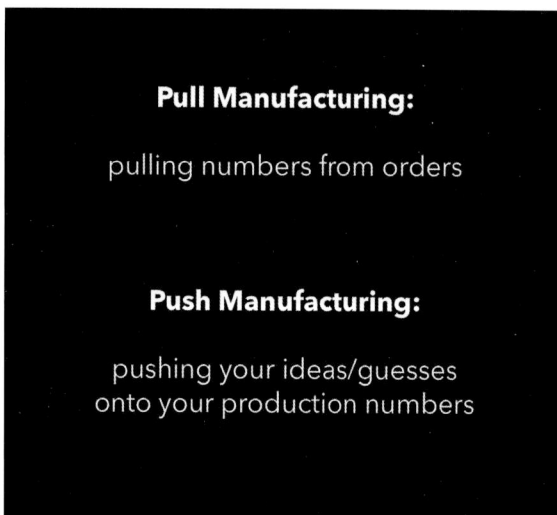

Pull Manufacturing:

pulling numbers from orders

Push Manufacturing:

pushing your ideas/guesses
onto your production numbers

FIGURE 2.17 This is how I remember the difference between push and pull manufacturing.

What If You Want to Do Both Wholesale and DTC?

Insert that "why not both?" GIF here.

I know you've seen brands sell both on their own sites and in other stores. It's possible, and probably something you should work toward. You will still be running things like a wholesale business. Instead of producing to order, you will produce more so you can stock your own stores. Some retail stores require a brand to have its own online presence and e-commerce site before they buy bulk from that brand.

Here's the most important rule of selling to both wholesale buyers and through your own stores: Do not undersell your stores.

Let's say you sell a dress to a store for $100 and the store marks it up to the standard 2.2x. Now it's $220 in the store. You can't sell it for $100 in your store to compete with your wholesale accounts. First of all, not only will that store never order from you again, but the news will spread to other stores and those stores won't order from you either.

Charge the same price in your store, spend some of the money on your own marketing and sales, and pocket the rest. That's why brands bother running their own stores, so they can make a little more money. Control over their brand image is also key.

What is Private Label?

Once upon a time, when I was a newbie designer, a chain of stores wanted to have their own brand in their shops but didn't want to handle product development and deal with production, you know, some of the hardest parts of running a design business. They would call up the company I worked at, and say, "Hey, can we get a bunch of style #2314 except change the collar and put our label in it?"

That's private label. That's when you order from a wholesaler, put your own branding and labeling on it, mark it up, and sell it in your storefronts. Some people don't make any changes, unlike the chain above. (The chain no longer exists, completely unrelated to their private label decisions.) Some companies design styles specifically to pitch to a prized private label client.

Consider it a compliment; it means the store loves the design and quality so much they're putting their money where their mouth is. Do you have to take the order? Maybe you don't want copies of your design under someone else's name. In that case, you might negotiate a design change, or color/fabrication change. Either way, it doesn't have to affect the rest of your business. It can be just another order. If they want exclusive sales of a specific style, demand a high minimum order in exchange.

Price Points

Part of your branding is keeping to a consistent price point that works with your customers' needs. Let's go over different price points in the industry so you can find your place.

The Fédération de la Haute Couture et de la Mode determines which fashion houses are eligible to be designated true Haute Couture houses. Couture pieces are handmade and of the utmost luxurious quality—and the prices reflect this. Brands include Schiaparelli, Dior, and Jean Paul Gaultier.

> *One of my pet peeves is people calling things couture when they're not, unless it's obviously tongue-in-cheek like the loungewear brand Juicy Couture.*

Designer and luxury price points are not the same. They're both very expensive, to be sure, but luxury brands must be well established with a global presence, often branched out into multiple fashion categories like shoes, perfume, and bags. Luxury is a step above, both in price and quality. Luxury brands include Hermes, Gucci, and Louis Vuitton.

Contemporary brands feature dresses that average $350–750 and are more youthful and fashion forward. Contemporary brands include Ganni, Nanushka, The Kooples, and Diane von Furstenberg.

On the least expensive end of the range, let's start with discounters or "off-price" stores like TJ Maxx, Ross Dress for Less, and Marshalls. These chains used to only sell samples, close-outs, discontinued items, and past-season or damaged goods, but more and more brands are now selling new designs to these stores' private label.

Outlets used to be where unsold inventory went to die/was offered at severe discounts. Now more and more brands are specifically designing and/or producing goods more cheaply for outlet stores.

> *Outlet stores only sell items from their brand, such as the Gucci outlet, or the Michael Kors outlet. Stores like Ross Dress for Less feature many brands.*

And then there's fast fashion. Fast fashion is a category of brands of poorly made simplified copies of runway looks. That's not my distaste showing. The founder of Zara, who is also the founder of fast fashion, has said publicly the whole point of Zara was giving runway looks to people who can't afford the runway prices. That's evolved into the big fast fashion companies copying anything popular. Fast fashion brands include H&M, Zara, and Shein.

What's in between the two ends is a bit murkier. Back in the good old days when we had a thriving middle class, we had middle categories that offered middle-quality goods at middle-of-the-road prices. "Juniors" was young, trendy, and cheap. "Moderate" was a little more expensive, a little higher quality. "Missy" was "moderate" but for older women in both styling and fit. "Better" was a contemporary price point for older women.

And then there are "Bridge" or "Diffusion" lines. These brands were designers' cheaper lines, a "bridge" between Designer and Contemporary. These brands included Marc by Marc Jacobs, REDValentino, Victoria by Victoria Beckham, Emporio Armani, DKNY, and Miu Miu.

These Bridge lines have all gone different directions. DKNY used to be significant enough to have its own runway shows but now has become cheaper and lower quality. Miu Miu has gone the other direction and is now a designer line on its own. REDValentino has officially closed. So has Marc by Marc Jacobs. Emporio Armani is still around, competing at a contemporary price point. There's no longer any trace of Victoria by Victoria Beckham; so much so that I'm starting to think I imagined the whole thing. (I didn't, I found a *Vogue* article about its launch in 2011. The internet is an absent-minded professor's best friend.)

Trade shows that used to sell Juniors, Moderate, Better, and Missy categories now call them "trend" and "young contemporary," but a lot of these offerings look like slightly more expensive fast fashion.

Market Research

Even if your plan is to start a brand in two years, you should start your market research now (**Figure 2.18, next page**). This is a plan for people who don't have the big bucks to hire a company to do extensive research for them.

Educate yourself on what's happening in the industry globally. Fashion has always been a barometer of a region's economic health. Pay attention

Get an overall feel for the entire industry.
Read the news, listen to podcasts.
How's the global economy? What's the state of the fashion industry?

Research your subsection of interest.
Read more news.
Read and watch interviews of people working in your niche.
Shop your market.

Identify problems to solve, holes to fill in the market.
Who are the people that need your clothes?

Strategize specific solutions.
What's your idea of beautiful?

Design clothes that incorporate these solutions.

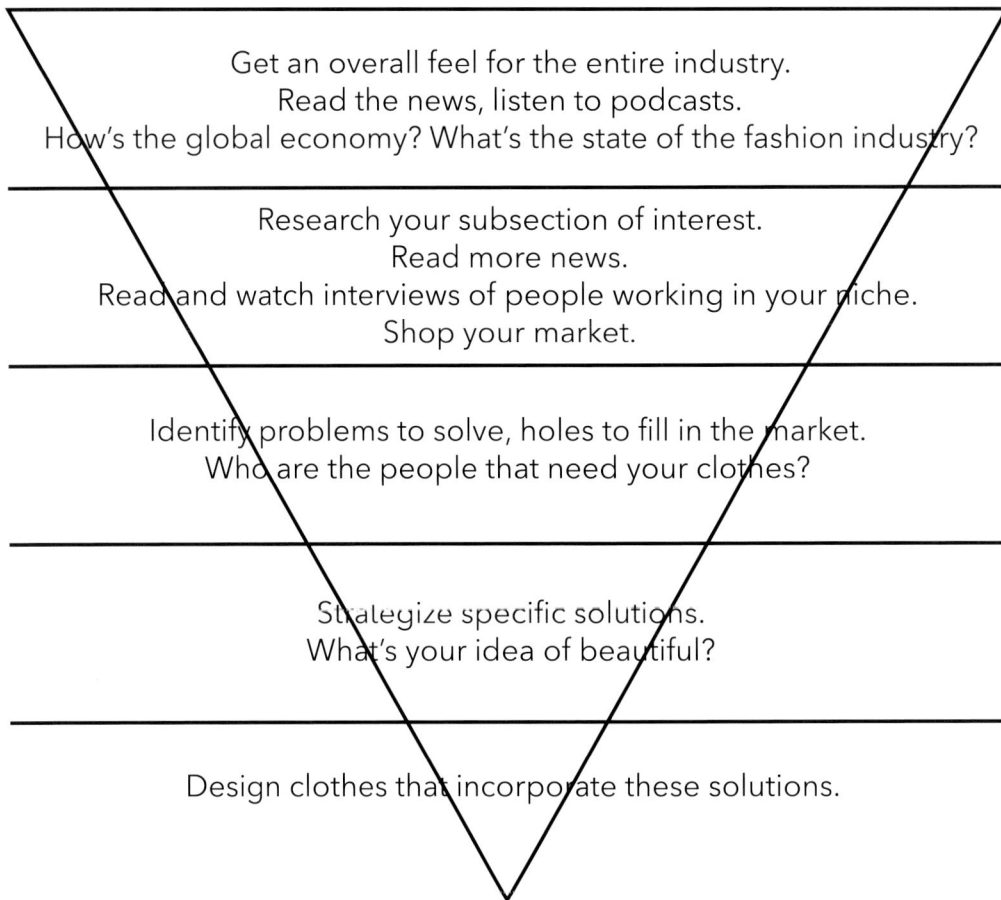

FIGURE 2.18 Don't @ me about my love of inverted triangles. It's a great visual of the broad-to-specific approach I teach.

to business and economic news. Subscribe to a fashion news site and commit to reading at least the headlines every day. Get knowledgeable about the fashion business, trends in both business and clothes, global economics, and how technology affects fashion and related industries.

Go shopping. The internet is a beautiful, beautiful thing, but sometimes you have to get off your bum, go to a store, and observe clothes and shoppers in the wild.

I get a lot of students who want to build a luxury brand but have no idea what luxury quality looks like. They think they know, but they don't. In this world of photo retouching, online shopping will not teach you much. You have to go look at a lot of thousand-dollar dresses before you can create your own thousand-dollar dresses to compete. And not only that, you also need to go look at thousand-dollar dresses from brands that aren't that famous. Famous brands really lean into that brand recognition to mark up their clothes. However, these big famous brands also have access to resources smaller brands can only dream about. Compare apples to apples.

Go check out the sales rack of stores. Grab the most discounted pieces and try to decipher why they didn't sell. Sewing quality? Itchy fabric? Awkward fit? Just plain ugliness? You can also check out the sales sections of websites, but again, there's nothing like holding a dress in your hands that gives you a more complete picture, a truer story—sans beautiful models, great lighting and styling, and pins behind the mannequin.

When you have a loose idea of what you may want to design, start talking to people who may be your target customer. Think you want to do childrenswear? Start talking to moms about what they hate about shopping for their kids. You're going to start hearing common stories and get a better idea of the childrenswear landscape.

Go into these conversations with an open mind; don't lead people into giving you the answers you're hoping for. Take notes, even (or especially) when they disagree with your opinions or preconceived notions.

Once you have more information to work with, create some surveys and circulate them. Join some mom groups and ask nicely if you can share a survey. Your surveys should include new questions you have and specific questions about some possible solutions you have to their shopping woes.

But What About Creativity?

I know what you're thinking. You might even be yelling at this book right now. What about creativity? What about my vision? I have beautiful things I need to share with the world, and I don't care about market research! OK. Go do it. Go make the most astonishingly incredible things the world hasn't seen yet. The fashion industry is happy to revel in bright new voices, but you have to have a sales plan to make enough money for another collection. You have to have a marketing plan so people will actually be able to find you and discover your talent. You have to make sure your quality is top notch, or no one will take your designs seriously. And don't worry, I have several chapters in this book devoted solely to pushing your creative envelope.

Understanding Quality and Analyzing the Competition

Two questions you should ask yourself are, "What is the highest level of quality I can achieve at my price point?" and, "What are the markers of quality in my category and price point?"

I have created a worksheet to help you analyze what's in the market to help you decide the answers to the above questions for yourself (**Figure 2.19**).

This is another one of those instances where the internet's offerings will fall short. You have to really look at these clothes up close, feel these clothes, try these clothes on.

FIGURE 2.19. RIGHT Design attracts the customer; quality keeps the customer.

Did you know that the vast majority of online returns get trashed? People think returns get restocked and resold but that's rarely the case. And the cheaper the item, the more likely it will get trashed instead of restocked. Please think about this before you make plans to order and return a dozen dresses.

Listen, it's a fashion school rite of passage to hunker down in a dressing room with a gown you couldn't afford in your wildest dreams to quickly scribble down your observations before the salesperson starts fake coughing outside the door. It's especially embarrassing when you know, and the store knows, and the store knows you know that your chubby self couldn't fit a leg into that size 2 you grabbed off the rack, but if baby Zoe could survive it, so can you.

Something you can do online is compare their store offerings and their runway shows. Google a brand to see what websites sell that brand. Look at what the brand sells in their own store, what wholesale buyers have ordered for their stores, and what showed on the runway to start learning patterns in what appeals to buyers.

PRODUCT ANALYSIS

Choose an item of the same type as your brand/project and analyze the construction by answering the questions below. Analyze at least one in your price point, one more expensive, and one less expensive. Take photos of the analysis process for your own reference.

1. Describe the product.

2. What is the price?

3. Fabric? Fiber content?

4. Knit, woven, hide, nonwoven?

5. Is the fabric high quality? Is the fabric soft? Itchy? Soft? Rough in a cool way or a bad way?

6. Is there a print? Is it well done? Solid dyes/pigments soaked into the fabric, no weird gaps or printed crookedly on the fabric?

7. Check the seams. Are they well sewn? Look for smooth, neat seams, not loose, gaping stitches, no weird bunching or puckering. The seams should be straight or clean curves, not wonky, rippling waves. Do the seams itch when the garment is worn or when you run your hand over them?

8. Are there any trims? Are zippers and buttons high quality and sewn on securely? Do zippers pull smoothly? Do the buttonhole stitches look neat and tight? Are hooks and eyes sewn on securely? Are snaps punched in without puckering the fabric?

9. Are there any embellishments? Run your hand over the beading. Does it feel like beads are about to fall loose? Are the embroidery stitches tight and smooth? With high-quality embroidery, you should not be able to see the fabric in between the threads. Are patches sewn on securely?

10. Are there pockets? Are they real or fake pockets? Are the pockets a decent size with strong construction?

11. Look inside. Is it lined? Is the lining fabric good quality? What's the lining's fiber content?

12. If not lined, how are the seams finished? Overlock? Hong Kong finish? Is the stitching neat and professional?

13. Try it on and analyze the fit. Or have a friend try it on. Does it pinch or rub anywhere? Does the fabric pull weirdly? Walk around and sit in it. Is it comfortable? Does the garment move with you?

14. Does the hangtag include repair extras like extra buttons or beads?

15. Is this product worth the price? Why or why not?

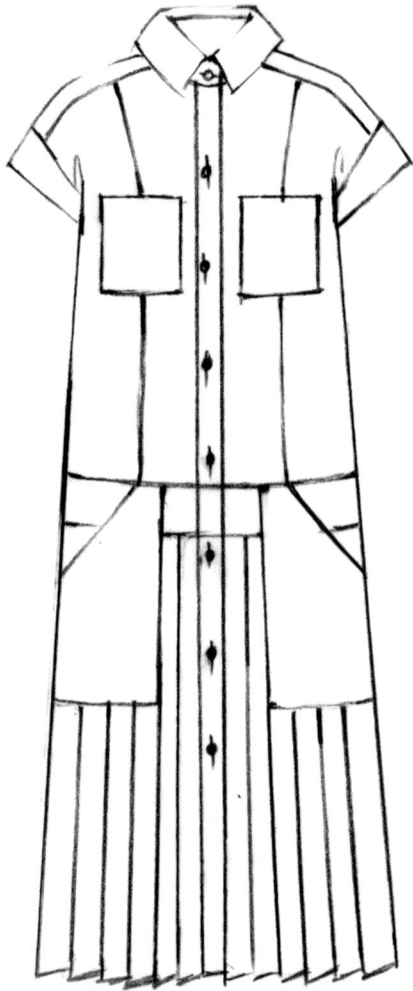

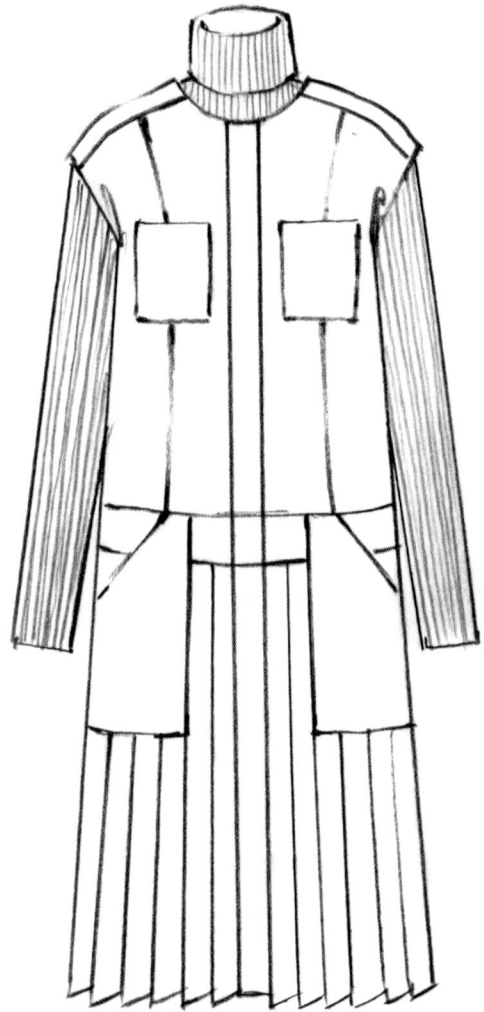

3

COLLECTION DIRECTION

What Season Are You Designing?

The season you are designing influences fabric choices, silhouettes, and garment categories (**Figure 3.1**). It would be highly impractical to design a summer collection with fur trimmed wool coats and quilted parkas or a winter collection consisting mainly of breezy linen dresses.

No, you can't change your mind midway through. That's not how this works. Now get back to work.

Here's a loose guide to help you design for your season (**Figure 3.2, next page**). This is by no means exhaustive of every fabric available.

Some things can be included in any season. Very few things are exclusive to one season. There are some things that should be used mostly in one season but can be used in small pop moments in other seasons. Sheer fabrics mostly belong in spring/summer, but can be used for details like overlays, insets, and ruffled trim for colder seasons. People wear sleeveless clothes all year, but they are far less likely to be worn alone in the winter. (Although, I will say, I grew up in Alaska and the second the temperature warmed up to a toasty 45 degrees Fahrenheit, the dads would bust out the jorts.) You can always make editorial statements like underwear as outerwear for any season, but your collection should be grounded in weather

	SPRING/SUMMER	ANY SEASON, DEPENDING ON WEIGHT/USAGE	FALL/WINTER
SILK	CHIFFON	CREPE	DUCHESS SATIN
	ORGANZA	DUPIONI	4 PLY CREPE
	GAZAR	CHARMEUSE	SILK JERSEY
	GAUZE	SILK TWILL	VELVET
	MOUSSELINE	JACQUARD	BROCADE
	SILK MUSLIN		
	GEORGETTE		
WOOL ALSO OTHER ANIMAL FIBERS LIKE CASHMERE	GAUZE DELAINE	WORSTEDS	WOOLENS
		GABARDINE	MELTON
		CREPE	BARATHEA
		TWEEDS	
CELLULOSIC (COTTON, LINEN, ETC)	VOILE	DENIM	DUCK
	GAUZE	LINEN	MOLESKIN
	BATISTE	SHIRTING	VELVETEEN
	CHAMBRAY	TSHIRT JERSEY	JACQUARD
	ORGANDY	SATEEN	
	SEERSUCKER	TWILL BOTTOMWEIGHT	
	CHEESECLOTH	CORDUROY	
		FRENCH TERRY	
SYNTHETICS* (NYLON, POLY, ETC) *MANY SYNTHETICS ARE CREATED TO MIMIC NATURAL FIBER FABRICS MORE CHEAPLY, LIKE SATIN AND GABARDINE.	NET/MESH	PVC	FLEECE
	RIPSTOP	LAMÉ	FAUX FUR
		ULTRASUEDE	SUEDETTE
		PERFORMANCE STRETCH FABRICS	
HIDES	MOST HIDES CAN BE TANNED IN DIFFERENT WEIGHTS FOR ANY SEASON.		

FIGURE 3.2. LEFT Consider this table a guide and not a set of hard and fast rules.

appropriate pieces also, like some great overcoats. You can include a mini skirt for a fall collection but also offer longer options.

And there are garment categories that are seasonless in terms of fabric choice, like lingerie and swimwear. Some fabric categories are also generally seasonless, like lace. Yes, there are some laces that look more summery and some that are heavier. You can use lace any time; the season appropriateness will be determined by usage.

Creating Your Own Direction

When you start working in the industry, the leadership will decide the direction of the collection, including the mood, the inspiration images, the colors, and the fabrics. As a designer, you will work on individual garments based off that direction to support the creative director's vision.

Some people love working this way; they flourish under set parameters, a box they can play in, bouncing against but never breaking through the walls. Possible hot take: Karl Lagerfeld was this type of designer. He flourished at Chanel, constantly toying with how far he could push the envelope within the Chanel house codes. His own eponymous label didn't have quite the same sizzle.

When you're on your own, you're on your own. You have to give yourself a directive, a game plan to stick to, so your resulting collection doesn't look all over the place.

Your design direction doesn't necessarily need to include sustainability if sustainability is already built into your brand values. You can be inspired by unhappy cigarette-smoking '70s housewives and create a collection with sustainable materials, using zero-waste cutting techniques, hiring an ethical manufacturer, and incorporating a secondhand program into your webstore. (What a vibe. Someone design this collection, stat.)

The following are some ideas on how to put together your own design brief. You will see that you can use these ideas again and again incorporating different time periods, different artists, and different words.

Design Brief 1: Two Become One

Pick two vastly different time periods. Choose some elements from each time period, and merge them into a cohesive, modern collection that doesn't look like costume design (**Figure 3.3**).

Each time period should be as precise as possible. Fashion moves very fast today, but there are times in history when people wore the same things for hundreds of years. Clothing in Western Europe didn't change all that much throughout the 14th century, so you can use that as one time period; but, if you pick an era from the 20th century, you have to pick a specific decade. Fashion in the '30s looked very different from fashion in the '20s. I wager the concept of microtrends are wholly a post-internet phenomenon.

You can and should select different countries as well. It is best if you use just a few elements from each time period and country, instead of trying to cram too many styles into one collection. We are being inspired, not copying or translating.

FIGURE 3.3. BELOW AND RIGHT Ancient Egypt meets rococo.

Examples: Merge elements from 1950s China and 1890s USA. Early 1400s France and modern-day Tokyo. The Inca Empire and 1970s Iran. 1920s Golden Age Hollywood and Mars 200 years in the future. Choose even smaller subcultures than what I've listed, such as the Teddy Boys, a mainly British subculture of 1950s and 1960s youth.

Pick up a costume history book at your local library and flip through until you spy something cool.

Design Brief 2: Master of Someone Else's Domain

Select a brand and pretend you have been hired to be their new creative director. Design a collection for this brand. How can you pay homage to the history of the brand while looking forward and creating something new? Start by studying the brand's history.

Example: Gucci has a history of craftsmanship, especially beautiful leather work. OG Gucci man, Guccio Gucci, used to work at the Savoy Hotel in London. He returned to Italy to make his own versions of the luxury luggage he saw at the hotel. Some of his earliest works included saddles and other accessories for horsemen. That's what inspired the horse-bit buckles and red and green strapping on his non-equestrian pieces, two things that continue to be Gucci's most famous emblems.

Can you whisper back to that heritage without making your designs look like you're reworking old pieces? Study how other Gucci designers have approached this dilemma, how they have given their own flair and flavor to Gucci. Ford, Giannini, Michele, and De Sarno have all taken that Gucci heritage and run with it, putting their own visual stamps on the house. Take notes on what you can bring to Gucci, how you can marry your aesthetic with Gucci's, and move them into the future (**Figure 3.4**).

Pick a house, any house, but maybe not your absolutely favorite house. Some students feel a little too precious about their favorites and have a hard time casting a critical view on the house's history

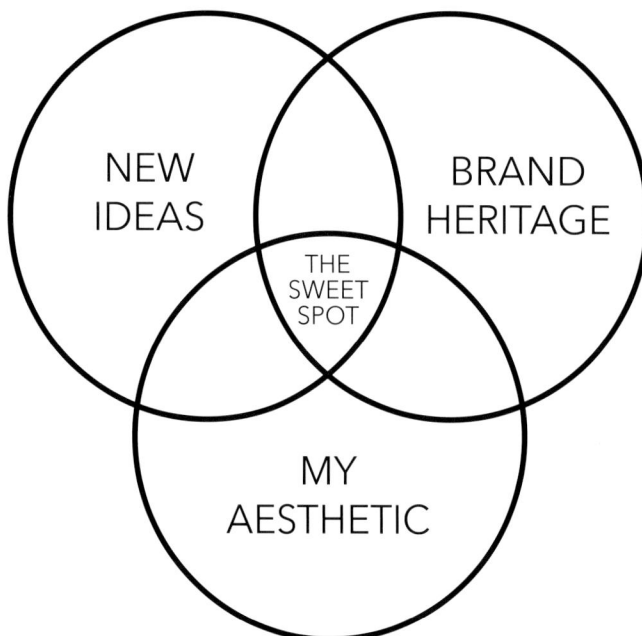

FIGURE 3.4 It's all about balance.

Design Brief 3: Unichromatic

Fine, unichromatic isn't a real word but monochromatic color schemes consist of the main color (red) and its tints (pink!), shades (maroon!), and tones (mauve!). When I say one color, I mean one, singular, all by itself, singing karaoke on a Tuesday night, all alone color.

Create a collection that is all one color (**Figure 3.5**). Use as few variations on the color as possible. If you pick blue, try to stick to one blue, instead of using lots of shades of blue. Create visual interest with textures, shapes, embellishments, fabric manipulations like smocking, pleats, quilting, and tucks. Bonus: Don't pick a neutral!

Double points if you choose one fabric. Try one shade of denim, smoky pale pink leather, orange corduroy, sage green linen—anything goes!

I am aware you can't just sell one color across your whole store. The point of this exercise is to learn how to create visual interest without relying on color. Ultimately, you will choose some other colors to merchandise out your collection.

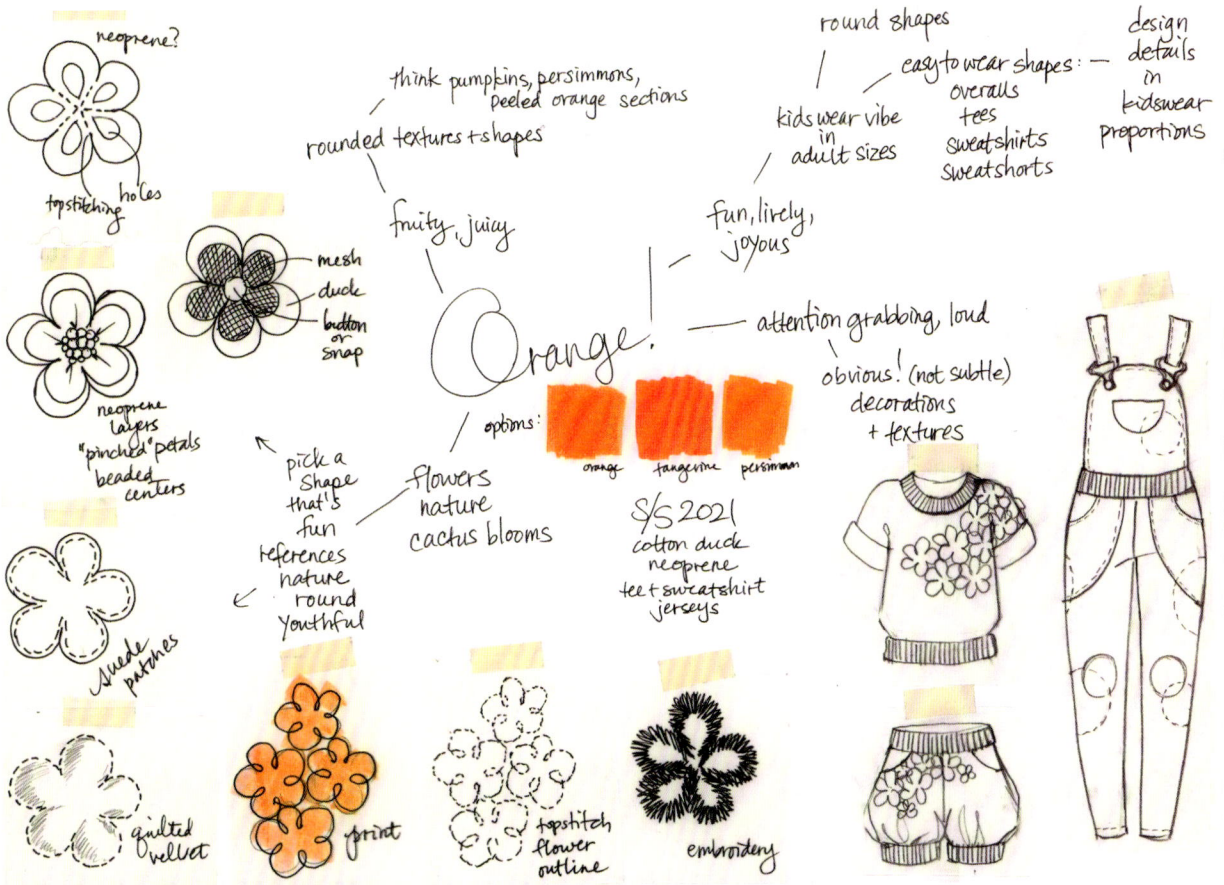

Design Brief 4: Fangirl It Out

Pick an artist and choose one to four of their works. Pull inspiration from these pieces and create a collection that doesn't look like a series of the artist's reproductions. Do not use too many works; focus and deep dive into a few key pieces. The artist does not have to be famous; the works do not have to be the artist's most well-known pieces.

Do not do anything obvious like screen-printing paintings onto t-shirts or embroidering parts of a painting onto a dress. Do not take things too literally. Go deeper. Research the meanings behind the works.

Take inspiration from Salvador Dali's melting clocks. Instead of making beaded clocks, think about elements falling apart, falling down, dissolving. Do not look at Degas's dancers and literally make dance costumes. Be inspired by the color palette, how many colors go into depicting white. Be inspired by the mood of his paintings and sculptures, the gracefulness.

Do not take Keith Haring's people and make it into a print. I mean, first of all, you'll likely be sued. Instead, be inspired by his bright colors, bold lines, political statements, his guerilla style of spreading his work. Take Picasso's *The Bull*. It's a series of 11 lithographs that study the process of abstraction. Do not make a print of bulls or make headdresses with antlers. Consider the meaning of a dress and the many ways you can abstract a dress in varying degrees of intensity.

Design Brief 5: Wordplay

Choose a book with a lot of text on every page. With your eyes closed, flip through the book and randomly point to a word. Design a collection inspired the definition of that word and what you think about when you read that word. Use a real paper book with pages. If you say you don't have a book, I don't believe you. You're literally reading one right now. (Or support your local library!)

This doesn't really work the same online or on an e-reader. You can try again if you land on more non-descriptive, sentence structure words like "and," "to," or "there." The best words are the ones you didn't know before, so your research is truly fresh.

FIGURE 3.6. BELOW This "preposterous" mindmap is indeed preposterous.

Or you can "cheat" and just pick a word you think is fascinating. My example project for this book is based on the word "syzygy."

Create a mind map with the word (**Figure 3.6**). Take the word as many places as you can. Take a branch of your mind map and use that as inspiration for your collection.

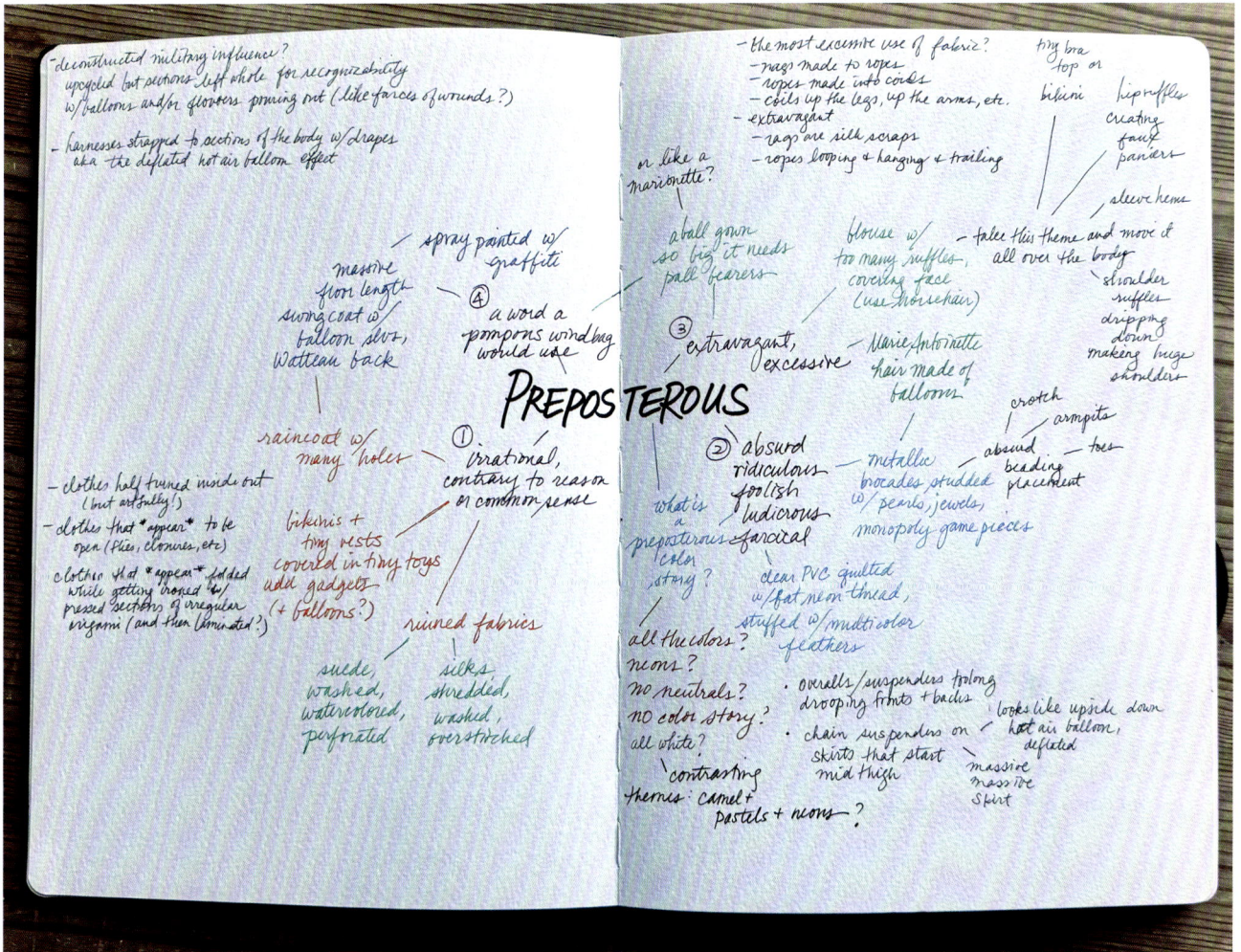

Design Brief 6: Modernizing History

Many of us are inspired by specific people, whether it's their style, lifestyle, or personality. Select a historical figure and design a wardrobe for them as if they lived in modern times. You can use some elements of that person's lifetime, but this is not about costume design. Focus more on this person's life achievements, personality, and lifestyle. Create a customer profile around this historical figure, and how they would live in the modern day.

Example: Let's pretend Harriet Tubman lived in modern-day America. Harriet Tubman (1822–1913) was an escaped slave and political activist who made over a dozen missions to rescue slaves in the 1850s. During the Civil War, she worked for the Union Army, and led a raid that liberated more than 700 slaves. Late in her life, she was active in the women's suffrage movement.

What kind of wardrobe would you build for her? How about an affordable, utilitarian everyday work wardrobe with lots of pockets? Easy to wear looks that includes some day-to-night looks? How about making the whole collection feminine without being fussy, using machine washable fabrics made of natural fibers? What details from the time period can you bring to present day without creating a costume? Portraits show Tubman in blouses with beautiful pleating, tucking, and shirring details and big, long, simple coats over her period-dictated long skirts. Her neck was usually covered by detachable collars or scarves. Think about incorporating these elements without making it look like costume design.

Design Brief 7: A Tourist in Your Own City

Visit the places your town is famous for that you're too busy living life to visit.

If you find the architecture inspiring, select one to four pieces of architecture that interests you. Analyze line, shape, form, color, texture, patterns. Analyze the mood and attitude of the buildings and how they interact with people. Is it a cozy, welcoming space or an awe-inspiring, grandiose presence? Translate your analysis into clothing design.

If you're designing a small collection (four to eight looks), choosing one style of architecture would make the most cohesive collection. If you're doing larger collections, you have more visual space to play with how different architecture styles can interact with each other.

Or hit a crowded area and go people watching. Take some notes or sketch some interesting characters. You don't have to pick the most stylish person—pick people you think seem interesting. Create a fake life story for this person. Develop a collection inspired by this character.

One day I saw this incredible sight. This very petite, slightly hunched over Asian grandma, wearing a massive, shiny, black, puffy, quilted short parka and a pair of what can only be described as flower-print pantaloons, was furiously riding a neon Huffy kid-size bicycle, not giving a single fluffernutter about the traffic. I fell in love immediately. In lieu of stalking her and asking her to adopt me and teach me her ways, I designed a collection inspired by her (**Figure 3.7, next pages**).

FIGURE 3.7. ABOVE AND RIGHT OG channel fans will
remember the moment I first clapped eyes on the badass
Asian grandma.

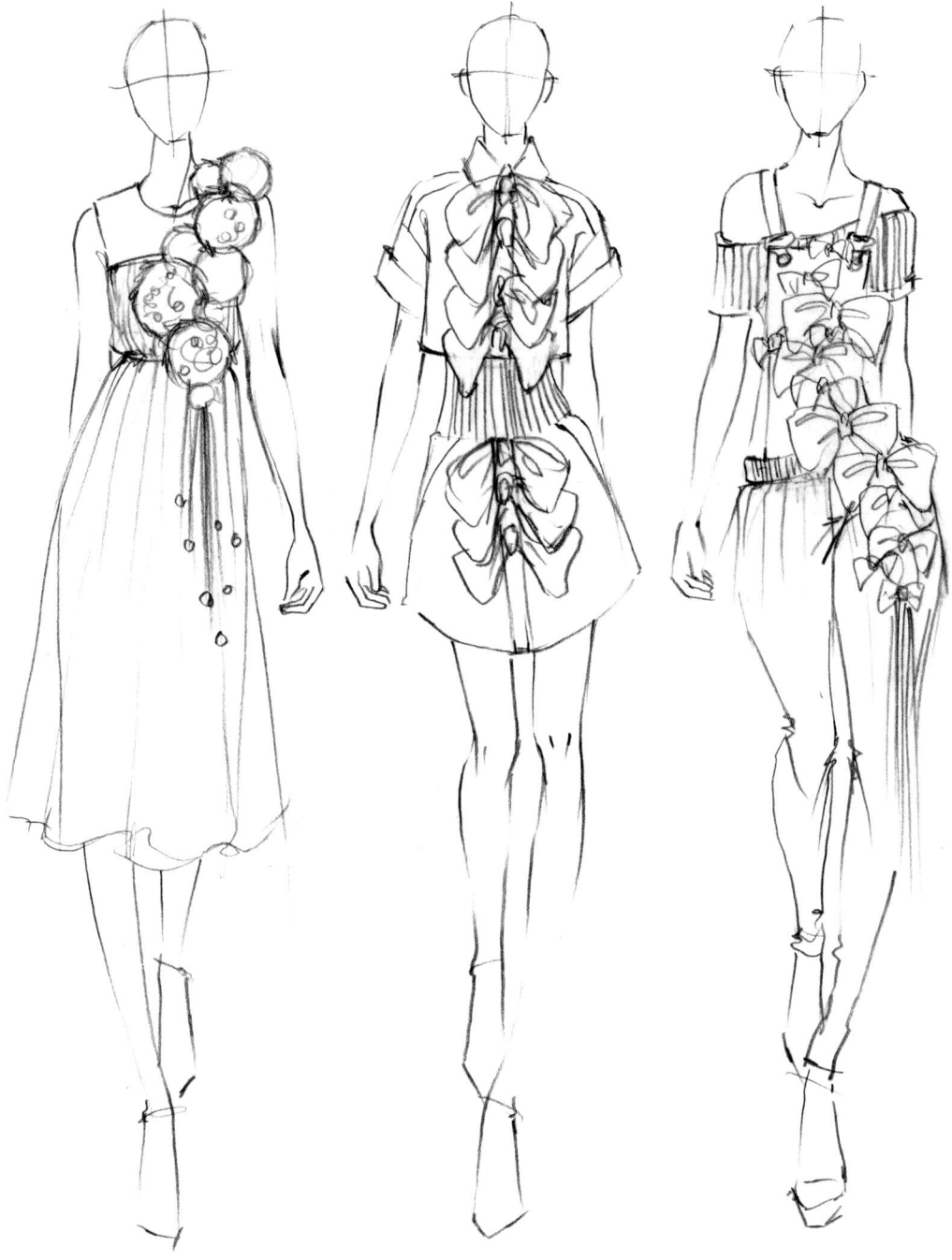

Design Brief 8: Deconstruct and Reconstruct

Buy three garments in a thrift store or pull three garments from your closet you'll never wear again (**Figure 3.8**). Take photos of them (front, back, side, and detail close-ups) for your mood board. Drape the garments onto your dress form in new ways over and over again. Situate them upside down and/or inside out on the dress form. Open up some seams. Also try combining two or three garments into one garment. Drape, fold, pin, photograph, and repeat over and over again in new ways. Print out your photos and use these drape experiments as inspiration for your collection. You can draw on your photos and expand upon the design, or you can layer tracing paper on top of your photos and draw out the design through simplifying and adjusting the drape.

FIGURE 3.8. BELOW Name a more iconic trio...I'll wait.

Design Brief 9: A Designer Designs a Design

A person does a thing. A toddler goes hiking. Grandpa learns ballet. A rap star joins a rock band. A woman travels the world. Make your own simple sentence of a person doing a thing.

A toddler goes hiking. You're not actually dressing toddlers or hikers. Take inspiration from childrenswear (fun colors, easy to wear shapes, soft fabrics, colorful prints) and merge them with the needs of hikers (pockets that zip close, windbreakers that fold very small, hoods, reflective patches, bungee cords).

Grandpa learns ballet. (Someone please make a tearjerker animation short with this idea.) Take inspiration from the needs of older people (easy closures, easy to pull on clothes, durable, machine washable, stain resistant) and merge them with the needs of ballerinas (close to the body, stretchy, moves with the body, nothing dangly that will catch while dancing).

Have fun making some sentences, get a little ridiculous, and run with it.

You can also merge two of the above directions to create your own twist. For my Syzygy project, I'm also going to incorporate elements of Design Brief 8: Deconstruct and Reconstruct. The word syzygy also refers to twins and complements, so I'm going to include the two coats, which are polar opposites from each other in design and function.

Desperately Seeking Inspiration

If none of these ideas appeal to you, here's a list of activities and places that might fire up some creative synapses.

◆ Visit different local museums and attend exhibitions not related to fashion. Many museums also have internet archives, video tours, and similar.

◆ Watch a movie, preferably a type of movie you don't usually see. Don't scroll on your phone. Re-costume the movie.

◆ Watch a TV show you've never seen before from a much older time and re-costume it as a modern show.

◆ Shop in stores you've never been to or are the opposite of your general tastes. Window shop for things you haven't been interested in before—random stuff like old clocks, military surplus, wigs, and party supplies.

Are you sensing a theme? Go look at things new to you.

- Spend some time in a fabric store and explore areas you often ignore.

- Visit stores that sell other clothes-making materials, in particular those you don't usually use: bead shops, yarn shops, craft shops, corsetry supply shops.

- Visit a candy specialty shop, the kind with big clear buckets of cool-looking treats. Put together a bag full of colors and textures that appeal to you. Take pics before you eat them all.

- Deep dive into a new hobby. After attending a 10-day indigo workshop in Japan, I'm still obsessed with and inspired by indigo dyeing techniques and boro to this day.

- Explore nature. Go on a hike, go camping (maybe glamping instead), take a drive through the woods, ride a train, visit a park or garden.

- Pull out your markers or colored pencils and select two or three colors you hate. Add two to four more colors to create a well-rounded color story and design around these colors.

- Think about a serviceperson you meet in your regular life, like a fast-food restaurant employee or package delivery person. Redesign their uniforms, taking into consideration their job responsibilities, weather, and logos. And you know, you should make them look a little cooler.

- Go to your local bookstore (or shop online) and hit the bargain bin. There are always some oddities in the bargain bin. Buy something fun and offbeat. This is how I discovered one of my favorite books, *Extraordinary Chickens*.

- Take a class at a junior college, community art center, or university extension program. These classes tend to be inexpensive if you're not taking them for college credit. The class doesn't have to be fashion related to get your creative juices flowing.

- Listen to a new or old favorite album. Pick a song and design and costume a music video for it, even if it's not music that usually doesn't use music videos, like opera or classical.

- Volunteer at a local event. Runway shows always need model dressers and other backstage help. Theater and opera productions always need a bit of help backstage or in wardrobe. Volunteer and get to know other people who enjoy making things. And the rush of events and shows can be very energizing and inspiring.

Mindmapping

You can mindmap before and/or after you gather your images. Pick a direction that appeals to you and start jotting down ideas. Think about time periods to explore, who your favorite artists are, where in your town the people watching is the best. Make notes on specifically where you can start your research, like the local library, somewebsite dot com, and a list of the best thrift shops in your area.

Once you've gathered your images or chosen your word, start taking notes. On what? Literally anything and everything even loosely related. Go back to the design brief and answer those questions. Let your mind wander past the answers to those questions and just keep writing and doodling. There is no bad idea at this point.

I googled "interesting words" and randomly picked syzygy without knowing what it meant just because the word aesthetically looked cool to me. When I looked it up, I got even more excited and immediately thought I could take this in a million different directions (**Figure 3.9, next page**). What can I say? I love weird words.

Don't get so angsty or precious about where your inspiration comes from; I promise you at least half of all fashion designers make up what their initial inspiration was in interviews to make themselves look cool. Be real with yourself about what actually gets your gears going.

During an interview, when asked yet again what my inspiration was, I told the journalist some wild story about a dream I had about frogs in the rain and pink clouds and smoking through my ears and then said, "KIDDING!" and she looked so disappointed I almost felt bad for joking around.

For those of you who wanted to start sketching right away, this is the time to scribble out those ideas rattling around in your head. Your brain can't generate new ideas when it's too busy trying to hold on to older ideas. Whew, if that's not a metaphor for life! But no really, I mean it literally. Declutter your brain. Draw it out. Get it out of your mind. You might return to it, but chances are, you'll have moved on to something new as you continue your design process.

quilted in a pattern not geometric — quilted organza, crepe back satin

RO+BG 2nd colorway

RV+YG — pink olive drab hunter green

ballcap covered in brooches

or double comps

knee socks, gym socks, fancy dress socks (mens)

explore merging 2 opposite garments:

1 mens military jacket + 1 womens emb. organza coat

complement any color scheme, obvi

maybe only in styling...

winter clothes? in summer fabrics

"pair of opposites united in their opposition"

but I've done a lot of that before...

lace gym shorts

category of clothes done in fabrics usually not suited

twins motif

extreme masc + femme mashup?

cotton? jersey corsets

intersex?

"humaphroditic dieties called syzygies"

athleisure in organza?

eveningwear in nylon ripstop? french terry?

Syzygy

"pair of oxen yoked together"

hauling motif? harness?

don't want to carry a bag

extravagant daywear!

"collinear configuration of 3 celestial bodies"

get a literal yoke, look @ shapes

scale?

pocket shapes

leggings, sweats, windbreakers, tees, tanks, but dramatic

3 layers of fabrics

groupings of 3

garters w/ o—o—o motif?

style lines

cording piping boning casing

tulle scrunched over cotton jersey w/ some embellishment

ruched organza over lace over btmwgt.

o — o — o

solar or lunar eclipse

sun — moon — earth

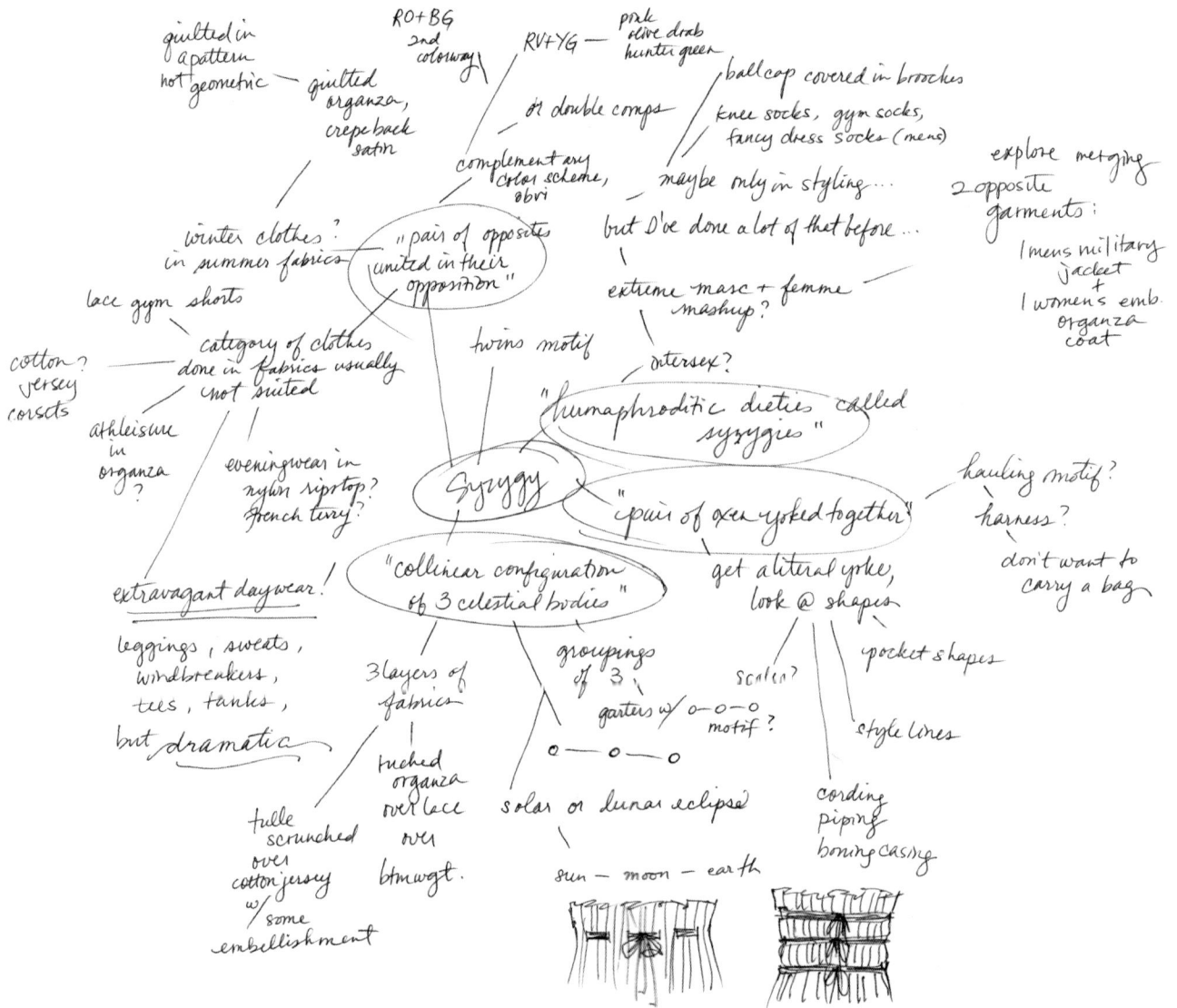

FIGURE 3.9 Syzygy can mean a lot of different things, apparently.

Gathering Inspiration Images, Research, and Sketchbook Development

Get your images together, whether it's your artist's paintings or photos of your thrifted garments. Go research past your initial inspiration, research topics you noted in your mind maps, and wander down those rabbit holes. Or you can sketch ideas from your initial inspiration mindmap.

Another thing you can do is buy something related to your inspiration to help you. I ordered a wooden oxen yoke miniature based off my initial syzygy research (**Figure 3.10**).

Start compiling your research notes and pictures in your sketchbook. You can use my Design Journal or whatever sketchbook you have.

PERFECTIONISM IS STUPID

First of all, don't worry about those perfect sketchbook pages posted on social media. Process is often messy. Perfectionism is stupid. It's so stupid, I did a whole series on my channel on how perfectionism is the opposite of progress. Perfectionism gets your panties in a twist and locks you up and doesn't allow you to try new things, make mistakes, learn from your mistakes, get over rejection, and develop a sense of humor about your work—all things you need in order to grow as a designer.

Get messy. It's literally just paper and pens. Everything is extremely low stakes right now. And yes, you can do everything digitally but just know, I'm side-eyeing you for being addicted to the CMD+Z function and not allowing yourself to actually get messy.

FIGURE 3.10 One of the definitions of syzygy is "yoked together."

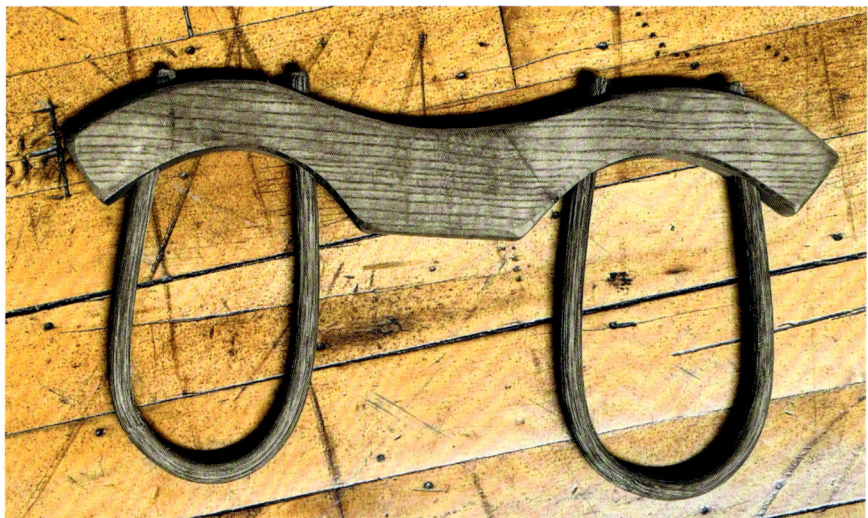

WHAT IS THE POINT OF SKETCHBOOK DEVELOPMENT?

Collaging your reference/inspiration images is all about forcing your brain to look at the images in new ways. I'm not going to literally put oxen yokes around my customers' necks.

I could give a class of 20 students the same starting point, same exact direction, same inspiration images and I would get 20 wildly different resulting collections. Everyone would take apart the images differently, put them back together again differently, compose them in the sketchbook differently, find different aspects fascinating, be inspired by different sections, and then translate them into different textures, fabrics, fabric manipulations, and shapes.

FIGURE 3.11A-C. BELOW AND RIGHT Sketchbook development collage pages from different projects.

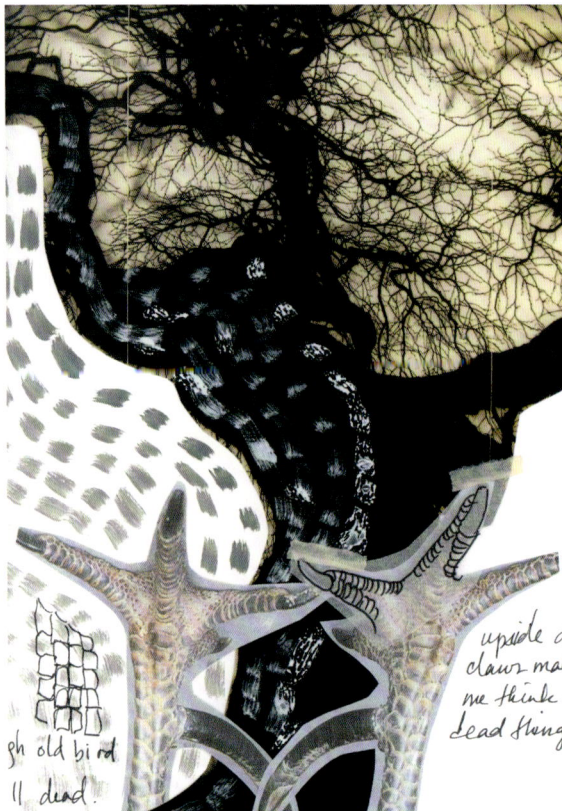

Simply staring into the void of your favorite painting will not help you.

But Zoe! I heard designers don't do this in the industry! Yeah, they don't have time to do this in the industry. A lot of what we do in the beginning serves to train you to do things much faster in the future. I cut things up and make collages in videos to show the learning process, but also to show you how I'm breaking down the image in my head. In real life, I look at an image and take it apart in my head and take some notes on what aspects I want to use. The more you practice the design process, the better you can deconstruct an image in your head, and the faster everything goes.

And feel free to revisit these pages and add/edit to your heart's content (**Figure 3.11a-g, opposite page and following pages**).

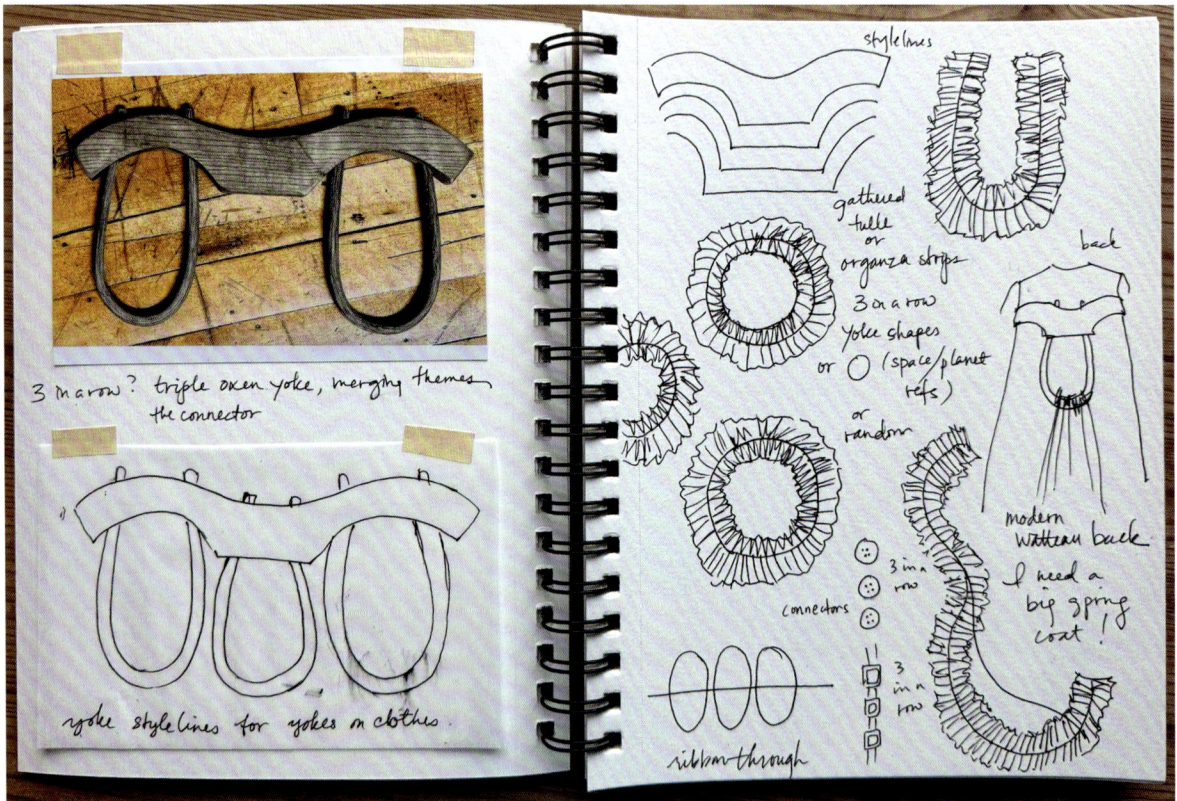

Handwritten notes on the sketches (left page):

3 in a row? triple oxen yoke, merging themes
the connector

yoke style lines for yokes on clothes.

Handwritten notes (right page):

stylelines

gathered
tulle
or
organza strips

3 in a row

yoke shapes
or ◯ (space/planet
refs)

or
random

back

modern
Watteau back

I need a
big spring
coat!

connectors

3 in a
row

3 in a
row

ribbon through

FIGURE 3.11D-G. ABOVE AND RIGHT These are some development pages I did for my Syzygy meets garment deconstruction project.

syzygy →

3 in a row!

soft
dreamy
fantasy

3 in a row!

3 tucks
in a row

watercolor tattoo over cotton lace or eyelet

3 in a
row!

3 in a
row!

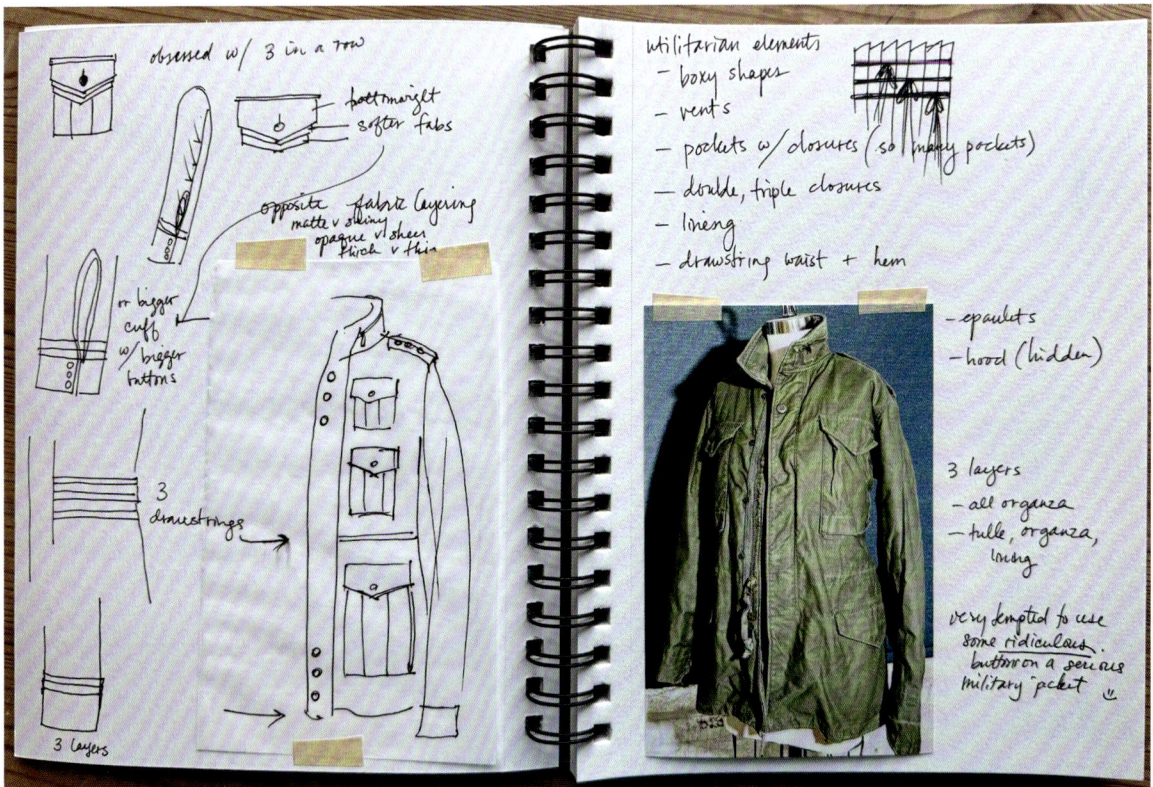

obsessed w/ 3 in a row

pott margit
softer fabs

opposite fabric layering
matte v shiny
opaque v sheer
thick v thin

or bigger
cuff
w/ bigger
buttons

3
drawstrings

3 layers

militarian elements
- boxy shapes
- vents
- pockets w/ closures (so many pockets)
- double, triple closures
- lining
- drawstring waist + hem

- epaulets
- hood (hidden)

3 layers
- all organza
- tulle, organza,
lining

very tempted to use
some ridiculous
buttons on a serious
military "pocket"

COLLAGING TECHNIQUES

Here's a list of possible techniques to get you started. Have fun!

◆ Make multiple copies of each picture. Cut them apart to focus on one section at a time.

◆ Blow up one or more of the above cut sections and add to the original picture to play with scale and layering.

◆ Take a cut-up section and lay out the multiples. Playing with repeats will start you thinking about the design of potential prints. We'll talk more about designing prints in chapter 5, but for now, play around with some initial concepts.

◆ Layer a piece of tracing paper on top and trace out interesting elements. Play with those elements. Think about those elements as silhouettes for clothes, motifs for embellishments, and shapes for sections of clothes like collars and sleeves.

◆ Layer two of the above tracings to see how the elements merge together and sketch out the results.

◆ Redraw the art with your own hand and see how your own line quality changes the look.

◆ Trace a small section of the art image. Remove the art image and freehand draw more, extending, expanding, and exploring.

Collection Planning

Fashion design sits at the intersection of art and commerce. It's necessary to think about your merchandising, which includes deciding how many pieces you'll make, which categories those garments will fall into, and how much they'll cost. Whether you're working on a portfolio project or a new brand's collection, I always advise to start small.

You'd be amazed at the short attention span of your average recruiter. Your resume has, on average, about 7 seconds to pique the interest of the recruiter, if you've passed the initial automated resume scanner most companies use. Design department managers and hiring managers are not going to sift through hundreds of sketches because you don't know how to edit. Showing you know how to edit is also a skill design directors are looking for.

For portfolios, I would recommend five to eight outfits per project, and about three to four projects. I detail portfolio project requirements in chapter 11.

Starting a company is expensive enough without investing in showcasing dozens of outfits. Very few have the funding to debut with a Fashion Week show with fifty looks. And it's not necessary. Throughout history, there have been many examples of successful brands that started with one garment or one fashion category.

Ralph Lauren started with neckties; Elsa Schiaparelli, a single trompe-l'oeil sweater; Chopova Lowena, kilts. Louis Vuitton, Hermes, Gucci, and countless others, old and new, started with one particular leather accessory. Prada was a luggage company until Miuccia Prada broke fashion with that little nylon backpack. Donna Karan became famous with her "7 Easy Pieces." Many successful intimates brands started with one great bra, one great panty. Diane Von Furstenburg had that wrap dress. Madeleine Vionnet only ever did dresses and the occasional coat. We don't think less of her because she never did a suit. Most people didn't know Tory Burch did anything other than those ballet flats for years and years. Did you know Tory Burch actually has a lot of cool shoes that are not those ballet flats?

Here are some example starter packs:

Start with five sweaters: at least three with long sleeves, include one turtleneck, one twinset, and one chunky cardigan.

Start with three amazing dresses. You might not even need three. In the early aughts, Robert Rodriguez's sheath midi dress with the sharp cowl/fold front and geometric cap sleeve was everywhere. It was *the dress* of 2003.

What's the difference between a sculpture and a dress? You gotta get a body in a dress. That's it. A dress can look like anything you could possibly imagine, you just have to figure out how to get it on a body.

Start with one beautifully tailored suit made available in a variety of prints.

Start with one amazing pair of jeans available in 2 different washes.

You get the idea.

What do you hate about shopping for jeans? Fix those problems in your future jeans.

Writing Out Your Direction

It's helpful to sum up your direction in a few focused sentences so you can refer to it when you start getting distracted by random sparkly things (**Figure. 3.12**). There are no official studies, but I'm fairly certain 73% of all fashion designers are hoarder magpies, 68% are distracted hamsters, and 31% are both.

The direction isn't about having all the design questions answered, it's about pointing your design team (or yourself) in a specific direction for research and development.

You will be adding to this direction as you put together your colors and fabrics.

FIGURE 3.12. BELOW This is going to be pinned to my corkboard, along with my Syzygy mindmap and original inspiration images.

Syzygy collection
Sp/summer
5-7 outfits
Extravagant daywear!
Themes: 2 things connected,
often opposites harmonizing
(complements)
Opposites such as gender expression,
utility, color, textures
strength in numbers
3 in a row motif

Day clothes fancier than evening
why wait for a special occasion to
look amazing

Customer: badass older women
who dress for themselves

4

COLOR

Brand Colors

Not to freak y'all out, but color is really important. Color plays a huge role in our purchasing decisions. What's the thing that catches your eye from across the street or across the store? A color you love to wear. You could try on a jacket and discover it fits great, makes you look almost amazing, all within your budget—but if it's not in the right color, you won't wear it. You might buy it, but it'll stay in the back of your closet.

Color is so key that if a fashion company has an excess in inventory of a specific colorway, sometimes they'll ship them off to get re-dyed into a new color before trying to sell them again.

Many brands are strategic in their color usage. Some have a brand color that permeates their products and packaging, like Tiffany blue, Hermes orange, and Schiaparelli shocking pink. Other brands don't have a signature color but a color palette they use so frequently it's part of their house codes. Simone Rocha uses black, white, and pink in every collection. Chanel is famous for using a lot of black and white. Thom Browne's runways are heavily grey. Christopher John Rogers splashes out a new rendition of a rainbow with every season.

As you work on your color stories, always consider your muse and customer, and what colors they will want to wear or are attracted to in an editorial sense.

> I just want to take a moment to implore all you magical, wonderful designers focused on sustainability to think in color: Your ethical, slow-fashion, upcycled, recycled, downcycled, deconstructed, reconstructed, organic clothes sewn by single moms making a livable wage can be any color you want. Sustainable clothes do not need to be a washed-out palette of dishwater greys and burlap browns. You can care about the earth in hot pink!

Color Vocabulary

Color is a subject you could study for years (and some people do!), but in lieu of that, here's a crash course on some important terms and concepts to help you pick colors for your fashion collection.

The color wheel is comprised of twelve colors (**Figure 4.2a**). You can consider the wheel the source from which you can make all other colors, except black. Black is theoretically the presence of all colors—but if you actually mix all colors, you get brown.

Every color can be defined by value, saturation, and temperature (**Figure 4.2b**). Value is the lightness or darkness of a color. Saturation is the brightness or intensity of the color. Temperature is how warm or cool the color is, which tells us the color's position on the color wheel. Blue is the coolest color. There is nothing you can add to blue that would make it cooler. When you get into greenish blues, you're adding yellow and making it warmer. When you go the opposite direction into purplish blues, you're also making it warmer by adding red. Orange, which is the direct opposite of blue, is the warmest color.

There are four main ways to desaturate colors (**Figure 4.3, next pages**).

And you can always create combos of the above (**Figure 4.4, next pages**).

Yes, this is how you create neutrals. And learning how different colors and neutrals are created helps designers reduce a lot of trial and error in creating color stories.

FIGURE 4.2A. RIGHT, TOP
The color wheel

FIGURE 4.2B. RIGHT, BELOW
VST: value, saturation, and temperature

V: medium
    (40%)
S: shade
    (+ black)
T: warm

V: light
    (30%)
S: very tinted
    (+ white)
T: cool

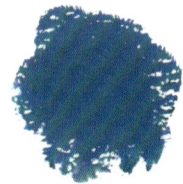

V: med-dark
    (60%)
S: subtle tone
    (+ grey)
T: cool

color + white = tint

color + black = shade

color + grey = tone

color + complement = mute

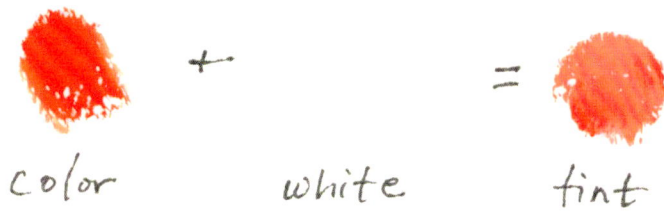

FIGURE 4.3. LEFT People use phrases like "shades of green" to mean all variations of green, but in color theory, the word "shades" has a more precise meaning.

FIGURE 4.4. BELOW Yes, we're learning color mixing 101 now.

color + complement + grey = tone of a mute

FIGURE 4.5. BELOW, LEFT
Monochromatic

FIGURE 4.6. BELOW, RIGHT
Analogous

Color stories, schemes, and palettes are all the same thing: a combination of colors put together to use in a design composition or product. I use the three terms interchangeably.

Color schemes are not hard and fast rules you have to follow. They are formulas that work and can help you create color stories for your fashion collection. The following are some of the most common color stories.

Monochromatic color schemes (**Figure 4.5**) are composed of tints, shades, and tones of a color. This is a very harmonious color story, as all the colors are similar to each other, but this is typically too narrow for a fashion collection. You want to offer your customers more options. You should offer every single garment you design in multiple colorways, except maybe some novelty, editorial piece, like a corset covered in rhinestones.

However, a monochromatic color scheme can make for an impactful presentation or portfolio illustration.

Analogous color schemes (**Figure 4.6**) are composed of two to five neighboring colors on the color wheel, and their tints, shades, and tones. They can offer the harmony of a monochromatic color scheme but with more variety.

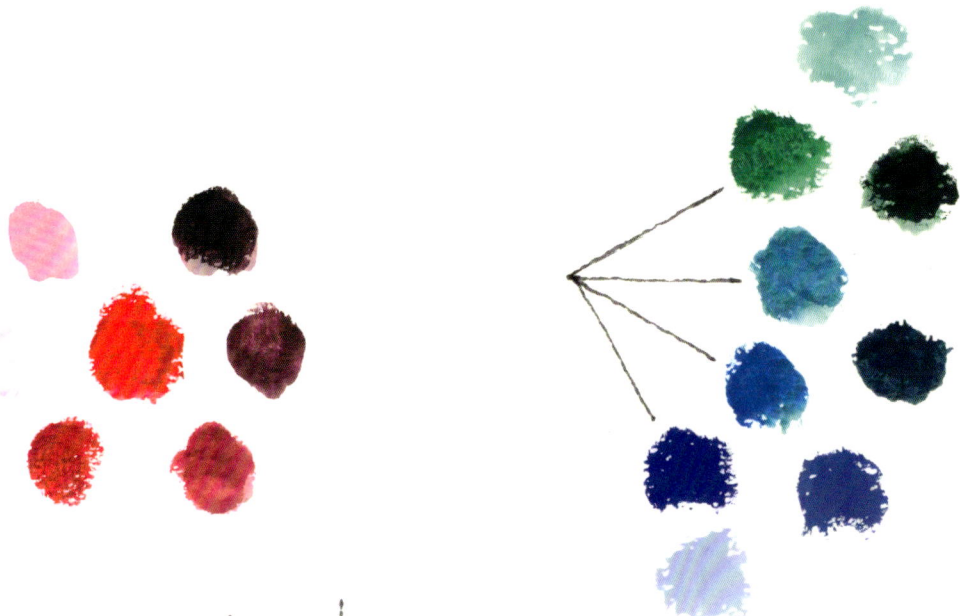

monochromatic color story

analogous
color story

complementary
color story

Split - complementary
color story

blue + orange = mute

blue + orange = near - mute

blue + orange = near - mute

FIGURE 4.7. FAR LEFT
Complementary

FIGURE 4.8. LEFT
Split-complementary at
full saturation

FIGURE 4.9. BELOW LEFT
Split-comp near-mutes,
which can include tints,
shades, and tones of near-
mutes. So many options!

FIGURE 4.10. BELOW
Triadic at full saturation
with some desaturated
options.

Complementary color schemes (**Figure 4.7**) are composed of opposites on the color wheel. The fact that they are each other's complement makes these colors pop more than any other combination, while harmonizing together. Complementary color schemes can include the tints, shades, tones, and mutes of each complement.

Compliments are nice things people say to you. Complements are two things that vibe so well that they complete each other. See what I did there? I am occasionally cringe and I'm ok with that.

Split-complementary color schemes (**Figure 4.8**) are a trio with one color and the neighbors of its complement. The complement of blue-green is red-orange, and blue-green's split complements are red and orange, the colors that sit on either side of red-orange. Complements create mutes and split-complements make near-mutes.

Split-complementary color schemes consist of the original trio, and their tints, shades, tones, and near-mutes (**Figure 4.9**).

Triadic color schemes (**Figure 4.10**) consist of three colors equidistant from each other on the color wheel, and their tints, shades, and tones. Do not include mutes or near-mutes because then you're introducing yet another color to the mix.

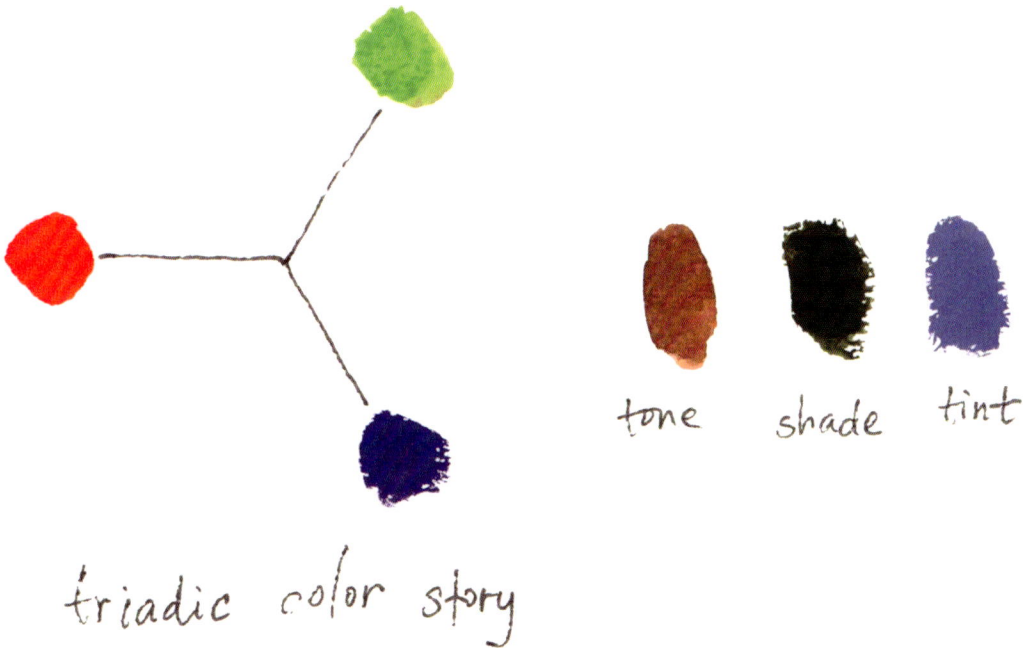

triadic color story

tone   shade   tint

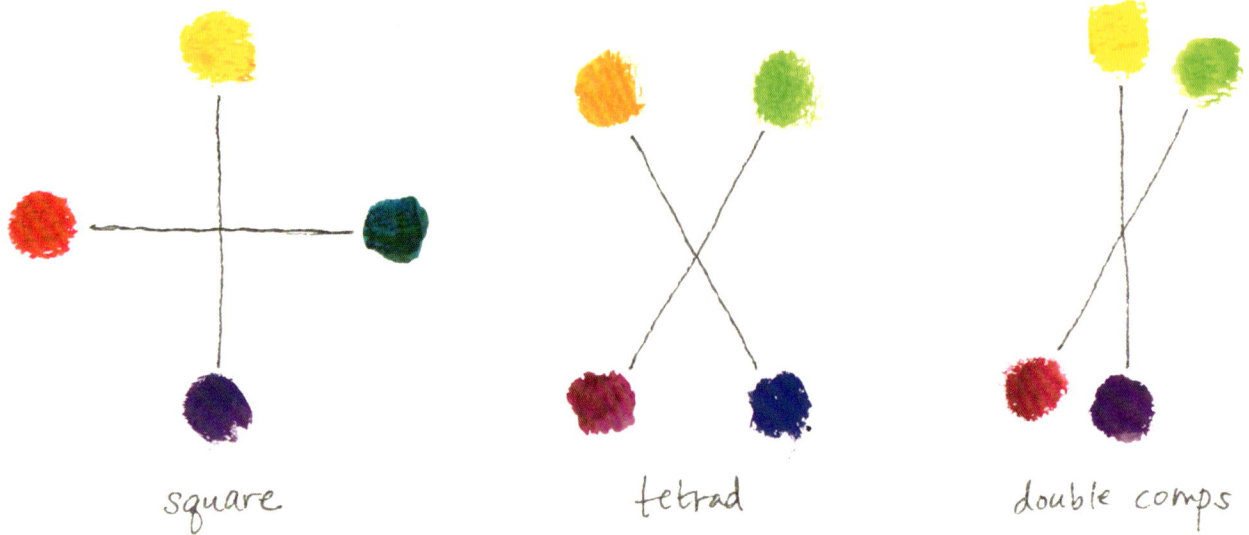

square   tetrad   double comps

If you're looking for a lot of variety, you can go for a square, tetrad, or what I call double-comps, when you use two pairs of complementary colors (**Figure 4.11**). You can use tints, shades, tones, and mutes with these four color combinations.

You can do a rainbow, I love a colorful collection, but you can give it some focus by choosing a type of rainbow. You can have a rainbow that leans towards jewel tones, or a pastels rainbow, or a fluorescent rainbow.

FIGURE 4.11. ABOVE
So many options!

FIGURE 4.12. RIGHT
Varying degrees of emphasis. What effect do you like best?

Principle of Design: Emphasis

Principles of design are taught in art schools all over the world, in curricula for all art and design disciplines, from graphic design to transportation design to fine art photography. I teach principles of design specifically as they pertain to fashion design, and I will address them individually throughout this book.

Emphasis is when you create a focal point of design using contrasts in color, texture, size, or any other element of design (**Figure 4.12**).

The principles of design are not the elements of design. The elements of design are color, value, line, shape, form, space, and texture. The principles of design include repetition, movement, rhythm, balance, unity, variety, and proportion.

When you put a circle of pearls on a black dress, your eye will zoom right to those pearls. The color and texture contrast makes that circle of pearls pop. That's an example of emphasis. You're emphasizing this embellishment by making it so different from the rest of the dress. If you put that same circle of pearls on a dress that is the same color as the pearls, the emphasis is much less strong. It will still show emphasis through texture, but much less so.

If you sprinkled these pearls evenly all over a dress of any color, there would be no emphasis because there is no focal point. (You can still have multiple points of emphasis, however. You could have two or three circles of pearls instead of just one.)

Here are some contrasts you can incorporate in your designs to create emphasis (**Figure 4.13, next page**).

DESCRIPTION	OPPOSITE	EXAMPLE
LARGE	SMALL	TIGHT BODICE WITH A BIG SKIRT
FLAT	3D	FABRIC FLOWERS VS PRINTED FABRIC
THICK	THIN	RUGBY STRIPES VS PINSTRIPES
MANY	FEW	SCATTERED BEADS VS CLUSTERS OF GEMS
SOFT	HARD	SLINKY DRESS UNDER A TAILORED JACKET
SMOOTH	ROUGH	SATIN WITH ALLIGATOR LEATHER
LIGHT	HEAVY	TULLE VS CHAINMAIL
LIGHT	DARK	WHITE BODICE WITH A DARK SKIRT
BRIGHT	MUTED	RED AND BURGUNDY, ORANGE AND BROWN
WARM	COOL	ORANGE AND BLUE, PASTEL PEACH AND SKY BLUE
TRANSPARENT	OPAQUE	CHIFFON AND SATIN
ORGANIC	GEOMETRIC	PRINT WITH FLOWERS OVER POLKA DOTS

Collection Planning: Color

If I had a dollar for every time someone asked me how many colors to have in a collection, I would be writing this book while on a flight to the Maldives.

And I know you'll hate the answer but here it is: it depends. It depends on the size of your collection, the category you're designing, and your customer.

Listen, design isn't arithmetic. 2+4 always equals 6, but designing two outfits doesn't always take exactly four colors.

First of all, do you have a customer who wants a lot of color options, or do they live in black and denim and white? Are you a colorful brand?

FIGURE 4.13. LEFT Pick a contrast, any contrast!

Second, even if someone wears a lot of color, people generally buy more colorful tops and dresses, and stick to neutrals for trousers and outerwear. Think about your category.

Third, your price point is also a factor. Most shoppers will invest in an expensive coat to wear for several winters if it's in a classic, not trendy, color.

Fourth, how old is your customer? Not to generalize, but to generalize, it's usually the very young and the very old who gravitate towards lots of bright color.

And last but not least, how big is your collection? And this is not always a factor. There are brands who show a lot of looks but keep the color story narrow.

Don't panic! I have a few exercises for you to figure out your color story.

Exercise 1: Analyzing Color Stories

Make a list of brands that you aspire to be in competition with, brands that cater to a similar customer, have a similar aesthetic vibe to yours. Back when I was in fashion school, my teachers would ask us, if Nordstrom bought your stuff, which designers would you want to hang with? Which section of Nordstrom would you fit?

From one of these brands, pick a fashion collection from which you admire the colors. Analyze the colors by answering the following questions. This will help you understand *why* you like the color stories so you can apply what you learned to future collections.

- **How many colors are used versus how many neutrals?**

- **What is the proportion of colors to neutrals used?**

These are two different questions. There could be a lot of bright colors and only two neutrals, but those two neutrals could be used for 75% of the looks.

Let's talk about wearable versus pop colors. Even bright colors can be wearable. Red is bright but popular and wearable. Lime green, not so much.

- **What's the balance of light versus dark colors? Wearable/classic versus pop colors?**

- **Do you think the colors match the fabrics?**

Maybe chartreuse looks great in a luminous silk charmeuse but cheap in a coarse linen?

◆ **Do you think the colors suit the season?**

If not, what would you change to make the colors suit the season better?

◆ **What kind of mood does the color story create?**

◆ **Do the colors elevate the designs or fight them?**

◆ **What about this collection's color story do you like or not like? What would you change?**

This analysis is also about figuring out what you gravitate toward.

Complete this analysis for at least three collections from different brands.

Exercise 2: Analyzing a Brand's Color Usage

Pick three to four fairly recent collections from one brand and analyze them, using the prompts from the previous exercise.

Compare the answers throughout the collection and note all the common threads.

◆ **What are the colors the brand uses every or almost every collection?**

These colors don't need to be identical; they can very similar, like how Simone Rocha always uses a light pink in each collection, but not always the exact same pink. She also uses olive drab of varying shades. Giambattista Valli's collections often feature different shades of red, pink, and light green.

◆ **Does the brand lean toward neutrals or colors? Wearable or pops? Light or dark?**

Most people associate The Row with neutrals, but they also love a pop or three of red in most collections. People also think of Rick Owens as heavy on black and grey, but his womenswear collections are often more colorful than you would think. He actually shows a lot of pinks.

◆ **Read reviews of the collections. Can you see the correlations between the designer's inspiration and the colors used? Do you think the colors work to express the mood the designer was going for?**

FIGURE 4.14. BELOW
Dusty rose looks slightly
different paired with dark,
medium, and light colors.

Exercise 3: Playing with Color Combinations

It's important that you not only pick a couple of great colors that express
your brand but also great companion colors. Colors actually look different
depending on what colors you put next to them (**Figure 4.14**).

Design a garment that requires two or more colors via elements like color
blocking, a print, significant embroideries or other embellishments, or
screenprint graphics. Sketch it out twice or make copies. Pick one color for
the main parts of the garment. Pick different colors for the secondary parts
of the garment. Observe how the main color changes based on what's next
to it.

What "works" depends on the effect you're going for. If you want the colors to pop, pick a contrasting color like your main color's complement (**Figure 4.15**). If you want the color blocking to create a more harmonious overall look, pick a color of similar value or temperature.

Moving into the next exercises, think about whether you want to create more harmonized looks or high-contrast looks.

FIGURE 4.15. BELOW Which color combo creates the most emphasis through contrast?

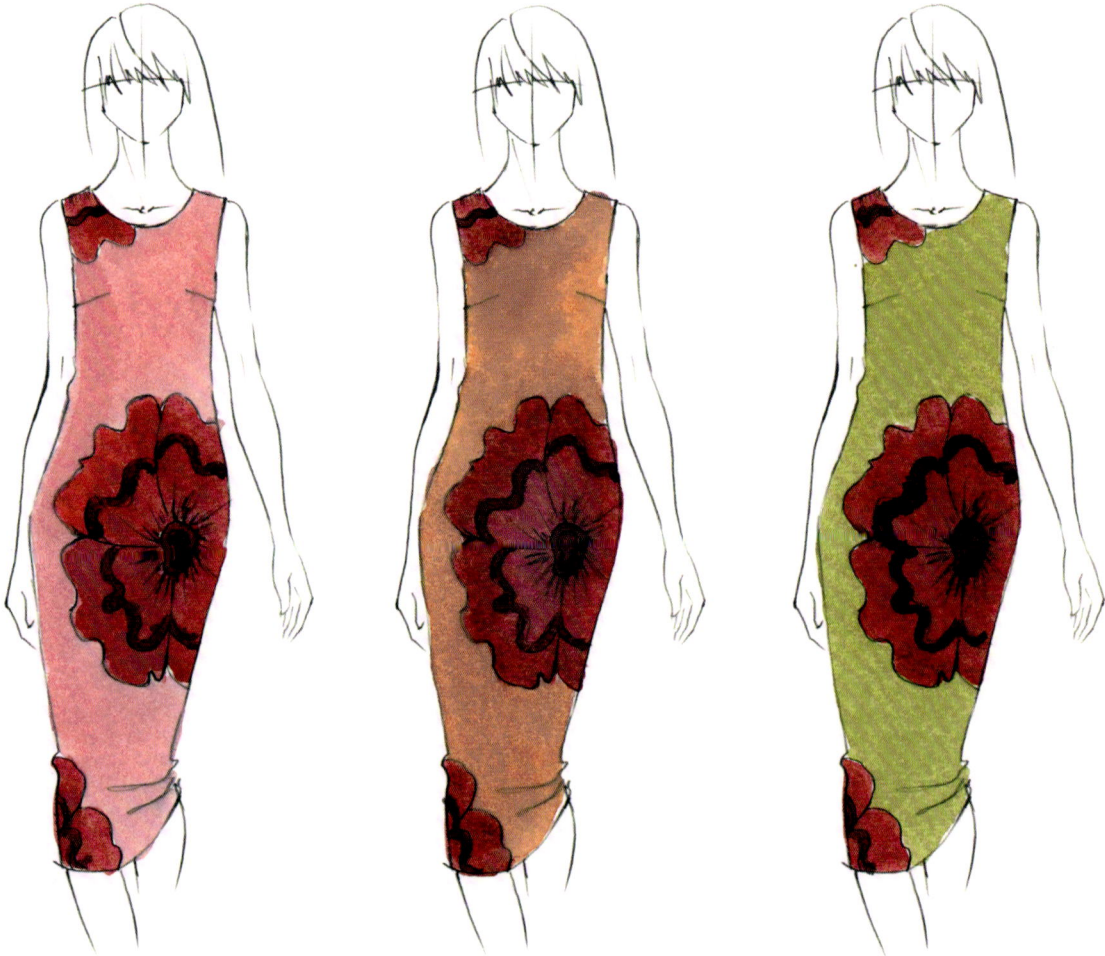

FIGURE 4.16. BELOW

Red-violet and yellow-
green. Remember when I
wrote in my mindmap that
complementary colors
were the obvious choice
for a word that means
"harmonizing opposites"?

Exercise 4: Colors from Your Inspiration

Refer back to your original inspiration to choose your colors. Do you have
to? Yes, that's the whole point of inspiration. It's supposed to inspire all the
visual aspects of your collection (**Figure 4.16**).

Look at the images and collages from your initial sketchbook and pull
all your favorite colors. Pick up to eight. Use markers or paint to make
big swatches of color. Colored pencils are slow to use but can be used in
a pinch. Or you can take your sketchbook to a paint store and get paint
chips. Cut your swatches into smaller little squares.

Use the color schemes defined earlier this chapter to create color stories.
Do at least three groupings (**Figure 4.17, next page**).

Another method is to create a deep dive color chart based off your original colors. This is especially helpful if you're new to studying color. Create
scales of tints, shades, tones, mutes, and near-mutes (**Figure 4.18, next
page**).

FIGURE 4.17. LEFT
My own color story options.
My direction practically
dictated complements, so I
stuck to exploring those.

FIGURE 4.18. BELOW
Not every color in your
collection has to be a
precise match to a color
found in your images. It's
about the general color
inspiration.

FIGURE 4.19. BELOW Use a window to isolate colors.

I have approximately 512% more markers than your average person. It can be quite thrifty and efficient to mix up a slew of colors in paints, pick your colors, and then buy markers in the precise colors you need for future renderings.

Create a color window by cutting a little square out in the middle of a folded bit of paper. I make and use these little paper windows all the time. Chances are if you ever catch me talking about a window, I'm not talking about home renovations. Move your window over your colors to pick the colors you want to use in your collection (**Figure 4.19**). Using the window helps you focus on individual colors.

Even with this exploration, your color story should still look like it relates back to your original inspiration.

Colors always look a little different depending on the texture of the fabric. At this point, I have a narrowed focus (bright and light cool pinks, black, white, and a variety of muted yellow-greens). I will shop for fabrics with these colors in mind. It's especially important for brands to source fabrics that will offer all the colors you need. You can custom dye fabrics, but do keep in mind the costs and time needed.

Exercise 5: Color Proportions

As you may have observed in earlier exercises, proportions of colors used in a collection can really change the overall mood. Using your favorite color story from the previous exercise, create three color proportions charts showing how you plan to use each color (**Figure 4.20**).

Here are some variations you can work on:

◆ Heavy on neutrals versus bright colors

◆ Heavy on light colors versus dark colors

◆ As evenly spread out as possible

◆ Three main neutrals with a lot of small pops

◆ Heavy on warm colors versus cool colors

Templates to help you organize your color exercises are available in the FSB Design Journal.

Your best color story from the previous exercise here:

most neutral + dark

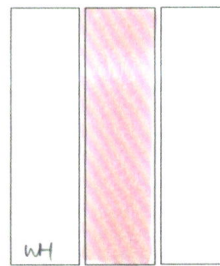

most colorful

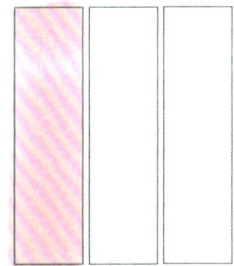

majority pink bits of greens

WHAT IS PANTONE?

Pantone is a company that provides color services for a variety of industries, including fashion. One of the key things Pantone does is provide a color indexing system. They assign numbers to colors and sell color catalogs full of these colors and their corresponding Pantone numbers. They create new colors all the time. Some brands have their own official Pantone color. Hermes (orange), Tiffany (blue), and Valentino (Pierpaolo pink) each have their own official Pantone color.

Once you've determined your color story, you can go through a Pantone color catalog and find the swatch (and its number) that's closest to it. You can go an extra step and order the fabric version of the color swatch. Colors change with texture changes.

You use this Pantone number when discussing colors with your vendors. It's far more precise to tell your dye house that you want your linen dyed Pantone number 16-2122 than "bright medium pink". You use this swatch and number as a guide to choose the right shade of pink for your trims, exact colors for your prints, and the closest shade of pink to order for zippers.

DYEING

Dyeing is done at different stages of the garment-making process for different effects.

You can dye fibers. You require different methods and different dyes for different fibers. This is also called stock dyeing.

With synthetics like polyester, the pigments are added to the polymer solution before being extruded. It looks a little like streams of colored liquid coming out of shower heads. These streams solidify and become the yarns that are woven into fabrics.

Yarn dyeing is used when you want to create patterns in the fabric in the weaving process. You use red and blue yarns to be woven into a red and blue jacquard instead of printing a red and blue design.

There's also piece dyeing. When you talk with a mill or distributer about getting a custom dyed roll of fabric, they are usually piece dyeing already woven or knit fabric. Or you can order a piece of PFD fabric and send it to the dye house of your choice.

PFD fabric is Prepared For Dyeing. PFD is also known as RFD (Ready for Dyeing). These fabrics are woven/knit, scoured, bleached, and equalized.

They don't have any dyes or finishes that could interfere with dyeing or printing.

Greige goods or greige fabric is woven and knit but not processed/prepared for dyeing. These fabrics are greige (grey/beige), not bleached white like PFDs.

PFD is Prepared For Dyeing. PDF stands for Portable Document Format and are computer files you read in Adobe Acrobat.

You can dye synthetics with a poly dye. If the fabric is 100% synthetic, it will dye the whole fabric one color. If the fabric is a synthetic/natural blend, the natural fibers stay white, creating a heathered effect. With cross dyeing, the synthetic fibers get dyed one color and the natural fibers get dyed another, which creates a multicolor heathered effect. Union dyeing dyes both synthetic and natural fibers together into one solid color.

You can also dye a garment after it's been completely sewn together. This is called garment dyeing. The garment is created using PFD fabrics. I used to know this designer who was known for making dresses out of different PFD fabrics. When she garment dyed them, the fabrics all took dyes at slightly different intensities which created a cool effect.

SUSTAINABILITY IN DYEING

Let's face it, dyeing isn't a particularly sustainable process. For one, it requires a ton of water. The process can release harmful chemicals into the water supply. But there are better, more sustainable options on the horizon that are becoming more and more widely available.

DyeCoo's carbon dioxide dyeing (CO_2 dyeing) uses no water, no process chemicals, and thus requires no wastewater treatment. It's energy efficient and saves time.

Raise your hand if you've heard me say, "Fabric technology is the future of fashion," at least three times.

Another growing arena is naturally colored cotton, instead of the original white. Yes, people are growing green cotton and brown cotton, instead of white cotton to dye later!

ColorZen uses a patented technology to treat cotton before it's dyed, which makes the dyeing process faster and uses 90% less water, 75% less energy, and 90% less chemicals.

There are new processes in which bacteria (yes, freaking bacteria!) is being used to dye fabrics. Bacterial dyes use less water. Several different companies are working on pigment producing bacteria and programming bacteria toward more sustainable dyeing means. Bacteria!

A company called Huue makes biosynthetic indigo blue for the denim industry that doesn't use petroleum, cyanide, formaldehyde, or reducing agents, eliminating a ton of water pollution.

Airdye uses dyes spread on a recyclable paper, transferring colors to textiles by heat. This method uses 90% less water and 85% less energy.

This isn't everything and more technologies are being developed every day. I'm actually hoping that dyeing technologies advance so much that this bit of info is outdated by the time you read this! Explore some options that work for you.

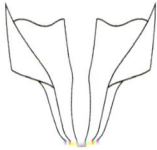

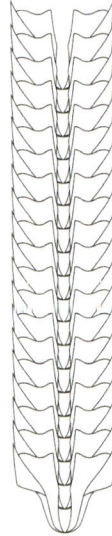

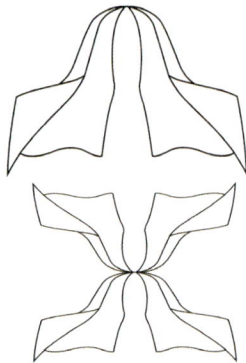

5

PRINT DEVELOPMENT AND SURFACE DESIGN

Classic Prints

FIGURE 5.1A. LEFT

Print explorations

I mean, you can hire someone to develop prints for you. Many companies have specific print designers. Freelancers abound in this category. Designers scroll Instagram looking for print designers. But in case you want to do it by yourself, or you don't have the cash to hire someone, let's go!

Friendly reminder that while I'm forced to make distinct chapters so you don't get lost, generally, color, print, and fabrics are sorted out around the same time, and decisions on one will affect another. Colors will come from the inspiration and direction; color combos and proportions will affect the print dev and vice versa; and fabric choices will be affected by the print.

Something that happens a lot, especially in print-driven or print-forward brands, is that the print(s) is developed first, and then the color story is pulled from the main colors in the print. Those colors are used for the solid color fabrics and simpler, complementary prints like stripes, plaids, and polka dots.

The Burberry plaid is a classic example of this. Many Burberry collections revolve around the original camel, black, red, and white of the classic Burberry plaid. Past collections have applied the plaid to many different fabrications and done in many sizes. The plaid has also been done in many other colorways.

Other brands have not one specific print but a category of prints as part of their house codes. Vivienne Westwood collections always feature tartans. Pucci's got their paisleys. McQueen is known for playing with houndstooth. Marimekko is known for their specific, recognizable style of graphic, simplified, colorful, often oversize florals and polka dots.

And other, other brands are not associated with specific prints but known for featuring great prints in each collection, like Dries Van Noten and Zimmermann.

Another category is monogram prints, which are used by very famous brands like Louis Vuitton, Gucci, and Dior. I wouldn't recommend using a monogram print until your brand is famous enough that people want to wear your brand name or initials all over their bodies.

Patterns That Aren't Prints

"Prints" is the term used to describe designs applied onto the surface of a fabric but there are also a lot of patterns that are woven into fabric instead. Jacquards are any pattern woven into the fabric, creating a raised surface texture in the fabric. Brocade is a type of jacquard; they're a little fancy and often feature metallic yarns. Damasks are reversible jacquards.

Any fabric in a pattern that is labeled "yarn-dyed" is also a pattern woven into the fabric. Yarn-dyed plaids are created by weaving one color of yarn going along the grain with other color yarns going along the cross grain. These are not made on jacquard looms and do not have a raised surface.

These patterns are harder to customize, as it involves the very construction of the fabric, and often requires larger minimum orders to achieve. But listen, if that's the effect you want, go for it.

Design Exercises to Develop Prints

◆ Take a slip of tracing paper, go through your inspiration images, and trace a cool section you see—the more abstract the better. Scan into Photoshop and play around with this tracing. Distort it, flip it, twist it, granulate it. Redraw in Illustrator and manipulate it, repeat it, or twirl it around. Have fun (**Figure 5.1a, shown previously**).

◆ Travel through life with a scrap of tracing paper and a soft lead pencil or colored pencil. Make rubbings of any interesting textures you come across (**Figure 5.1b**). Translate the textures into patterns.

FIGURE 5.1B. Print explorations

- Spend a couple of hours absentmindedly making marks on paper (**Figure 5.1c**). Look at your inspiration images for a while and then put them away. Play some music or watch a show that fits the vibe of your project.

- Take photos of interesting negative shapes or pull negative shapes from your inspiration and play (**Figure 5.1d**).

Image © Vincent Van Gogh

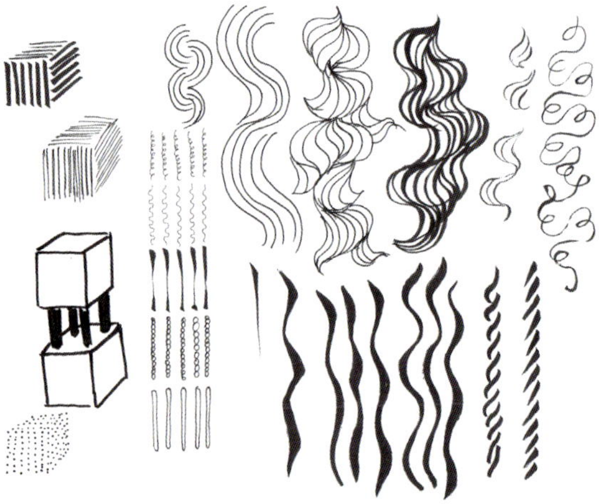

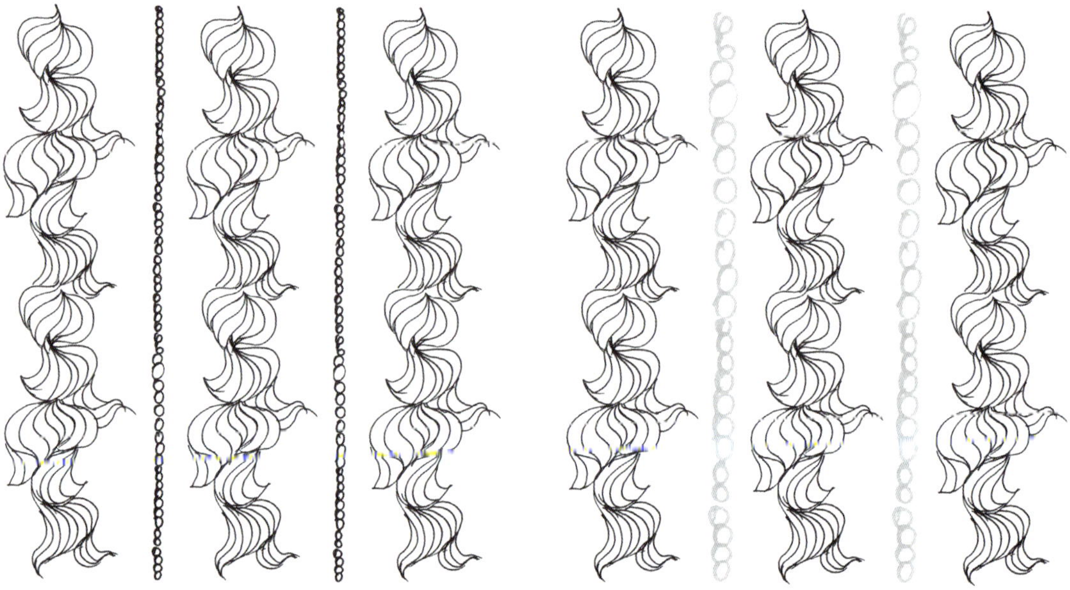

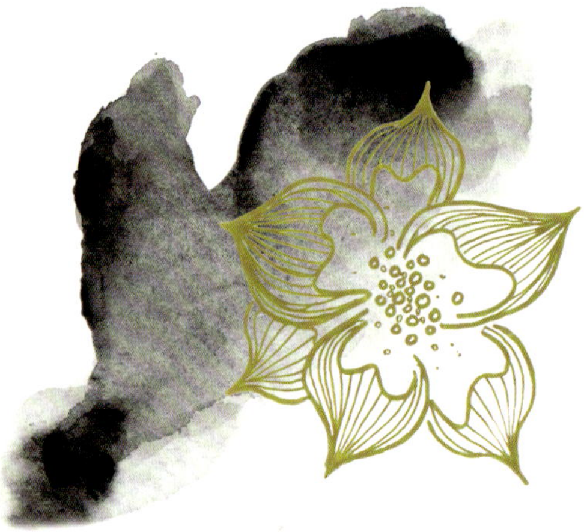

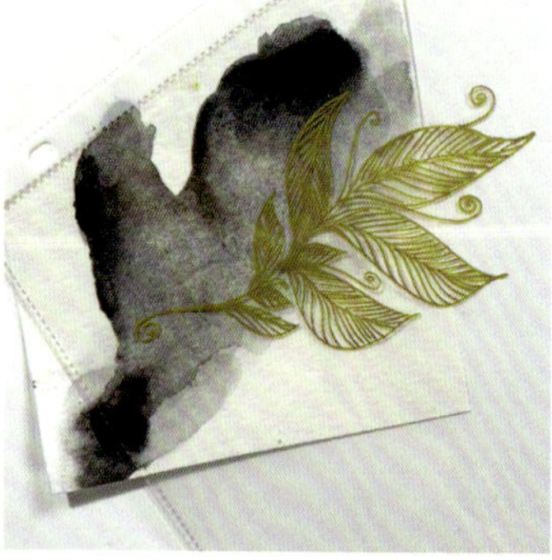

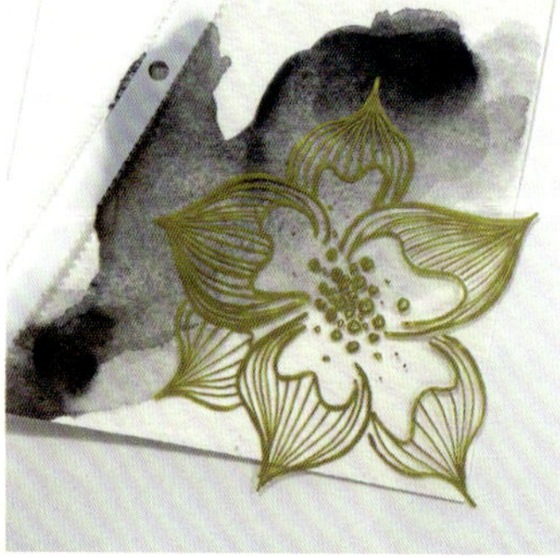

FIGURE 5.1E–G. LEFT, BELOW
Print explorations

◆ Choose one of the prints you designed and overlap it with a classic pattern like polka dots, stripes, plaid, or check. Or you can layer two of the prints you developed (**Figure 5.1e**). I like drawing on plastic page protectors and layering them on top of other illustrations (**Figure 5f**).

◆ Cut out a little shape of a dress out of cardstock. Put your cut-out in front of interesting images to see if that will inspire a print (**Figure 5.1g**). I call this the Reverse Paper Doll.

Draw out your prints precisely in Adobe Illustrator and thank me in the morning. Creating clear vector art of your design will help you copy and paste and make a million versions, revise and edit, play with repeats and directions. Above all, it will save your work in formats your fabric printer will accept.

Explore Pattern Directions

The direction of the print affects the overall look.

You can have a one-direction pattern, where the pattern only looks "correct" in one direction. Your garment pattern pieces have to be cut in all one direction in order to look right (**Figure 5.2**).

You can have a two-direction pattern, where the pattern looks "correct" in two directions. You can cut the pattern in either direction on the fabric.

You can have a four-direction pattern, which you can cut any which way on the fabric, and it gives a really different look than a two-direction pattern.

FIGURE 5.2. BELOW

Pattern directions

ONE DIRECTION

TWO DIRECTION

FOUR DIRECTION OR ALL DIRECTION

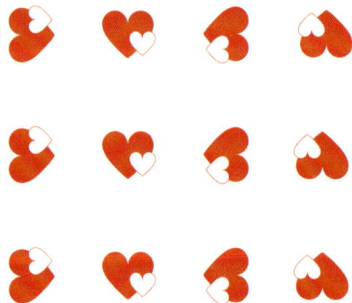

FIGURE 5.3. BELOW The most common pattern repeats

Explore Pattern Repeats

Given the same design motif, you can create a lot of different looks with different repeats. **Figure 5.3** shows some common pattern repeats.

Then think about putting a direction and a repeat together, as in **Figure 5.4, next pages**.

BLOCK REPEAT

HALF DROP REPEAT

BRICK REPEAT

ALLOVER LAYOUT

"Allover" layouts are when the design is scaled up very large so that it is printed only once per yard of fabric. The design is so large, you only see it once on a garment, making it look like a non-repeating design.

DIAMOND LAYOUT

STRIPE LAYOUT

DOT LAYOUT

HALF DROP TWO DIRECTION

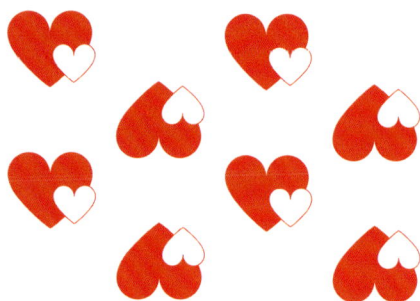

BLOCK FOUR DIRECTION

STRIPE TWO DIRECTION

BRICK TWO DIRECTION

Regardless of which repeat and layout you choose, consider how much negative space you leave in between objects. How objects are spaced greatly impacts the final print.

FIGURE 5.4. ABOVE AND OPPOSITE PAGE This is a lot easier if you took my earlier advice to draw this out in Adobe Illustrator.

HOW TO CREATE A SEAMLESS PATTERN

Sometimes you will want a print that doesn't look like an orderly repeating pattern but more complex, organic, or random.

The best way to accomplish is to design a pattern with many elements set in a square or rectangle in a block repeat. The key is to have some elements expand past the borders of the design and continue them on the other side.

On the left is the rough draft hand drawing of a print I designed many years ago. To create a seamless look, some fairies (and all background elements) are cropped and continued on the other side.

Do you see in my rough draft the edges don't match perfectly? The avoid this, draw past the edge and then copy and paste to the other side. Using this example, I should have drawn the blue hair fairy completely and copied it to the other side.

Explore Pattern Scale

Now that you have a design motif, a direction, and a repeat, you should think about the size of the pattern in relation to the body.

Use a figure template or even a photo of a person in a swimsuit and layer the pattern onto the figure in Photoshop or Illustrator (**Figure 5.5**). Sheer out the pattern if it helps you visualize.

FIGURE 5.5. BELOW Playing with scale

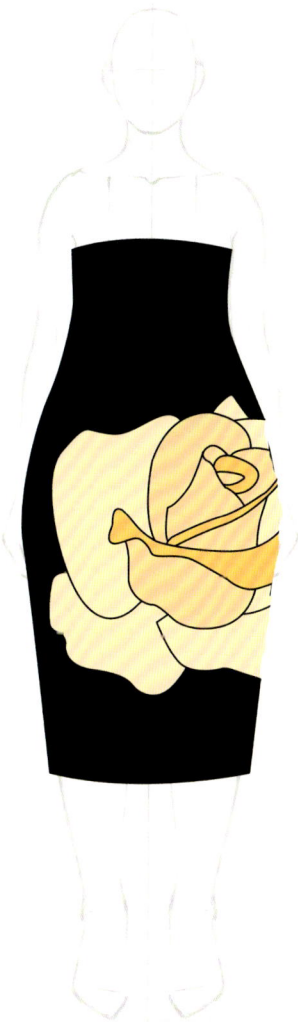

You can also have two prints that are based on the same base design. You can take the flower you designed and create a large-scale print and then create a ditsy print with itty bitty versions of the same flower.

A ditsy pattern is a print in which the design motif is very small in scale and the repeat appears scattered or random, like someone took all the teeny tiny flowers and threw them up in the air.

What Are Placement Prints?

Placement prints are when you print a design on fabric in such a way that you can place the design on the body in a particular way (**Figure 5.6**). They are also called placed prints or engineered prints.

Listen. Do we love a placed print? Of course we do. Does it waste a ton more fabric? Yes, it does. Does it mean you can never use it in a sustainable way? No. We can work around it. You can create a zero-waste pattern so the whole pattern is a big rectangle anyway. You can create a way to use the scrap. I've heard of companies that wove scrap into new fabric. You can create more geometric patterns. Find inspiration in patterns of traditional costumes, as they are often more geometric. Traditional Japanese kimono patterns are a series of rectangles, with very little wasted fabric.

Border Prints and Panel Prints

Border prints have designs printed along one or both selvedges of the fabric (**Figure 5.7**). Both borders can have the same design or different designs. The middle can be yet a different design or a solid. You can have a lot of fun playing around with a border print.

Panel prints have designs repeating in big blocks along the selvedge (**Figure 5.8**). Like placement prints and border prints, you have to be strategic in how you use them, but they can be well worth the effort.

Designing with Grainlines

This is one of those moments where it really comes in handy to understand the basics of garment construction when designing.

When you understand how grainlines work, you can design with stripes and all kinds of plaids. Most large panels of clothes need to be cut on the straight grain, but some can be cut on the bias to feature a diagonal stripe on some sections. Pockets, cuffs, button plackets, waistbands, and collars are popular spots where cutting on the cross or the bias is an option. Shirt yokes are traditionally cut on the cross grain so stripes can be horizontal or also on bias here.

See pages 232–233 for grainline diagrams.

Pattern Colors

Once you've developed a few prints you like, start applying colorways. Start with your color story and make combinations with those colors, depending on how many colors you need for your print to work.

You can also add some colors, but the bulk of your colors should remain your original color story and shades of those original colors. If your colors include red, brown, and orange, you can include a few different tints, shades, and tones of red, brown, and orange to flesh out your print while still staying true to your original color story.

Test your colorways with the scale on your figure templates again.

FIGURE 5.7. RIGHT
Border print

FIGURE 5.8. BELOW Panel prints are essentially a very large-scale pattern that takes up the entire width of the fabric.

Spin-off Embellishments

Pull elements from your finished pattern to create all kinds of other design elements for your garments. You can:

◆ Make graphics for screenprints, appliques, embroideries, beaded designs, and patches

◆ Create debossings or embossings

◆ Make the print three-dimensional, such as turning a flower print into fabric flowers

◆ Simplify the print design and turn it into a quilting pattern

◆ Use the print design as inspiration for patterns in decorative stitches like smocking

◆ Combine two or more of the above, such as beading a quilted fabric or sewing flowers onto a flower print

DEbossing is when the design is DEpressed into the fabric. EMbossing is when the design is raised like an EMbroidery.

When I was a wee baby designer over twenty years ago, I was assigned to design a print. It was the first day of my first real full-time design job right after fashion school. My boss plopped a stack of books in front of me and told me she wanted a print inspired by art deco, vintage kimono, and old psychedelic rock posters (**Figure 5.9a**).

My boss liked my fairy print so much we pulled elements for appliques and embroideries and screenprints (**Figure 5.9b-d, next pages**).

And then after all that, my boss liked the print so much we decided to do a spin-off print of bubbles that were a blend of polka dots and the bubbles I included in the original fairy print (**Figure 5.10, next pages**).

Examine your print and take notes on how to make the 2-D into 3-D (**Figure 5.11, next pages**).

FIGURE 5.9A. RIGHT

I hand drew the original fairy print, which in retrospect was bonkers and incredibly inefficient. Did I mention I was a total newb and not that fast on Illustrator yet?

eva FORTUNE SPRING I 2004 COLLECTION

FIGURE 5.9B–D. BOTTOM
Do you see how we pulled the solid colors from those used in the fairy print for a cohesive look?

FIGURE 5.10. RIGHT
I think we called this the galaxy print.

FIGURE 5.11. BOTTOM
I'm sure you can think of even more ideas than I did.

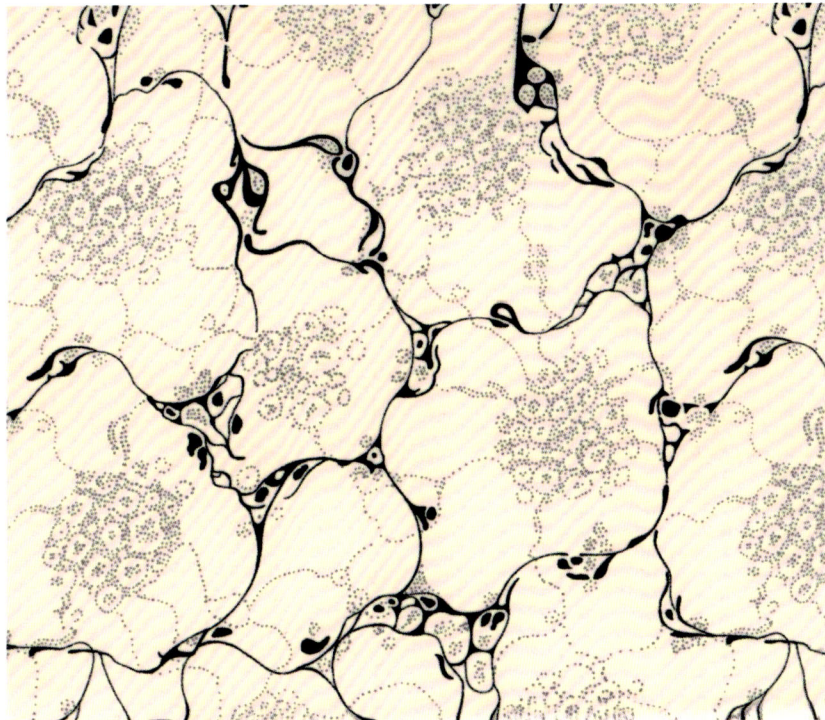

black lines OR → quilting pattern?
as beading? w/blk topstitch
(caviar beads)

silver
caviar beading?
w/feathers nestled
under beads
(everything scaled up?)

cluster of
pearls?

* embroider
blk + grey designs

Principle of Design: Pattern and Repetition

Pattern and repetition involve repeating designs in a way that entices the viewer's eye to move around the whole of the composition. Instead of having splashy beading in one section, beading is scattered across a dress so your eye looks all over the garment.

There are four kinds of repetition that you can play around with in fashion.

Repetition is taking the same thing and repeating it exactly over and over again. In fashion, this is basically print design or embellishments that are done in a repeating pattern, such as a beaded fabric.

Motif is similar to repetition in that you have several elements that are similar to each other but are not identical, and are not arranged in a precise repeating pattern.

An example of this is rows of fringe in different lengths hung all over a dress (**Figure 5.12**).

Tessellation is a type of repetition, but the shapes tile together to be perfectly interlocking. The most common tessellation in fashion is houndstooth (**Figure 5.13**).

Tiny scale houndstooth is called puppytooth! Adorbs.

Tessellation, like repetition, can be done in print design but also done in 3-D objects like beads or literal tiles.

Ambiguity is when you have a lot of different elements (they don't even have to be that similar) that follow an umbrella concept. These elements are sprayed out evenly to keep the eye moving all over the composition. Remember when Carey Mulligan went to the Oscars in that black Prada gown that had all those little sewing tools sewn all over it in a seemingly haphazard way? Classic example. A current trend is wearing over a dozen brooches scattered across a sweater. Another great example of ambiguity.

FIGURE 5.12. RIGHT
I would not be able to stop shimmying in a dress like this.

FIGURE 5.13. FAR RIGHT
See page 237 for a houndstooth rendering tutorial.

PIGSUEDE

6

FABRIC

Basic Vocabulary

FIGURE 6.1. LEFT Hangers and color cards. Cards with a big swatch of fabric and several alternate color options below used to be called headers, but are now called hangers. You can get these hangers and color cards from wholesale fabric reps.

For designers, fabric is everything. If there's one subject you can never learn enough about, it's fabric. If there's one subject you should devote all your extra time to learn more about, it's fabric. Stop asking me which marker brand is the best and go test some fabrics. Let's start with some basic vocab.

This is chapter 6, but some designers start here. Fabric guides them, inspires them, and they put together the rest of their direction and colors around a special fabric.

Fiber and **fabric** are not the same thing. To define a fabric, you need the fiber content and the construction. Sateen is a cotton fabric constructed in a satin weave. It's a cotton satin.

Fiber is like flour. Flour can make bread if you bake it, flour can make pancakes if you fry it in a pan, and flour can make doughnuts if you fry it in oil. But you can't eat spoonfuls of flour on its own without getting sick. It's not really a food by itself. I'm pretty sure it's the reason you're not supposed to eat big spoonfuls of raw cookie dough. You have to do something with it. Same with silk. You can have endless tangles of silk strands, but they won't do you any good until you weave them into chiffons or knit them into silk jerseys.

There are several categories of fibers.

119

Cellulosic fibers are from plants, such as cotton, hemp, flax, linen, jute, and ramie.

You can find organic versions of these cellulosic fibers, meaning the plants were grown using more sustainable farming practices such as specific pesticide use and crop rotation.

Rayon/viscose fabrics are made from wood or bamboo and are categorized as manufactured cellulosic fiber fabrics because of their highly chemical processes. Companies are currently developing new, less toxic processes to make rayon and rayon-like fibers more sustainable. These fibers include lyocell and modal.

You can't get high from wearing hemp. This is no lingering THC on the surface of hemp fabrics that will soak into your skin to get you high. There is no THC powder that sloughs off the surface of hemp for you to inhale and get high. I'm sure if someone wanted to, they could develop such fabrics, in a region where that's legally allowed, and market it and sell it at a premium. But no one is getting you high for free. No one is selling you regular, ordinary, untreated hemp to sneakily get you high.

Manmade/manufactured/synthetic fibers are petroleum products: polyester, nylon, acrylic, acetate.

There are blends too, created to optimize the pros and reduce the cons of each fiber. A cotton poly blend is cotton fibers wrapped around a long polyester filament fiber. The soft feel of cotton is next to your skin, while the polyester makes the fabric stronger and cheaper. However, the polyester also reduces the breathability of the fabric and makes the fabric harder to recycle.

Synthetic fibers can be recycled, but it's a complicated process. It's debatable whether or not the efforts are worth it. Separating blends for recycling is even more difficult. Technology on recycling synthetics is ever-changing so it's hard to write something definitive here. I recommend you look up options yourself.

Adding stretch to a fabric might make it easier to fit and to wear but be careful how much elastane you add. Any more than 5% elastane makes a fabric no longer biodegradable.

P.S. Spandex and elastane are the same thing. People in the US usually use the term spandex and Europeans usually use the term elastane. Lycra is a brand name for spandex.

Protein/animal fibers are from animals: wool, silk, cashmere, vicuna, mohair, alpaca.

Animal hides are not in the fibers category because the hide is being used whole, not broken apart and woven or knit to create the fabric. This category includes furs, leather, suede, and shearling. Shearling is when the hide has a finished leather or suede on one side and some form of hairs or fur on the other.

Fabrics made by weaving strips of leather together exist, but that is a new and different material entirely. That is more of a fabric manipulation created with leather.

Common animal hides include cow, goat, pig, and lamb. Cowskins are very large, and the texture and drape differ greatly depending on where on the animal the skin is from. Cow plonge is from the belly of the animal and usually much softer than regular cowskin. Exotic animal hides like snake and alligator are most often lambskin embossed with the textures of exotic animals. Yes, accessories made from these embossed lambskins are stamped with the words "genuine leather" because technically lambskin is still genuine leather. Some animals like pig and goat are more often used for suedes, not leathers.

The debate on the sustainability of leather rages on and entire books are written on it. I can't go over everything here, but I do want to touch on chrome versus vegetable tanning.

Tanning is the process of turning raw skin into a leather ready to cut and sew. Chrome tanning uses a lot of chemicals, creates toxic wastewater, and the resulting leather doesn't wear as well or last as long as vegetable tanned leathers. Vegetable tanning results in a more natural look, creates a more durable leather, and the process is more eco-friendly. Vegetable tanning is more expensive, however.

There's no beating around the bush when it comes to fur. Real fur kills animals and faux fur kills the planet with further use of plastics. Technology developing faux fur from organic sources is in its very early research and development stages! I am always low key looking for more news on this.

Nonwovens are neither woven, knit, or organically grown like hides. This is a catchall category that includes materials like PVC, which is plastic that is melted and formed into sheets, and felt, which consists of fibers that are swirled around and matted.

I'm not sure where to place faux leathers. Marketing companies would probably like me to put them in the animal hides category, as they are made to mimic leathers as much as possible, but they are technically in the nonwoven category.

Speaking of marketing, let's touch on purchasing faux leathers. Companies are applying the label "vegan leather" to anything that is leather-like. Many of these materials are straight up plastics (any material whose name starts with "poly," like polyester and polyurethane). However, a new category of leather-type materials made from plants is emerging. This category includes materials made from mushrooms, pineapple harvest waste, cacti, or fruit peels. Be careful when you see the label "vegan leather" and double check the material content.

All the above types of materials can make a multitude of different fabrics in a variety of weights, and levels of softness and opacity. Almost all types of materials can be suitable for any season, depending on the construction and weight.

Bottomweights are fabrics that are heavy enough to make pants, skirts, and jackets.

Topweights are fabrics that are light enough to make shirts and blouses.

Dressweights are fabrics appropriate for dresses. I find this term a little loosey goosey, since you can make dresses out of denim and out of chiffon.

Novelty fabrics are those special, often expensive, often embellished fabrics that are only used for a few pieces in a collection. These can be any weight, from any fiber category.

There are no specific weights for what constitutes a bottomweight because that depends on the season you're designing, and possibly the region's climate, if you're focused on a product for a very specific customer or activity. A winter denim for LA is a lot lighter than a winter denim for Amsterdam.

Learning About Fabrics

Nothing beats touching real fabrics when trying to learn fabrics. You can read fabric books with pictures and descriptions of fabrics. You can buy swatch books with the swatches labeled. See the bibliography in the back for my recommendations. No sponsored content here. I'm sure my publisher wishes someone else footed the bill for my advance but nope, we're just out here raw-dogging life and paying for stuff by ourselves.

Something I recommend to everyone is to hit a fabric store. Read the info on the ends of the rolls and feel the fabrics. Pull some out, pick it up with two fingers to see if the fabric drapes smoothly or is stiff and crinkly. Feel the surface.

Test for give/stretch. Does it stretch along the selvedge, along the cross grain, and/or the bias? Is this because there's a percentage of spandex in the fabric or because it's a loose weave or knit?

Compare polyester chiffons, taffetas, and satins side by side with silk chiffons and satins. Polyesters tend to be shinier, while silks are more softly luminous. Polyesters tend to be stiffer in drape.

Check out the cut edge. Does it fray/unravel easily? Don't pull too many yarns out. That's just damaging product that doesn't belong to you.

Think about what kinds of things you can make with the fabric. Is it heavy enough for coats? Or great for slinky evening gowns?

> *The right side of the fabric is whatever side you want to use. Most fabrics have an obvious right side, like prints, velvet, and anything shiny. Always swatch the fabric for your swatch card, pattern card, and tech packs, with a special note on which side you're using for the right side. With some fabrics, this is especially important. Crepe-backed satin can just as easily be satin-backed crepe.*

Exercise to Analyze Fabric Stories

Pick a fashion collection in which you admire the fabrics. For best results, choose a collection that's the second most recent so you can examine the collection both on the runway and in stores. Analyze the fabrics and put them in categories. Answer the questions below to help you in your analysis, but also take notes on anything of special interest to you.

Don't pick huge brands who put eighty looks on the runway each season. Their fabric usage is not relatable to you right now.

First, check out the collection on the runway.

1. How many looks are in the collection? How many bottomweights are being used? How many topweights? How many dressweights or novelties? Identify as many as you can, even if your notes read, "very

soft-looking fuzzy knit?" or "white suiting that's a little shiny." You'll learn more as you study, but quite frankly, the best way to identify fabrics is to look at them up close and touch them. Don't feel bad if you can't tell what something is precisely from a runway photo. And you can also tell your fabric sales rep you're looking for suiting for blazers that's a little bit shiny.

2. How many colors does each fabric come in?

3. Are any fabrics used in an unexpected way? What do I mean? Anything that makes you think, "Hey, that was unexpected. I didn't know you could/should/were able to do that!"

4. Do any fabrics show special techniques such as laser cutting, allover embroideries, beading, or special finishes? Describe as best you can, even if you don't know the precise techniques or what they're called.

5. What is the ratio of special developed/embellished fabrics to plain/ simple/right off-the-roll fabrics being used?

Next, look for the collection in stores. Look at the brand's website, look them up under the Google Shopping tab to find where else they are selling, and look up those listings. You will find more information on colors available and fiber content. If possible, try to find some pieces in stores and feel the fabrics. Keep adding what you learn to the questions above.

Exercise to Analyze a Brand's Fabric Usage

Pick three recent collections all from one brand and analyze them like the previous exercise. Make note of frequently used fabrics, again, even if you can only identify it as "slightly shiny suiting." Maybe you will find they consistently use this SSS.

Remember to pick a smaller brand that produces smaller collections. These exercises can get unwieldly with too many looks.

Do these exercises with different brands that you admire, that you aspire to be your competition, to get a feel for a framework of fabric usage. This is helpful, too, if you decide to start a brand in a single garment category, like knit sweaters or jackets.

FIGURE 6.2. BELOW

Picking Your Fabrics

Pull textures from your inspiration images (you can see mine in **Figure 6.2**). Make notes on what kinds of garments you're designing and what season you're designing. If you're doing coats, swatch a few options. If you know you want to do blouses, think about what a good winter blouse fabric would be versus a summer blouse fabric. Note what your customer loves and hates to wear.

Also note which fabrics get a print and which fabrics get which colors. I'm probably not going to print a wool Melton coat fabric, as the fuzzy texture would interrupt the print, but I could possibly print a silk charmeuse for my dresses. Someone else might love a fuzzy effect on their print. Now I'm thinking about how a print could look printed on a fuzzy wool. Hmm…

cotton lace
silk organzas
linen (bottomweight)
silk crepe
cotton twill (bottomweight)
eyelet
10oz denim
4 ply silk crepe
silk charmeuse (about 16mm)
cotton laces
tulles

Every single garment you design should be made available in multiple colorways, except possibly a very special novelty, like an allover beading. You're not going to pour all that time, money, and effort into the product development of a jacket just for it not to sell because no one liked that shade of green you picked. Also offer it in a neutral like black or white, and a more popular brighter color like red or pink. Of course, what works depends on the garment. Many people like pink tops, but pink pants are more niche. When you shop for fabrics, make sure they come in all the colors you need.

Brands have a lot of other considerations in choosing fabrics such as cost, country of origin (shipping logistics and taxes), MOQ (minimum order quantities), and customization options. Make sure you address these concerns with your fabric sales reps.

Not every fabric needs to stand alone. Think about how you can layer fabrics for either structural reasons or purely aesthetic reasons.

Underlining is not the same thing as lining. When you line a coat, you make the coat shell (outside fabric) out of one fabric, and then you make the coat lining in another fabric, and then sew the shell and lining together. When you draft a pattern for this coat, the pattern pieces are all different.

When you underline a coat, you cut out the same pattern pieces of two different fabrics and stitch them together so the two layers of fabric function as one piece of fabric. Then the coat is sewn together. After that, you might want a separate lining to sit under those layers for either warmth, structure, or a clean interior.

Think about making a lace coat. Most laces don't have enough structure and warmth to make a proper coat, but you could underline the coat with a more suitable coat material like a tweed. Tweed can be scratchy, so maybe you line the whole thing with a Bemberg.

You can also think about underlining purely for the look. Whatever coat fabric you layer under the lace will affect the overall look (**Figure 6.3**). You don't have to stop there. You could stitch through both layers with a contrast thread that picks up the color of the coat fabric and highlights the shape of the flowers in the lace.

You could layer tulle on top of wool suiting, scrunching the tulle strategically. You could layer net over French terry, stitching the two together with little bar tacks. You could cut up a fabric and apply it to another fabric, like stitching leather strips onto denim.

Consider how to create your own fabric by knitting or weaving something other than threads or yarn, such as ribbon, elastics, zippers, bungee cords, leather strips, zip ties, wires, or strands of candy (**Figure 6.4**).

Finalizing Your Fabric Story

How many fabrics you need depends entirely on what you're designing. If you're designing an eight-outfit collection for your portfolio, you'll want approximately three to four topweights, two to three bottomweights, and a novelty. You never want to use a fabric only one time in a collection this size, even your novelty (**Figure 6.5, next page**).

This is just a guideline. Please remember that a lot of design is preference, aesthetic, and gut instinct, with only a dash of math. If your style is layered maximalism, you're probably going to need a lot more fabrics.

If you're designing a spring/summer collection, you could have a couple of dressweights that work for tops, dresses, and jackets. If you're designing a fall/winter collection, you might want to add a heavy-duty coatweight fabric.

When people contact me about starting a brand, I always recommend that they start small. That can mean a single garment category like jeans, or a focus on a type of fabric, like chunky cut-and-sew knit sweaters and dresses.

FIGURE 6.5 Bottomweights: heavy linen and cotton twill. Topweights/dressweights: organza, 4-ply crepe, charmeuse, and cotton lace. Tulle to be used for appliques/trim only.

Sourcing For Portfolios

If you're making a project for a portfolio, you should acquire enough fabric to cut up into multiple good-sized swatches and make some fabric manipulation samples. You can seek out retail stores or jobbers. Jobbers buy leftovers, in bulk, from design houses, mills, distributers, or anyone who is looking to offload excess inventory, and then sell them to you. Some jobbers will even label the fabrics with the designer they got it from. I wouldn't use something instantly recognizable. As a designer, I want to source solid color fabrics and design my own prints. An exception would be classic patterns, such as tweeds or tartans.

Sourcing For Brands

Almost every designer I know who has started a brand has had that moment when they realize they can order anything they see at the tradeshow and go nuts. They get distracted by every shiny bauble. They order sample yardage of fabrics too expensive for their price point, or fabrics that make no sense for their brand, leading to the stages of grief once they get back to the office.

Shock: I can't believe I did this!

Anger: Why did I do this?

Denial: I didn't do this. There must have been some mistake that has nothing to do with me. I must have done my cost sheets wrong. I can definitely afford these fabrics.

Acceptance: We either create the weirdest collection ever or put together a Wall of Shame for the office so we never do this again.

Let's get organized. We've done some studying, some design research, some mindmapping, some messing around. Now it's time to buckle down and make some decisions.

You need to do a preliminary cost sheet so you can determine what price range of fabrics you can afford for your brand's price point. Imagine a baseline project and write out some basics.

Let's say you want to make women's coveralls that are utilitarian but still cute. We start with the price you want your coveralls to sell. Pretend you want to go wholesale. Let's pretend you're aiming for your coveralls to cost $300 in stores to individual customers. Standard retail markup is 2.2, which means the store buys your coveralls, multiples your wholesale price 2.2x to get their retail price.

If your goal is $300 coveralls, your wholesale price has to be 300/2.2=$136.

You also have to make money, so you should aim for the cost of the garment to be around half your wholesale price, which is $68.

Now, this is a very loose ratio, but you want to think about one-third of your cost for materials, one-third for garment labor, and one-third for miscellaneous (taxes, overhead, shipping, etc.).

Now you have about $23 for your materials. Yay, $23/yd is a lot of money! But, no. What do you need for your coveralls? The self fabric. Maybe not lining, but definitely a pocketing. Some kind of closure like zippers or snaps. Zippers are surprisingly expensive. Interfacing to structure collars and cuffs. Do you want an elastic or drawstring waistband? So now maybe you have $13 left for fabric. Coveralls will require more yardage per unit than, say, a bikini. You may need anywhere from two-four yards, depending on the silhouette you're designing and the width of the fabric. Incorporate that into your math. Now you have a very general starting point for the price range of the fabrics you need to source.

I cannot stress enough how loosey goosey this math is and how it's purely so you can have some pricing/costing framework to start from. You should absolutely do a real cost sheet with real prices, shipping costs, taxes, etc.

FIGURE 6.6. RIGHT Most companies continue to sell the same fabrics season after season, excluding special prints and novelties, so it's important to keep track of swatches for possible future use.

At this point, you've come far enough in the design process that you have a good idea of what you're looking for and what price range you should stick to. Now you need to know where to get your materials.

Once you've started sourcing, keep track of your fabrics and related information for this collection and future collections. Here's a swatch card template to help you (**Figure 6.6**).

TRADESHOWS

For the fashion industry, there are two types of tradeshows. One type is for sourcing fabrics, trim, and production facilities; the other is for sales reps to sell clothes and accessories to wholesale buyers. Some, like the Magic show in Vegas and New York, do both.

I always recommend that new brands attend fabric tradeshows. You do need credentials, like a business license, to attend them, but you can check out multiple sources at the same time, get a feel for the variety available, practice talking to vendors, collect swatches and color cards, and compare prices. There are tradeshows all over the world, all year long. Do a quick online search for something local before investing in a major trip to attend something big like Magic or Première Vision.

Mills make fabric. When you buy directly from a mill, the price might be lower but the minimums will generally be higher.

Converters buy greige goods from mills and "finish" them. This can mean dyeing, printing, or adding waterproofing, to name a few options.

Importers do just that: they import fabrics so you don't have to deal with the shipping and taxes headache. They stock them in a more local warehouse and create in-stock programs for designers to shop from.

All three of the above can set up booths at textile tradeshows with sample yardage, rows and rows of hangers, and color cards. A hanger is a folded card with a large swatch hanging from it. The card will include pertinent ordering information as well as smaller swatches of different available colors. Color cards include small swatches of every available colorway and are usually made for fabrics that come in many colors, such as linings. You can ask for hangers and color cards but expect to pay a small fee.

fabric name:
fiber content:
description:

width:
vendor:
price & date:
colors:
notes:

fabric name:
fiber content:
description:

width:
vendor:
price & date:
colors:
notes:

fabric name:
fiber content:
description:

width:
vendor:
price & date:
colors:
notes:

Jobbers do not show at tradeshows; they run brick-and-mortar shops and/or online stores. The infamous Mood Fabrics is a jobber. As mentioned above, jobbers buy cast-offs and sell them to individual shoppers. You do not need a business license to shop at a jobber. I do not recommend using a jobber for business except for a few use cases. Jobbers are great places to window shop and get some quarter yards to play with. Take these pieces to fabric sales reps to give them examples of what you're looking for. A picture's worth a thousand words and a swatch is worth two thousand.

Jobbers generally can't restock, but they will likely have several sources for basics like muslin, plain cotton fabrics in common colors, black silk crepe, things like that. Jobbers are also great when you want to buy some cheap fabric and experiment. What's the difference between messing around and conducting a science experiment? It's science when you write things down! Experiment and catalog your results for future reference.

QUESTIONS TO ASK FABRIC SALES REPS

◆ What is the MOQ (minimum order quantity)?

◆ How wide is the fabric? This will factor hugely in how much yardage you'll need.

◆ What colors are available? If your color isn't available, ask them if they custom dye or sell PFD goods.

◆ Where do the fabrics ship from?

◆ Do they have an in-stock program? Some companies keep certain fabrics and colors in stock. These fabrics will often have zero or very low MOQs and are generally readily available to ship to you.

◆ If not, what's the turnaround time for made to order fabrics?

DEADSTOCK

Deadstock is fabric inventory that no one wants anymore. Deadstock can come from the fabric mills that made it, the converter who finished it, or the designer who ordered it once upon a time and never used it. People started selling deadstock to individuals and smaller brands. Deadstock was once considered a great sustainable alternative to using resources to create more new things. There are rumors that not all deadstock is actually deadstock—some companies have been discovered to be deliberately over-producing so they can sell to the deadstock market. You have been warned; buyer beware.

beaded ribcage
crinoline cage
w/ many sheer
open front skirts
worn w/ panties
garterbelt
thigh highs

7

DRAWING, DRAPING, AND EARLY DESIGN

Is It Time to Sketch Yet?

Yes! Are you excited? Gold stars for every student who patiently slogged through six chapters without skipping ahead.

Set up your workspace! Have your inspiration images, colors, fabrics, and prints in front of you so you are designing with these elements constantly reminding your brain. I don't know about you, but I'm a little bit of an "out of sight, out of mind" sort of person, so I find this design board or sketch-book very helpful.

Have fun. Brainstorm, jot everything down, even if it's a section of a gar-ment. No bad ideas at this stage; you can edit later. Refer back to your sketchbook development for ideas on shapes to use.

Use a figure template or flat template for efficiency (**Figure 7.1**). Designers don't have time to resketch the whole body every time they have a good idea. Using templates help you work on consistent proportions in relation to the body, in relation to other designs you sketch, in relation to other parts of the garment.

I like to pick figures that relate to what I'm designing. I use plus-size figures if I'm designing plus. If I'm designing activewear, I like to use figures in action poses, like legs akimbo or walking poses. Walking poses are overall my favorite because it forces you to think about how your clothes will look and feel in motion. I like using larger templates to design intimates and swimwear. My Design Journal has plenty of templates for you to play with.

Can't Sketch?

I mean, most people can, with some practice. But if you're feeling stuck, try drawing flats, which are often easier to draw than clothes on bodies. You don't have to worry about drape lines and wrinkles. Flats are supposed to be drawn as if you laid down a garment on a table as flatly as possible. The only drape lines you add should be related to construction like gathers and ruffles. I encourage you to use a ruler to get your lines and angles accurate (**Figure 7.2**).

Designing on flats is actually really great because it forces you to create visual interest through some other means, like texture, print, or embellishment. When the drawing is boring, you have to make the design interesting!

In the industry, flats are done in Adobe Illustrator and added to tech packs in the product development process. They are the technical drawings of clothes, and the correct proportion of sleeve to bodice and the correct spacing of buttons are far, far more important than line quality or how the blouse falls on the body. Again, use a template to help you.

Hate Paper?

Some people are really good at digital drawing but are not good at paper and pencil. Try sketching on a tablet. Gotta love that undo button, am I right? No. In a perfect world, I would allot a certain number of undos per drawing to prevent students from relying too much on it and get used to committing to a line. But I digress.

Don't draw flats in Procreate. Procreate creates raster files like Photoshop, not vector files like Illustrator. Flats should always be drawn in a vector format. Did you ever notice you can blow up a pen tool line drawing in Illustrator and it stays sharp and crisp? You want that. Drawings blown up in Photoshop eventually get fuzzy depending on the dots per inch.

FIGURE 7.2. RIGHT An outfit on a body and the same outfit as flats.

leather patch

cotton gauze sweater

extra layer
(not seamed piece)

leather bandeau
bra corset

linen mini
w/ leather suspenders

bones @ bust,
ss, cb

ss railroad zip

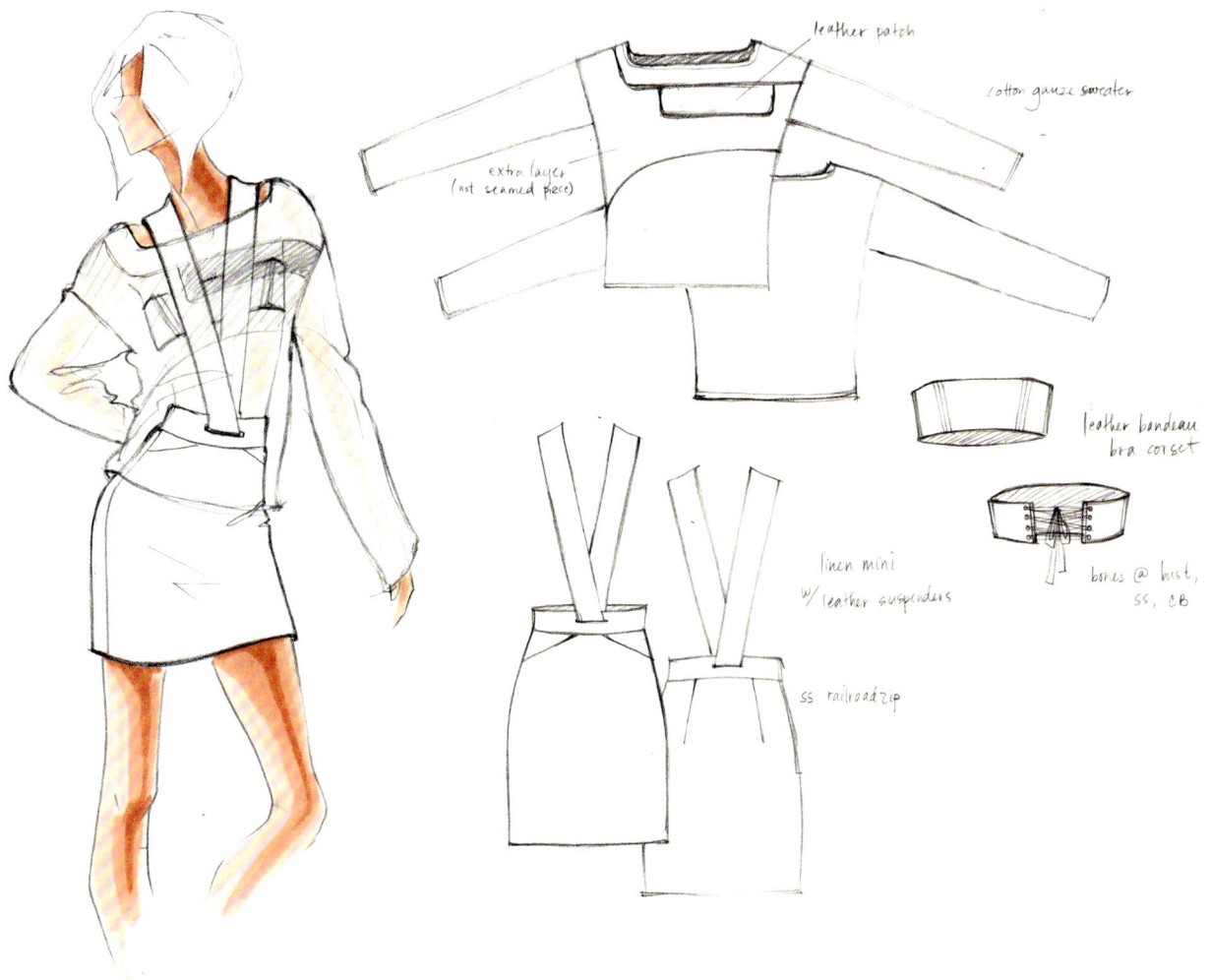

Principle of Design: Proportion

Proportion is a simple concept but worth mentioning. Proportion has its absolute claws in everything.

Proportion is not size, it's the size of something in relation to another thing. This translates to a lot of different design considerations in fashion.

Proportion can mean the general boxiness of a coat or dress in relation to the body. Proportions can mean where the waist sits on a dress, creating a 50/50 proportion versus an 80/20 proportion (**Figure 7.3, next page**). One of the key reasons I recommend designing on a figure or flats template is I want you to design with the body in mind, always.

Proportion means the size of the sleeves compared to the bodice. How does the vibe of the dress change when you go from little flutter sleeves to long sleeves? Think about how the whole dress can change when you change the proportion of the collar (even if it's the same shape!) or the scale of buttons on a blouse or jacket.

Proportion can mean the amount of embellishment on a garment, too. How does the overall look change when you encrust an entire dress in crystals as opposed to sprinkling a few crystals all over? What happens when you choose large gems over tiny seed pearls?

As you design, remember: a new design doesn't mean a whole new idea from scratch. You can and *should* rework the same dress several times, exploring different proportions.

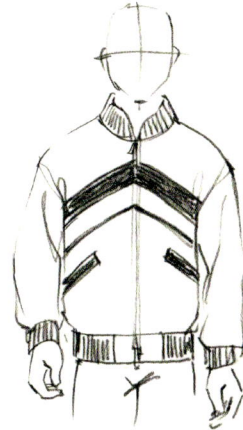

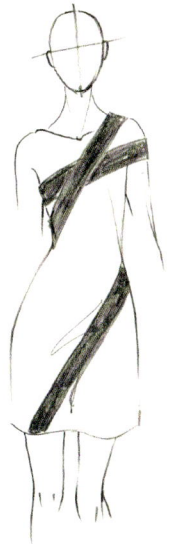

FIGURE 7.4. ABOVE This was a random boat I rode in Japan. I grabbed a fat marker and played with the lines.

Shape Versus Silhouette

Aren't shapes and silhouettes the same thing? Nope. Silhouettes are the outer shape of the whole garment, like an A-line skirt or cocoon coat. Yes, that's a skirt that angles out like the letter A and a coat with a round elongated shape like a cocoon.

Shapes can be applied to the shapes of collars, the shapes of pockets, the shapes of buttons, the curve of style lines, formation of beading, designs in a print—any part of the garment.

Design Exercises to Explore Shape

This section covers design exercises that incorporate both 2-D and 3-D work. Is every design exercise for every designer? No, which is why there are so many. Do I think I'm a genius and you should try each and every one in this book at least once? Maybe.

Refer to your sketchbook and isolate shapes and lines that you liked from your inspiration images. Use them to build your silhouettes and interior shapes (**Figure 7.4**).

Turn style lines into sections of garments with different fabrics, colors, textures, and prints (**Figure 7.5, next page**).

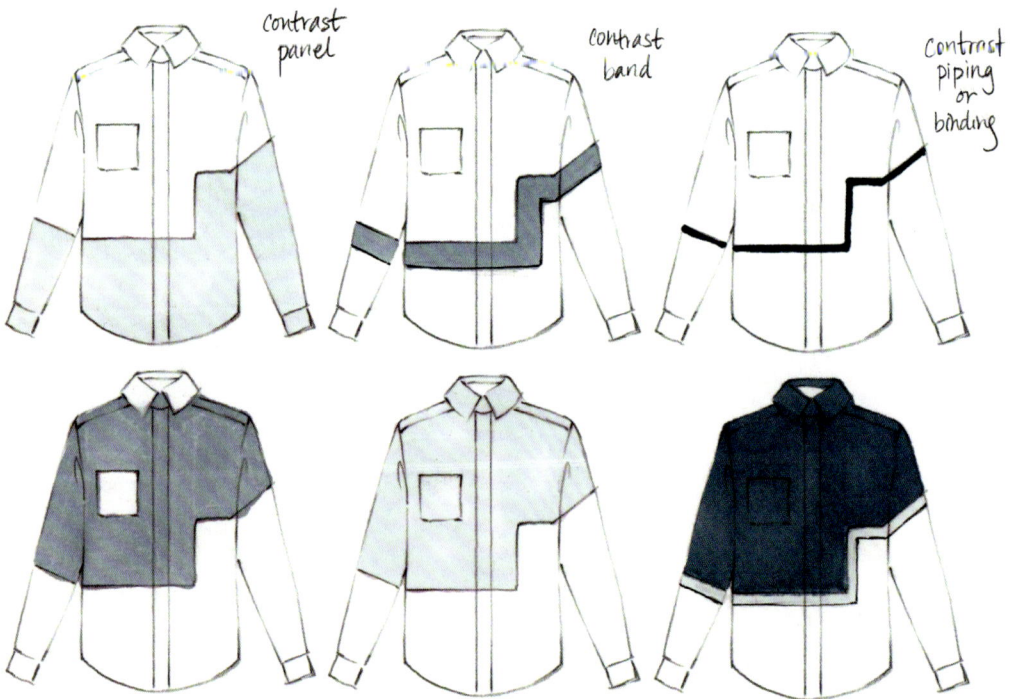

contrast panel

contrast band

contrast piping or binding

FIGURE 7.5. LEFT Fun fact,
I love trains.

FIGURE 7.6. RIGHT Rose
print made huge.

Blow up shapes from your print and use them to create shapes and style lines in your garment (**Figure 7.6**).

Create style lines across a garment inspired by letters of the alphabet (**Figure 7.7, next page**). Use whatever letter from any language you use. Use letters as inspiration, twist letters around, blow them up huge, play with the letters so you're not just making a monogram print.

Create and draw out an element. This element can be anything: a heart, a bow, a constellation of stars. Design garments incorporating that element (1) in the silhouette; (2) repeating the element in a smaller scale within the garment; and (3) scaled down very, very small and used as an embellishment (**Figure 7.8. next page**). This is a great time to play with a motif you're considering for a house code. What's a motif that's important to you?

FIGURE 7.7. ABOVE The literal ABCs of design

FIGURE 7.8. LEFT I recently read a trend report that bows are "back." Am I doing trends right???

FIGURE 7.9A-B Sometimes just part of an idea is enough to get you going.

Drape a section, not a whole garment, in muslin on your dress form. Take a photo of the drape on the dress form. Print out the photo and expand upon the drape in different ways (**Figure 7.9a-b**).

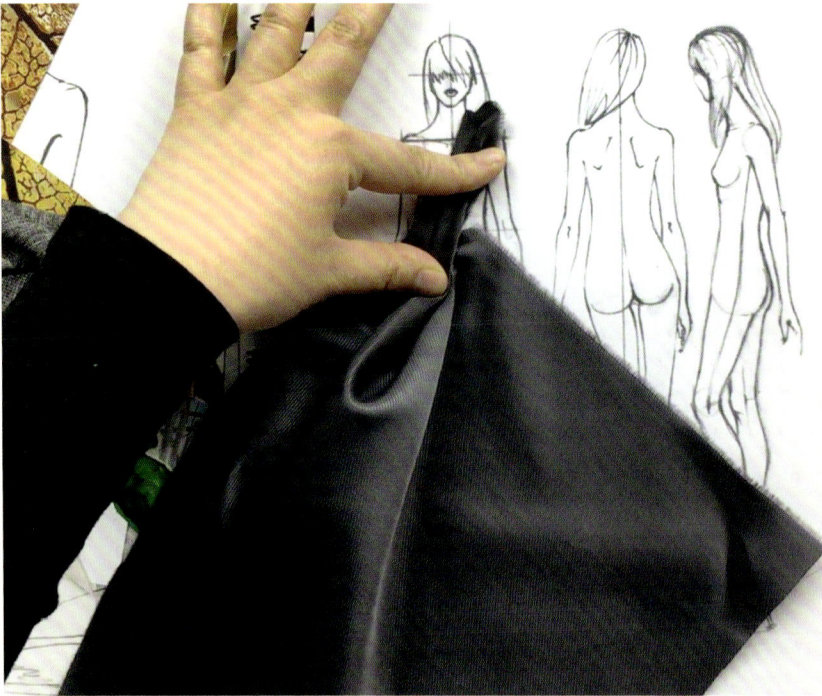

FIGURE 7.10 Don't have a tripod? Bribe a sibling or kid into holding the camera for you.

A half form is great for draping exercises; all the play, half the fabric usage. Madeleine Vionnet, the mother of us all, draped all her designs on a half-size form. For precise draping for bodice blocks and testing patterns, I would recommend a full-size form. If you can only afford one, go with the full size.

Drape even smaller. Take a 12x12" (30x30cm) piece of fabric and create drapes on top of a figure template. Take photos. Better yet, take video, and take screenshots of your favorite drapes (**Figure 7.10**).

Pin twill tape to your dress form inspired by shapes found in your inspiration images. Drape partial or full garments using the twill tape as guides for style lines.

Twill tape can be sticky like actually tape or just very thin ribbon. I like to use the ribbon type on my dress form because I don't like the sticky residue tape can leave behind. I like to use the sticky tape on muslins/toiles, because there are fewer pins to prick the fit model.

Drape identical toiles in vastly different fabrics. This is also an excellent exercise to study fabrics. Try a light, stiff organza versus a heavy, slinky matte jersey. Try a thin, sharp cotton shirting versus a soft, spongy wool

FIGURE 7.11 Feel free to get buck wild and oh, I don't know, even join two garments together.

Melton or felt. Try draping with your final fabric or a similar, cheaper alternative.

Another great fabric learning exercise is to drape identical designs on a form with one using the straight grain and another on the bias.

Cutting on the bias means the center front or center back is not parallel to the selvedge but at a 45-degree angle. Cutting on the bias adds ease, drape, and a slinkier look not achieved on the straight grain. The bias-cut drape can fit over curves smoothly without a lot of darts, depending on where your seams are, but bias cut can also use up a lot of fabric.

Cut a big geometric shape out of muslin. You can use a shape from your inspiration images. If you want to explore zero waste cutting, make sure this piece is a big rectangle or triangle using the entire width of your fabric. Drape on a dress form with this shape. You can cut slices into the fabric but try not to cut off pieces of fabric. If you cut away pieces of fabric, try to incorporate them back into the design as pockets, patches, or embellishments.

Drape a garment, pinning, cutting gathering, and adding twill tape lines to create something new (**Figure 7.11**).

Hate Staring at a Blank Piece of Paper?

◆ Some people feel more flow when they're correcting or editing. Try taking some photos of garments and editing or redesigning them. You can also edit your own old designs, whether to update the style or to practice and improve on your own design skills.

◆ Try using something you don't wear anymore. Why don't you wear it anymore? Fix it.

◆ Take apart two dresses. You can pick them apart at the seams or cut them up however suits your fancy. Put the pieces back together on your dress form in a new way. Throw away as little as possible.

◆ Many feel inspired by fabric itself. There's nothing that says you can't drape in your final fabric. I mean, it can get expensive, depending on what your final fabric is, but you can try looking for cheaper versions that are more similar to your final fabric than muslin. Maybe draping in muslin feels daunting because it's too blank.

◆ Start with a big piece of fabric and apply some fabric manipulations to it to start. Fold the fabric up into rows of pleats or tucks or ruffles or panels of smocking. Drape this piece on the form.

Even if these exercises don't relate exactly to your current project, they can get your creative juices flowing far faster than staring at a blank piece of paper. The point is to use what's in front of you to start experimenting and trying new things. Different things work for different design minds.

Drawing Clothes on Bodies versus Flats

Every designer, regardless of who they work for, should have some basic sketching skills, purely as a form of visual communication. A picture is worth a thousand words, especially when trying to communicate with people you don't share a common language with.

The following pages go over how to draw some basic garments, both on a figure and on the flat.

FIGURE 7.12 These ellipses show how clothes should wrap around bodies: stripes on fitted garments, hems, waistbands.

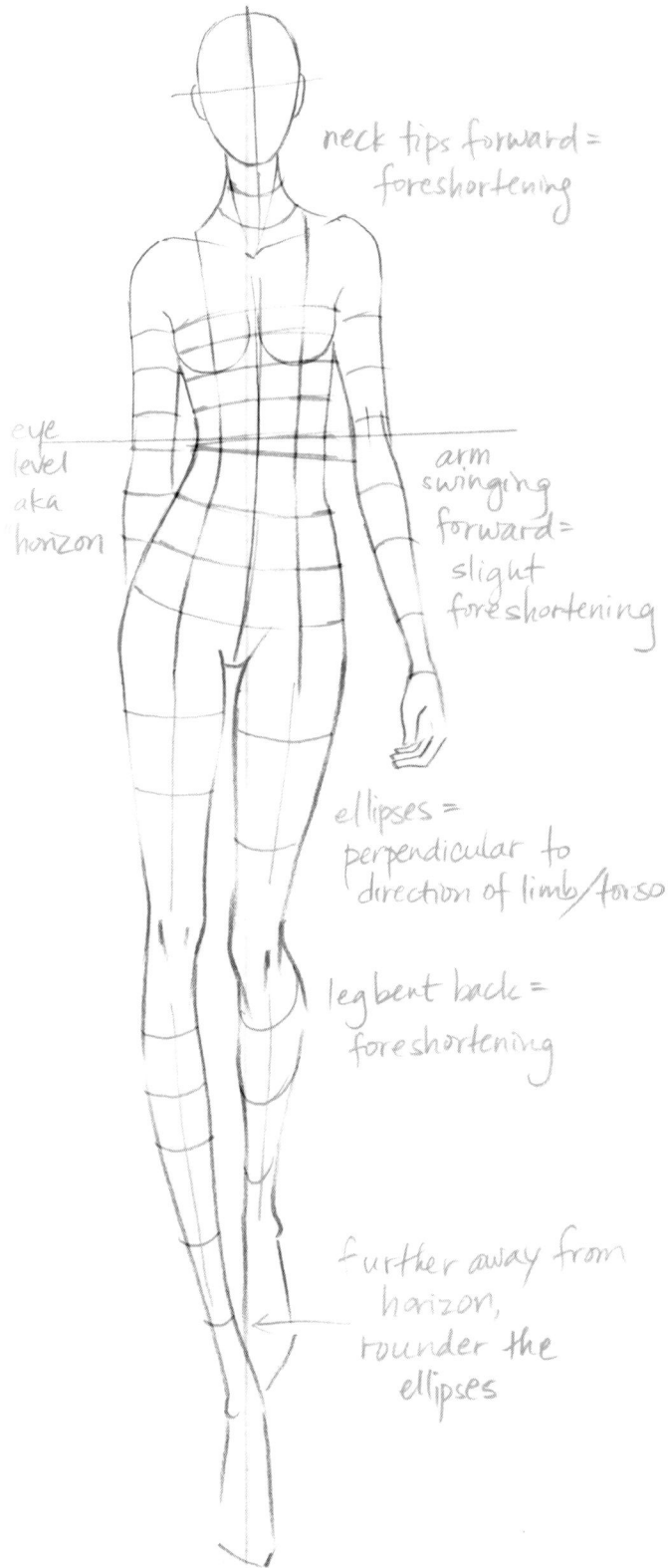

neck tips forward = foreshortening

eye level aka horizon

arm swinging forward = slight foreshortening

ellipses = perpendicular to direction of limb/torso

leg bent back = foreshortening

further away from horizon, rounder the ellipses

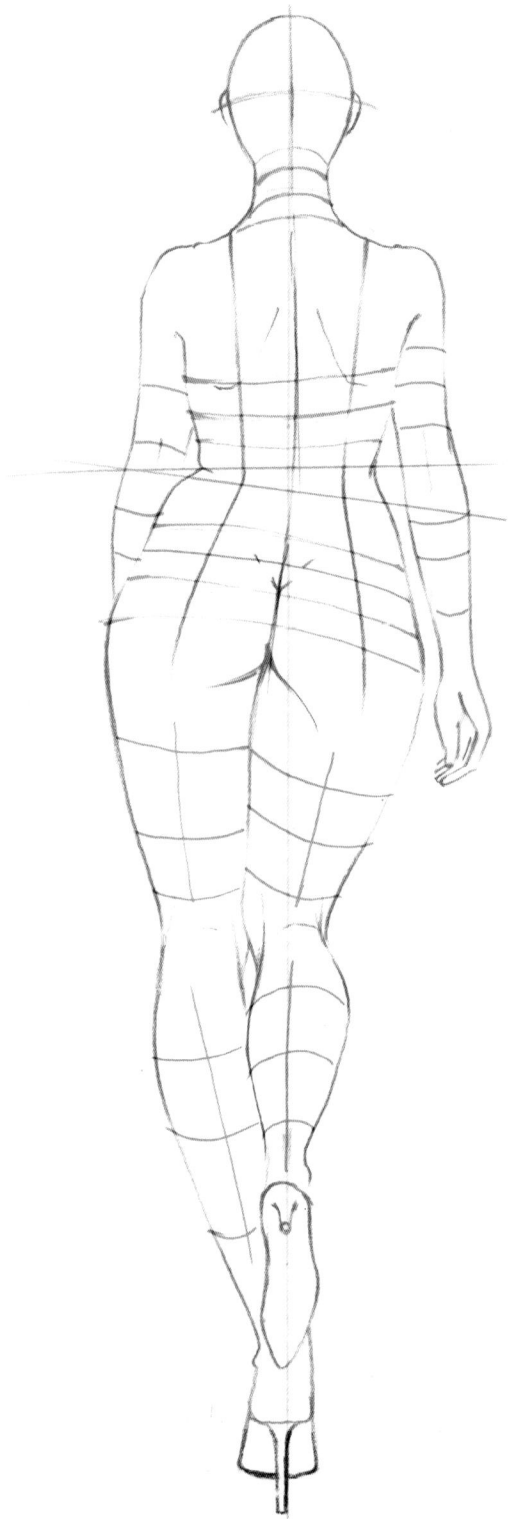

FIGURE 7.13 All ellipses should sit 90 degrees from the direction of the body part: center front, center back, side seam, direction of a limb.

under the tummy, over the butt

lifted leg: ellipses turn up

tight clothes

armpits always squish the fabric

can't make pants w/out center front + back seams

wrinkles at joints

hems + wrinkles follow direction of ellipses

flat = no curved hems no wrinkles no drape lines

pants waists usually constructed lower in front

even laid flat, pants crotches have a bit of fold per its pattern

this is also a skirt

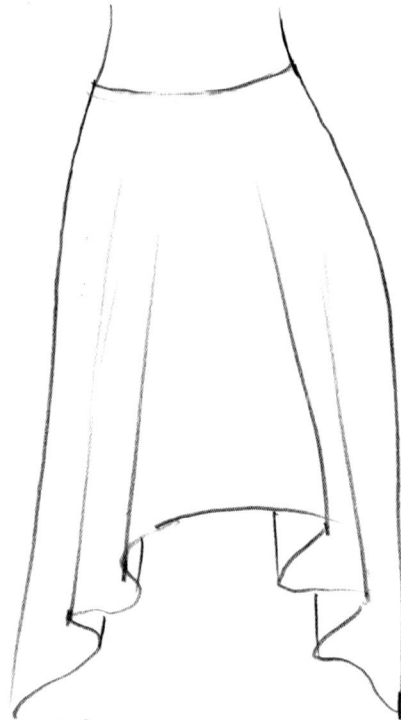

a-line skirt =
curved hem is
the construction

this is a
handkerchief hem
skirt

circle skirt =
no gathers @ waist,
fullness @ hem

circle ruffles = flources

lighter fabric

dirndl =
gathers @ top

stiffer fabric

the angle of the hem =
angle of last fitted place

it's usually the waist.

full skirts + ruffle flats drawn like they hang

open coats = shoulders

bigger shirts = shoulders

circle skirt pattern is literally a circle

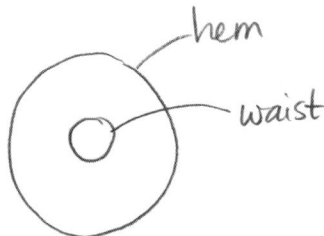

hem

waist

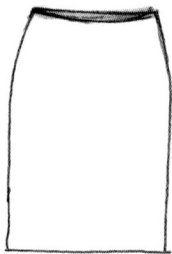

use ellipses to
bring a pencil skirt
to life

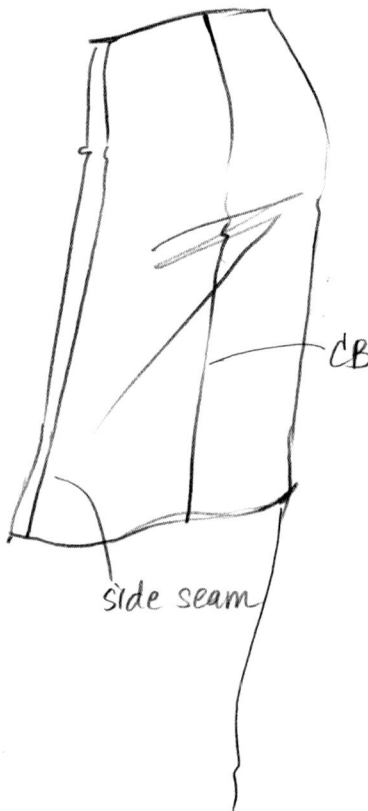

CB

side seam

FIGURE 7.17. LEFT It can help to design on the flat. When the drawing is boring, you have to make the design interesting.

FIGURE 7.18. RIGHT Yes, I'm aware "pants" means underwear in British English. Pretend I wrote "trousers" every time I wrote "pants."

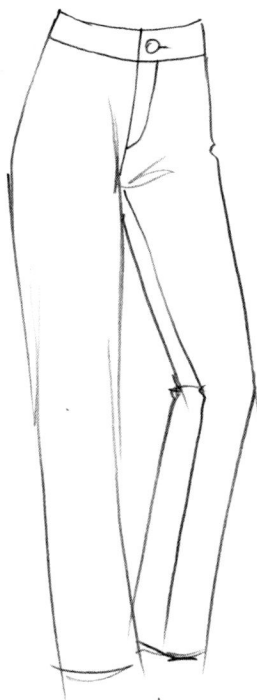

straight leg

flares +
bootcut

skinny jean

wide leg

even flat
crotches fold
over a bit,
thus the
little slash

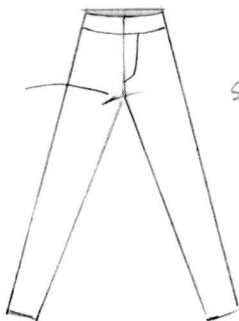

straight
leg

skinny
jean
or
legging

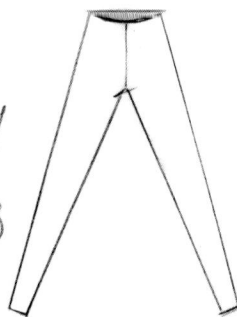

flats of
casual pants
usually drawn
legs apart,
dressier pants
usually drawn
legs together

all pants need
Center front + back
Seams for
construction

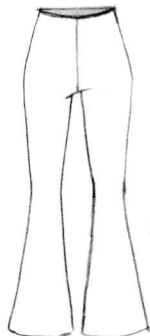

curved hems
like a-line
skirts

yes,
use a ruler
to draw
flats

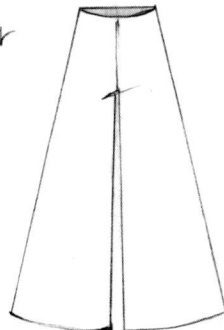

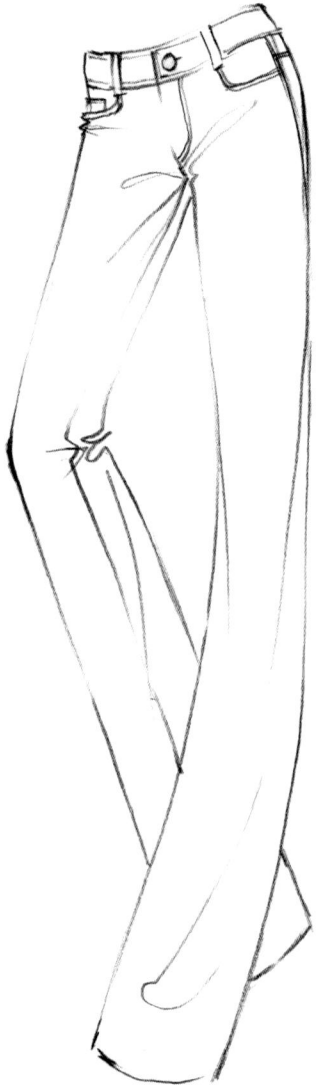

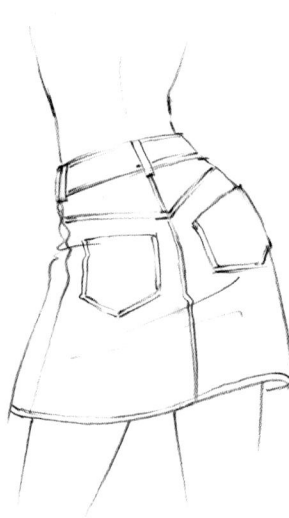

jeans are a
style w/
various silhouettes,
featuring
CB yoke + patch
pockets, curved
front pockets,
a lot of topstitching,
welt seams,
metal shank
button,
metal rivets
reinforcing corners

FIGURE 7.19. LEFT Once upon a time, I asked in a video what the current name for super short cut-off jeans were. I grew up calling them Daisy Dukes. Some people call them booty shorts, some people call them things that are more...adult.

FIGURE 7.20. RIGHT Use a flicking motion to draw gathers. Start at the top and flick down/up. You want that tapered line.

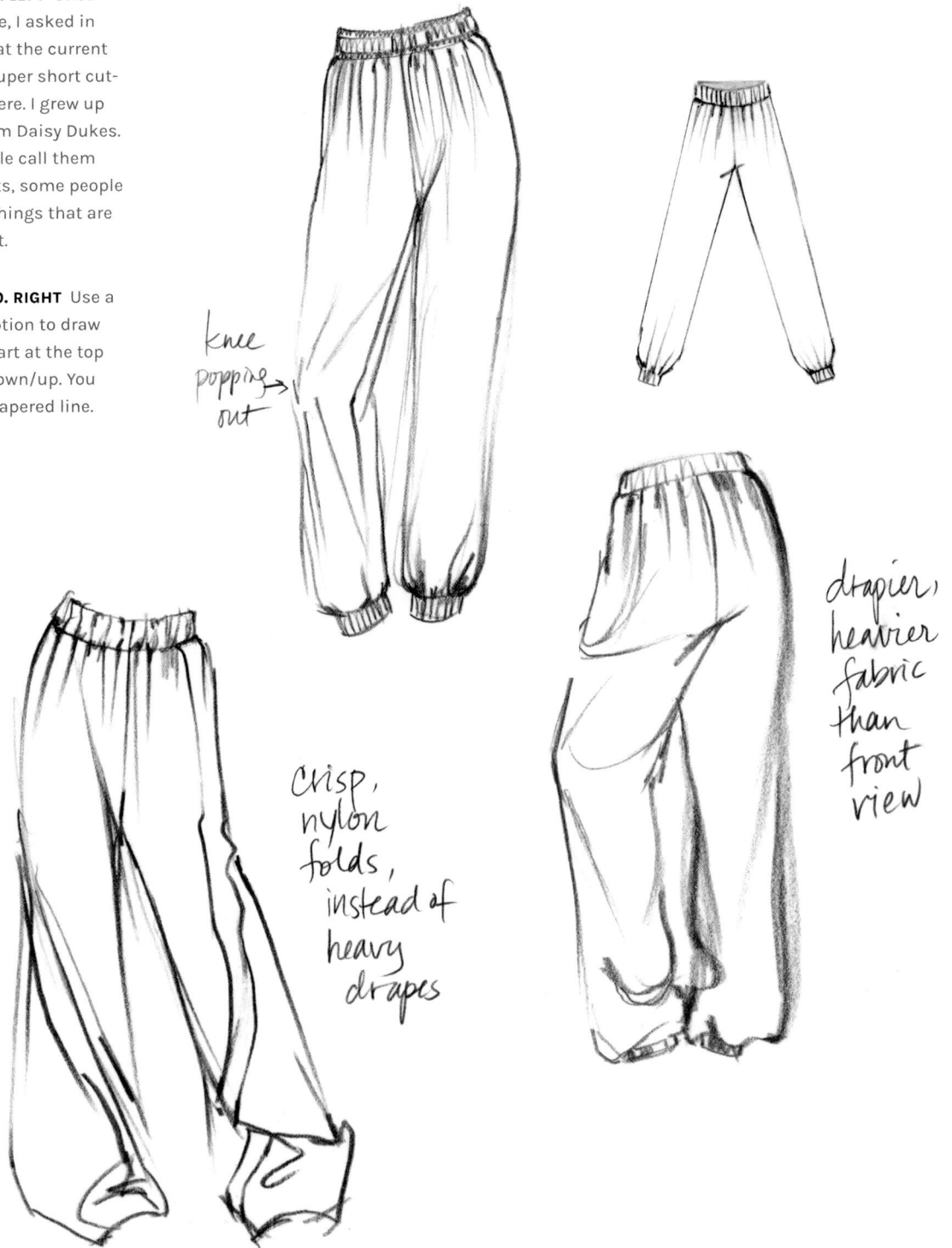

knee popping out

crisp, nylon folds, instead of heavy drapes

drapier, heavier fabric than front view

side seam

inseam

who has disco fever?

love a sharp, crisp crease

if they're in the front, they're also in the back

skinny vs straight leg

bootcut vs bellbottom

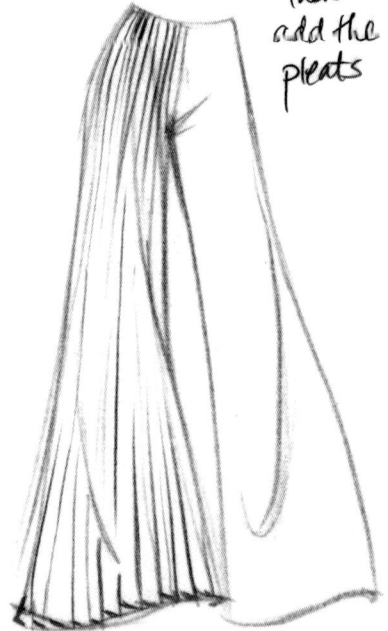

draw the basic shape, then add the pleats

FIGURE 7.21. LEFT Pants were the hardest for me to learn, back in the day. Don't worry if drawing pants doesn't come naturally to you. Long, fluid, but precise lines are difficult.

FIGURE 7.22. RIGHT Any sort of boxy, loose-fit tee, even if it's not as oversize as these, will be a big T-shaped flat. That's why they're called t-shirts.

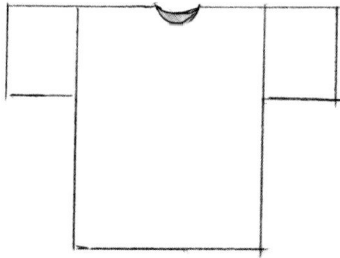

gravity = tension from shoulders

folds inside elbows of every bent arm

Soft, round drapes = something slinky, like a rayon shirting.

sharp crinkles + creases = a crisp cotton shirting

women's blazers = right over left

men's = opposite

buttons sit center front, not the jacket edge

peat

shawl

notch

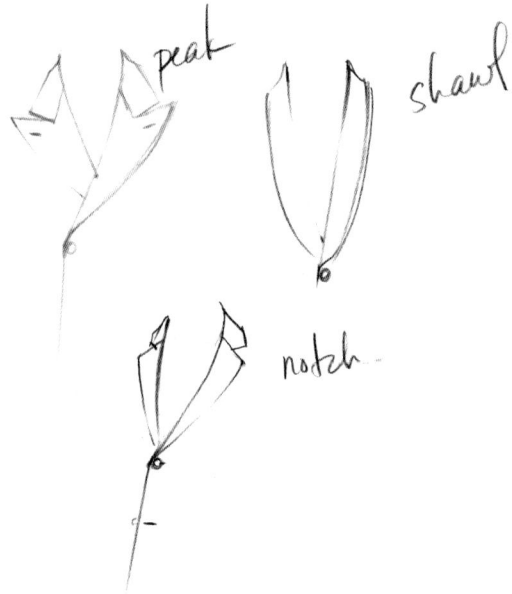

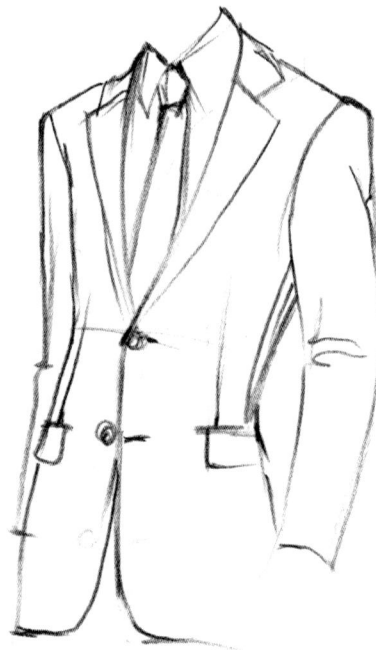

formal dressing "rules" state you leave the bottom button open on 2- 3-button blazers

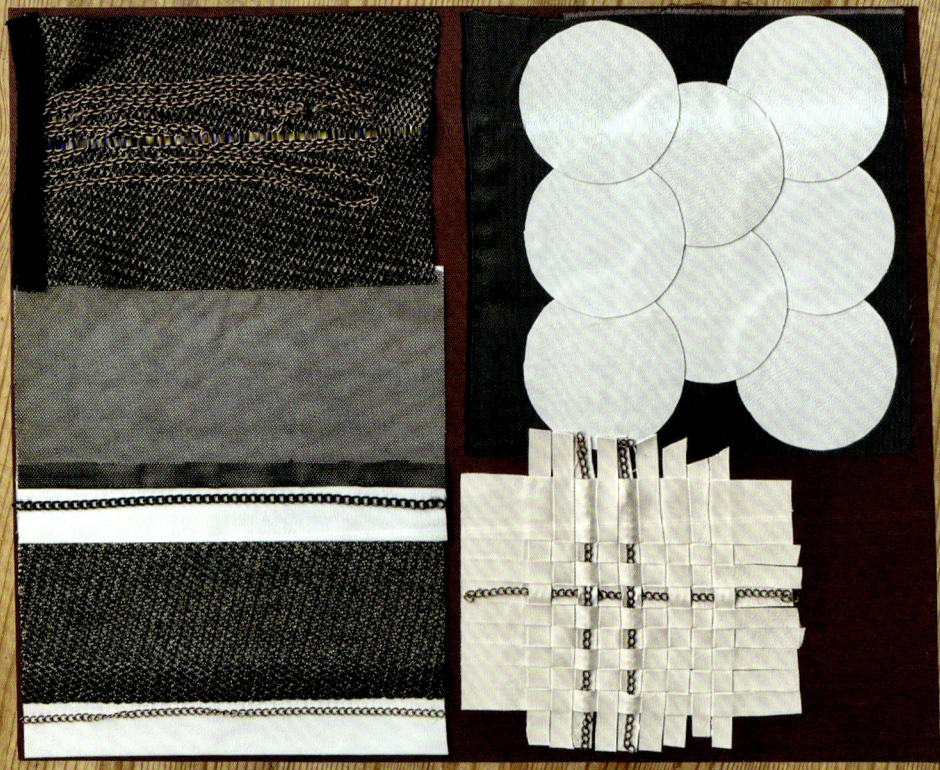

8

3-D DEVELOPMENT

Fabric Manipulation and Embellishment

This category covers doing anything to fabric to change its appearance or texture. Fabric manipulations can include, but are not limited to, darts, pleats, tucks, smocking, shell smocking, gathering/shirring/ruching, flounces, ruffles, padding, and quilting.

Darts can be placed pretty much anywhere on a garment, whether it's to manipulate fit or purely as decoration. There are so many different kinds of pleats it boggles my mind. Google different kinds of pleats. Pleats just mean folding permanently or semi-permanently in fabric. You can fold fabric in a million ways. Pleats can be simple folds like an accordion. Pleats can also be folded into an accordion and then zigzagged across the accordion folds. Please consult a professional before you steam burn yourself.

While you're at it, google tucks. Tucks are narrow folds that are sewn down. There are a million ways to tuck fabric, too. You can tuck one way and then tuck the tucks across the other way into a checkerboard.

Quilting can be done in whatever pattern a machine will allow. You can stuff fabric with as much quilting as you want to produce a very thin, light effect or a fat, stuffed turkey effect. But you know, in a cute way.

Flounces and ruffles can be literally any width and length you want. And you can layer them endlessly. And nearly any fabric can be ruffled, some more than others.

163

Fabric manipulations are different from embellishment, even though some people lump them all together. Embellishments are things applied on top of fabric to decorate the surface. These include embroidery, beading, sequins, paillettes, appliqué and patches, decorative topstitching, and adding trims like lace edging, fringe, piping, or cording.

Did you know there are such things as biodegradable sequins and glitter made from cellulose? Which is good because there's a plastic glitter ban across the EU.

You can embroider with threads, which is the most commonly known way, but you can also include beads, feathers, and whatever doodads that can be sewn down. There are a lot of things that are functional but can be used as trim or embellishment, such as zippers, buttons, buckles, grommets/eyelets, lacing/ribbons, and rivets.

Go through your sketchbook and make notes on what can be translated into fabric manipulations and/or embellishments. Pick up a book to learn how to embroider, seek out a class, or you can always sketch out your ideas and consult professionals.

Exercises to Design 3-D Effects

Go buy some stuff and play! Go buy some yardage and fold it up, cut it up, sew it up. Go buy some beads and splay them out on a table and try arranging them in cool ways. Take photos and try again. Have your inspiration images in front of you so you're constantly referencing them, and those images are helping your brain.

Refer back to the exercises for designing prints in chapter 5 and apply them to fabric manipulations and embellishments (**Figure 8.2**). Refer also to the section on spin-off embellishments.

Cut up copies of your original inspiration and apply them to figure templates. Imagine the many ways those images can be translated in pleating and beading.

I once met a woman who worked at a fairly large, well-known womenswear company. Her entire job was to take beading designs and map them out precisely on grids. She graduated from my alma mater with a degree in fashion design and this type of work suited her desire for order nicely.

Working With Scrap

Necessity is the mother of invention. Your brain can surprise you when pushed to its creative limits.

Go back to your notes and think about how you can be more sustainable in your materials and processes. Let's think about how you can use scrap in ways that look artful, not amateur.

One option is to use larger scraps of leather, suede, or nonwoven materials like felt to cut smaller pattern pieces. These materials have no grain, they are not woven or knit in a specific direction, so they can be cut up any which way. You can use these to cut pockets or more subtle details like a collar stand or under collar, or inside coat cuffs.

Explore options where you use the fabric in such a way that the grainline doesn't matter.

◆ I know of a company that used to buy large scrap from cutting factories and use that fabric to cut into strips and weave them into new fabrics. To be clear, they didn't do this themselves by hand, they hired a weaving company.

◆ I know of a different company that uses scrap to stitch cool fabric collages to the fronts of their shirts.

◆ Explore patchworking. You can sew pieces together to create a new fabric. *Jogakbo* is a Korean style of traditional patchwork that includes but also goes beyond a series of squares.

◆ You can use small pieces to make fabric flowers.

◆ You can also use small pieces to create appliqués.

◆ You can also use small pieces to make covered buttons.

◆ I've seen some cool effects with using scraps as stuffing in quilted fabrics, using sheer fabrics to show the colors inside. You can design around using scrap of a specific color story. The double effect is you use up scrap in a pretty easy way while also not using polyfill.

◆ I mean you could shred scrap and use it as regular quilting stuffing too, with regular opaque fabric. This effect would probably be better with a thicker fabric, to smooth out any lumps.

◆ You can make small accessories to either sell or include as a gift with purchase, such as scrunchies or bookmarks.

If you work with an aesthetic that fits, you can include a scrap with your purchase for mending. You know how beaded dresses often include a tiny baggie with spare beads and a bit of thread? You can sell your jeans with a square or two of denim for patching. You can post mending instructions on your website or social media, which is a handy way to get people to visit your site again. Maybe you can include patches of fun fabrics for mending kids' clothes.

Linings

Linings serve both the aesthetics and function of the garment and should not be a sloppy afterthought. A good lining elevates the quality and perceived value of a garment. A good lining can elevate the design as well. Arguably the top function of linings is to cover the mess of raw edges and inner construction with something beautiful. Consider hanger appeal.

> *Hanger appeal is an industry term to describe how good a garment looks on the hanger. The vast majority of garments are displayed on hangers, not humans or mannequins, so hanger appeal is important.*

Linings add warmth. For winter coats, think about flannels and woolens. Sleeve linings should always be slippery so shirt sleeves of any fabric can slide into coat sleeves easily. You can line a coat with flannel in the body and something slippery in the sleeves. You can coordinate patterns and textures and solids to create a beautiful interior.

Linings add longevity to a garment by supporting the shell fabric and lending it strength. Lined garments crinkle less, as the extra thickness makes it harder to fold sharply. Lining protects the shell from your body's oils and sweat.

> *Have you considered adding a little armpit gusset either inside or outside the lining for extra sweat absorption and better armhole fit?*

Match lining fiber content with your shell fiber content. Don't line a silk dress or wool jacket with a polyester lining! You will lose some of the benefits of silk or wool with a polyester lining, like silk and wool's breathability. Opt for a less expensive, thin silk like habutai.

You don't have to do a fiber-to-fiber match. You can just stick to categories, like using cellulose fabrics like cotton and linen for other cellulose fabric shells.

Alternatively, if you're trying to design something very lightweight, you must pay special attention to the shapes of facings and how seams are finished.

Pockets

I will never skip an opportunity to climb up on my pockets soapbox. Give us all the pockets! Design a beautiful interior with gorgeous linings in colors that coordinate well with your shell fabric, with some big, roomy pockets. Put pockets on the inside and on the outside! Cell phones are getting bigger every year!

There are a lot of different kinds of pockets, for both the inside and outside of garments: welt pockets, patch pockets, on-seam pockets, slash pockets, and bellows pockets; pockets with flaps, buttons, pleats, or Velcro; pockets for your butt, pockets for your chest, pockets to hide a hood, pockets for warming your hands. Pockets are where aesthetic meets function. Explore!

All The Trimmings

The word "trim" in fashion means pretty much anything on the garment that's not a type of fabric (self, lining, interfacing). Trim is the fringe on a shawl; trim is buttons, zippers, and snaps that close the jacket; trim is aglets on shoelaces.

You may have heard of the term "CMT" in fashion. CMT stands for Cut Make Trim. CMT factories cut the fabric, sew the garment, and trim, which is the rest of it, to finish a garment. CMT price is the cost to cut, make, and trim the garment.

When designing a portfolio project, you don't have to design every lining, but showing one example lining on a coat or jacket would show your thoroughness as a designer. If you find an incredible fabric for a great contrast lining, you can include the swatch on your boards. Include trim on your boards that are pertinent to the design. A very special lace trim you've gathered into ruffles you use throughout the collection? Get that swatch. Little white buttons on a button-down shirt? Eh. We already know what those look like.

Making Samples

Start making samples of any design elements you want to test before you make a whole complete garment sample. It saves a lot of time and a lot of materials to test the artwork and small sections of the garment beforehand.

Some manipulations and embellishments should be sent out to professionals who specialize in these services. There are companies devoted to pleating, embroidery, debossing, and more. Create the artwork for the embroidery and get a sample done from a professional embroidery house. Your artwork should be drawn in a vector format. Send out yardage of your final fabric to get it professionally pleated so that the folds will hold permanently.

There are also companies that create patches and companies that apply appliqués to fabric. Patches are one single piece with all the design elements on that one piece. Appliqués are a design constructed by a series of fabric pieces sewn onto a background fabric.

If you're making a portfolio project, you should still make final art for your embroidery to include on your boards and test out some pleats in muslin. Samples you make will help recruiters visualize your designs better, and you will show them that you know a thing or two about how a design gets made.

Remember when I said the design process was a zigzag? Some designers start with playing with fabric in this way. Some designs will get rushed into development at this stage, or even earlier, because the team or the leadership loves it so much. Is this a good idea? Eh, I think your instinct for this kind of thing gets better over time with experience. But in the end, if you have to ditch this design for the sake of a better collection on the whole, so be it.

9

MERCHANDISING AND EDITING

Merchandising

What is merchandising? Are we just verbing a noun? Ok, first of all, verbing a noun is a real thing; it's called a gerund. Second, merchandising in the fashion industry involves making sure a collection is market ready. Merchandising is part of designing and also part of editing.

Looking at previous sales, fashion merchandisers analyze which silhouettes, fits, fabrications, and colorways have sold well and not sold well, and how this data should be incorporated in future collections.

You should absolutely repeat your best-selling whatever. Something that oddly surprises students and clients is how much design houses repeat silhouettes, fabrics, and colors, even if they're not a category-specific brand like a denim house.

Another aspect of merchandising is making sure you have a variety of styles for your customer. Not all your tops should be sleeveless. Not all your skirts should be maxis. Throw in a couple of different lengths. Edit out styles that are too similar to each other. The smaller a collection, the more you want to show a lot of ideas while keeping the collection cohesive.

Get organized. Divide your designs into categories and make sure you are designing an assortment within each category. I've developed some exercises to help you expand and merchandise your collection.

Principles of Design: Unity and Variety

Technically unity and variety are two different principles, but they really go hand in hand when applied to fashion collections. Even if your whole collection is five sweaters, you want them to follow a theme (unity) while offering different styles within that theme (variety).

Unity is the harmony and cohesiveness between all the moving parts in a design or group of designs. Each garment's individual elements should harmonize together, the outfit should harmonize together, and all the outfits in the collection should harmonize together.

Variety is using different design elements and motifs in different configurations to grab the viewer's attention, hold the viewer's attention, and move the viewer's eye through the clothes and through the collection.

Together, it's the balance of unity and variety that create cohesive, well-merchandised collections.

Under the unity umbrella, you need to harmonize the collection within itself, have a consistent mood throughout, a color story, a fabric story, a series of shapes. Even if you have Christopher John Rogers' style color use, full of rainbows, there's always a *type* of rainbow. One collection he uses a rainbow of jewel tones, another he uses a rainbow of fluorescent colors.

For unity, you use the same fabrics over and over again throughout the collection. Emphasize the trends you want people to pay attention to, like that Miu Miu collection with the sparkly spanky pants. They did several renditions so it's not this random outlier, it's a statement to be made—a statement we paid attention to.

Another part of unity is cohesion within the brand. All your collections for a brand should look like they belong to the brand.

Variety is what makes everything seem exciting, not like we're seeing the same thing over and over again. Variety is the fresh new thing each season, the different details blouse to blouse.

Exercises to Help You Expand Out Your Designs

Exercise 1: Musical Chairs

Design a garment and identify the design elements that make that dress special, such as contrast godets, a pattern of stitching, or sheer panels. Apply those elements to a jacket. And then pants. And then a top (**Figure 9.1a. next page**). Move the element to different parts of similar pairs of leggings (**Figure 9.1b, next page**). You should recognize this sort of design rotation; it's very common.

Exercise 2: Hokey Pokey

Design a garment and then remove an element. Adjust the design to balance it as necessary. Maybe you remove the collar and finish the neckline with some topstitching or binding. Take the new design and add a new element. That's three designs related to each other. Take the third design and remove a different element. Keep going (**Figure 9.2, next pages**).

This exercise works great when you want to deconstruct a classic, like a motorcycle jacket, shirt dress, or trench coat. You definitely want to start with a more complex design with a lot of elements.

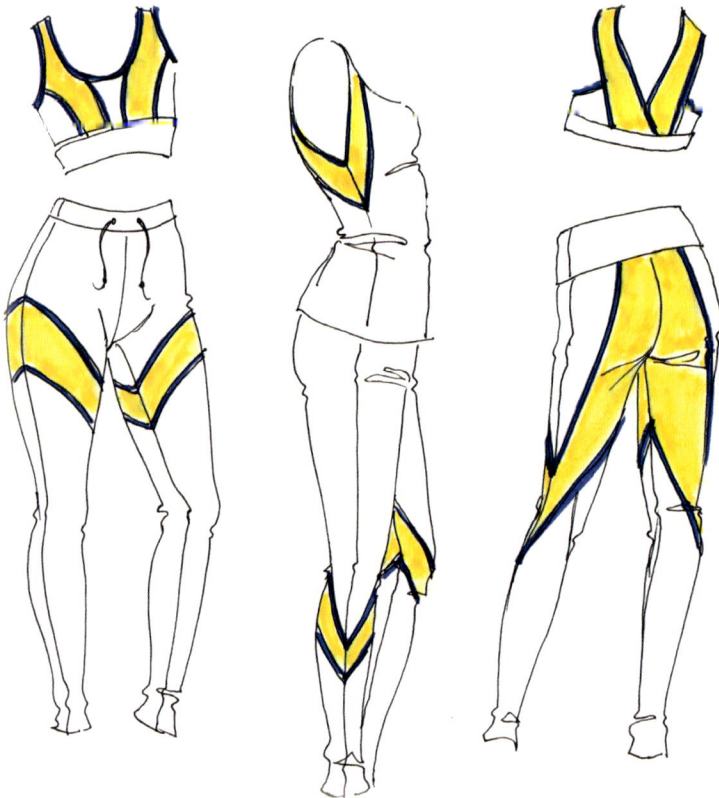

FIGURE 9.1A-B. ABOVE AND LEFT Play musical chairs with your design element.

FIGURE 9.2. BELOW
Play hokey pokey with your
design elements.

Exercise 3: Fun for the Whole Family!

Design a garment and then adjust the garment for a younger customer, such as shortening the skirt. Adjust the original design for a grandma. Adjust the original design for the opposite gender. Adjust it again for a kid. Adjust it so it's more cutesy. Adjust it so it's more grown up and sophisticated. Adjust it for whoever your customer isn't (**Figure 9.3**).

What's the point of this? Understanding how to dress different customers will help you stay on track with your customer. This is for the next time you're at a fitting and think, "Why does this dress look matronly? How do I make this look more youthful?"

FIGURE 9.3. BELOW Mom gets a skirt! Grandma gets a skirt! Baby gets a skirt!

Exercise 4: Fashion Plates

Select four previously designed garments. Choose the same category (all dresses, all jackets, etc.). Cut them apart and make four new garments with the pieces (**Figure 9.4**). The aim is to have some part of each of the four previous garments in each new garment. The point is to push you to use the same design elements and motifs in a new way. Do you remember the '80s toy Fashion Plates? Like that.

FIGURE 9.4. RIGHT You can also split up designs into quadrants instead, for more avant-garde looks.

Exercise 5: Mind Meld

Grab two very different designs and merge them together in varying degrees. For example, take a trench coat and a sweater. Add an element of the sweater to the trench. Add an element of the trench to the sweater. Add several trench elements to the sweater. Keep going until you have a variety of garments that include both trench and sweater elements (**Figure 9.5**).

Exercise 6: Teamwork Makes the Dream Work

Sort your designs or design elements into groups. Or teams. I have several groups here (**Figure 9.6a-c, next pages**). One group is inspired by aprons. I have another I call "Drapes and Stripes." One group is inspired by pockets and boro patches (using scrap). They are all part of one larger collection, so they follow the same color, fabric, and print story.

You can group by fabrics or category, meaning all your leather jackets and coats share similar design details like buckles and triple needle topstitching and all your cotton button-down shirts play with intricate pintucks and pleats. This is very practical because not all design details work for every fabrication.

drawstrings
adjusting
fit

floral
linen

FIGURE 9.6A–B. LEFT AND RIGHT Remember my love of clusters? Clusters of patches, clusters of lines, clusters of pockets—I can't stop, even when I'm not thinking about it at the time!

FIGURE 9.6C. LEFT Red rover, red rover, send boro patches right over.

This is actually similar to how larger design companies function. Designers are divided by category. I have a friend who used to be the design director of the boys and men knit bottoms division at their company. (Think basketball shorts and track pants.) Yes, that means there was a design director of the boys and men woven bottoms division too. (Think cargo pants and gym shorts.) And a design director of the girls and women knit bottoms division. The bigger the company, the more divisions.

If your project or company focuses on only one or two categories, you can pretty much group however you want. When you design in groups, several things can happen. You can find one group is the strongest or your favorite. (Those two are not always the same.) This is the best option for small collections.

You may also find that you start merging the groups, like adding boro patches to aprons and stripes to your boro-inspired dresses. You will add cohesiveness overall. See previous Mind Meld exercise.

Exercise 7: The Price is Right

Design variations of a garment to accommodate different price points. It's important to practice making designs more cost efficient or more luxurious. To reduce cost, think about how to reduce fabric usage, like making ruffles less full, ribbons a bit narrower and shorter, and finding subtle spots to replace expensive laces with cheaper solid cotton blouseweights (**Figure 9.7, next page**). To increase a design's perceived value, think about adding embellishments and using fine seam finishes.

Exercises to Help You Edit and Merchandise

Exercise 1: Analyze a Designer

Pick a designer or brand and pick several seasons of collections (a variety of seasons—spring, fall, resort, pre-fall) over several years. Scroll through and study them. Start jotting down design elements you see and make three lists:

1.   Elements you see throughout only one collection

2.   Elements you see in many collections

3.   Elements you see very rarely or only once

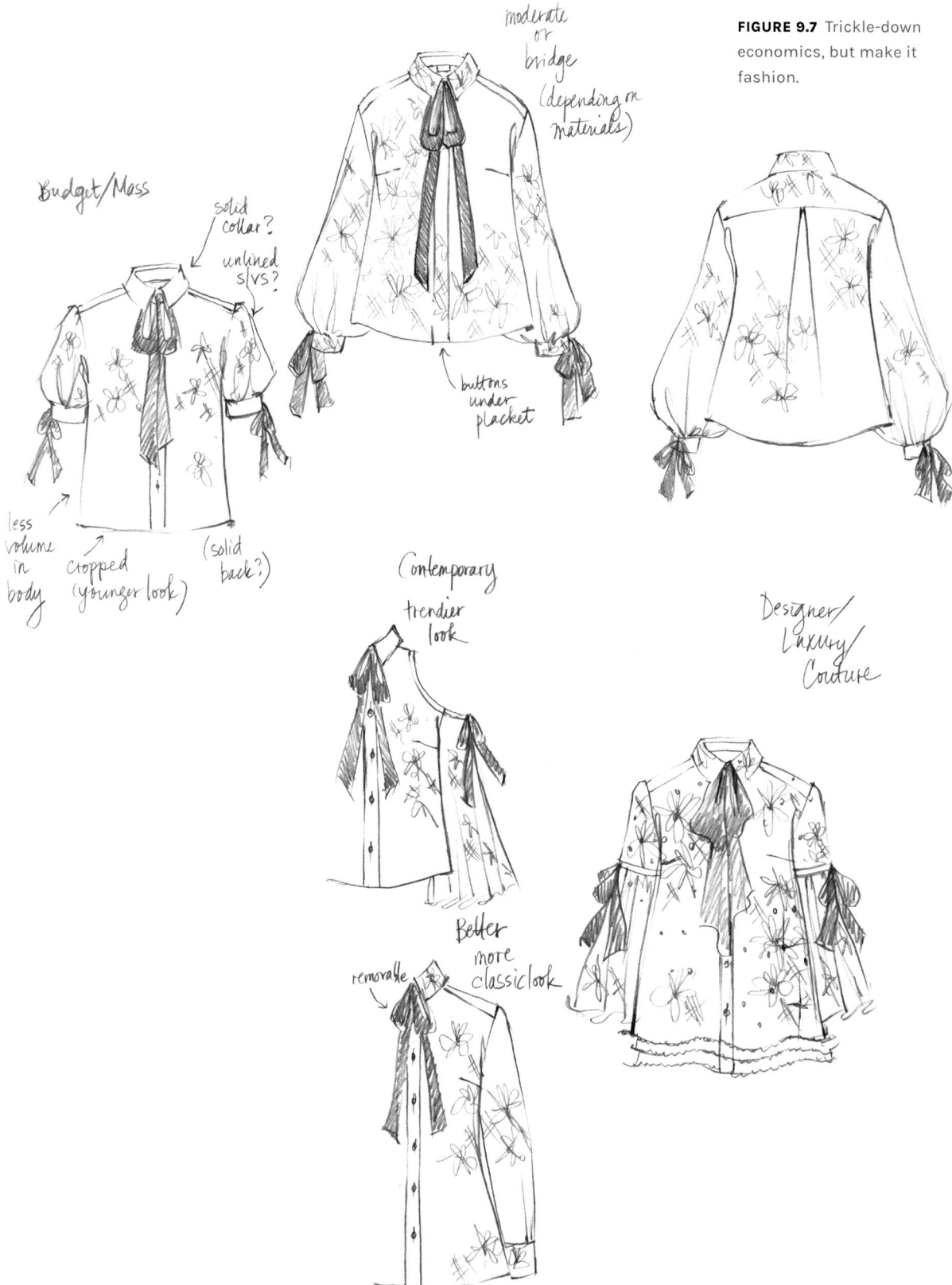

moderate
or
bridge
(depending on
materials)

FIGURE 9.7 Trickle-down economics, but make it fashion.

Budget/Mass

solid
collar?

unlined
s/vs?

buttons
under
placket

less
volume
in
body

cropped
(younger look)

(solid
back?)

Contemporary

trendier
look

Designer/
Luxury/
Couture

Better
more
classic look

removable

These elements can be a specific silhouette or shape, a certain hem, a color story, a motif (like bows)—so many things. Just look for repeats.

Run this analysis on a few different designers you admire so you can learn about how brands merchandise their collections (and what their house codes are).

Exercise 2: Edit Someone Else's Collection

Sometimes we feel a little precious about our work and find it difficult to "trash" things. I know because I've been there. Select a collection and download the photos. Open them up in Photoshop. Take out all the outfits that don't work. Try pairing tops with different bottoms to make new outfits. Practice editing out half the looks to make a more cohesive collection of the best pieces that still show variety.

Call me a hoarder if you want, but I never throw old designs away. I squirrel them away for a rainy day just in case. Oh, crap, I am a hoarder.

Exercise 3: Edit an Older Collection of Your Own

Pull out all the sketches from an older collection of your own, including the designs that you edited out before. Again, you may feel less precious about an older collection. Re-edit and re-merchandise your collection. Fresh, better-developed eyes can create a better collection off old designs with some minor alterations.

Organizing for Presentation

Whether that presentation is portfolio boards, a runway show, or a series of lookbook photos, you want to present your collection in the best light possible.

Gather up all the sketches from your project. Make a set of copies. Cut all the copies in half and tape them together again creating new combinations of tops and bottoms. Pair different jackets and coats with different outfits. Layer in new ways (**Figure 9.8, next page**).

If your collection is well merchandised, each of your tops should coordinate well with several different bottoms and vice versa. Each jacket or coat should work with several outfits.

You may think this is about styling outfits, but this comes before that. If you have a random blouse that doesn't work with anything else in your collection, don't even bother making a sample. If it's still amazing, make like a Zoe-esque trash panda and pocket it for another day.

Again, pay attention to creating a cohesive collection that still offers visual variety. And while the point isn't styling, this exercise will help with styling for your presentation without making your model try on 3,921 outfit variations.

The last consideration is which color to present each garment in. Every garment, except for the occasional editorial piece, should be offered in multiple colorways. Gather up all your sketches and make a set of miniature copies. Color your garments quickly (**Figure 9.9**). Check to see which colors from your color story look good on which garment. This step is especially important for garments with any color blocking. Set up your outfits in a lineup for a practice presentation.

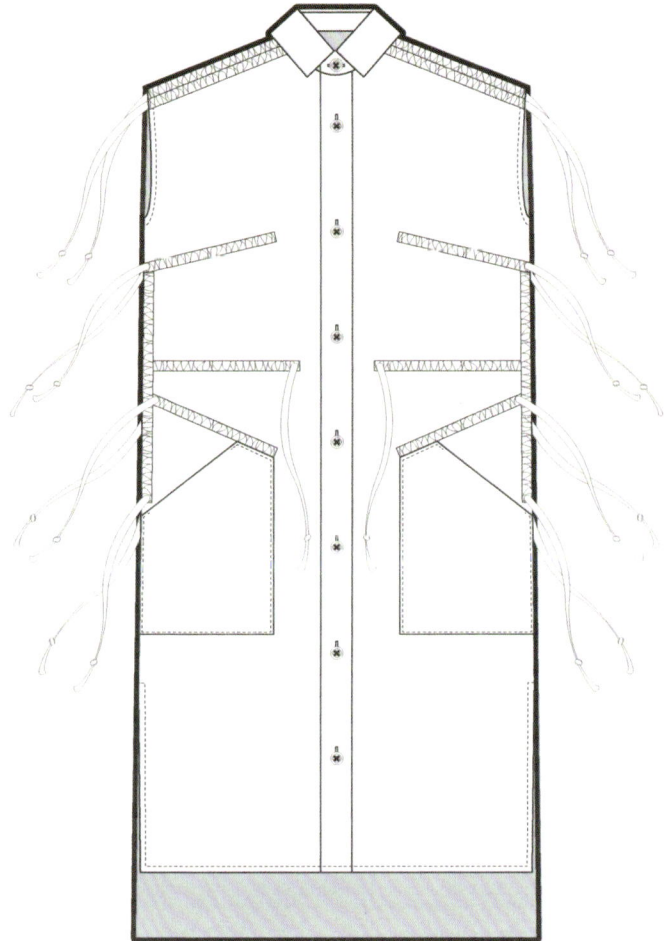

10

BEYOND DESIGN PROCESS FOR BRANDS

A Brief Summary of Product Development

Prod dev is the process used to create the garment you've designed.

Once you've finished designing, brands don't need fancy mood boards or illustrations. You should have a board that clearly communicates the direction, color story, and fabrics to your team. They don't need to be perfect. Clarity over everything. Create this board even if you're a team of one. It will keep you on track when you're making 289 decisions.

Once you've edited your sketches down, you need to draw flats, which are technical sketches of clothes. Even if you design with flats, clean them up to be symmetrical, even, and detailed.

Flats are called flats because you're supposed to draw the clothes as if they were laid flat on a table. You can practice by laying your clothes out as flatly and neatly as possible on a table and drawing them.

Sketching for designers is about communication. Flats are the clearest way to sketch, as the drawing will be uncluttered with drape lines. Only draw drape lines when they designate construction (**Figure 10.1**).

Flats should be drawn in Adobe Illustrator. Do not use Photoshop. You need a vector-based program to draw clean lines that you can scale up and down. If you run your own brand and you're good at sketching by hand, hand flats are OK. It's also OK to learn how to draw flats before you transfer those skills to Illustrator. You can scan in your hand-drawn flats and trace them in Illustrator. Many designers learn this way.

Whether you draw digitally or by hand, you should use a flats template. It will help you keep your shapes and proportions accurate and consistent across all your flats. This is important to communicate whether something is fitted or baggy for the same customer (**Figure 10.2**).

The next step is to make tech packs, which should include your flats.

Tech packs are a series of documents that detail exactly how to create the design. Tech packs include the flat, including close-ups of details, lists of materials used, and measurements.

At smaller companies, tech packs are often created in Microsoft Excel. At bigger companies, they use PLM (product lifecycle management) software.

Every company is different; sometimes designers do the flats, sometimes tech designers do the final flats in Illustrator. Sometimes designers do the whole tech pack, sometimes designers pass on flats to tech designers to do the tech pack.

If you're designing on your own, you could also hire a tech designer to do your flats and/or tech packs.

Once your tech packs are done, they are passed off to a pattern maker and sample maker for the first pattern and sample. Samples are fit on fit models, corrections on made on the patterns, new samples are made. Lather, rinse, and repeat until the sample is perfect.

FIGURE 10.2. RIGHT Use the template to design your fit. Notice how the collars are the same but one is very big and boxy and the other is boxy but a much closer fit?

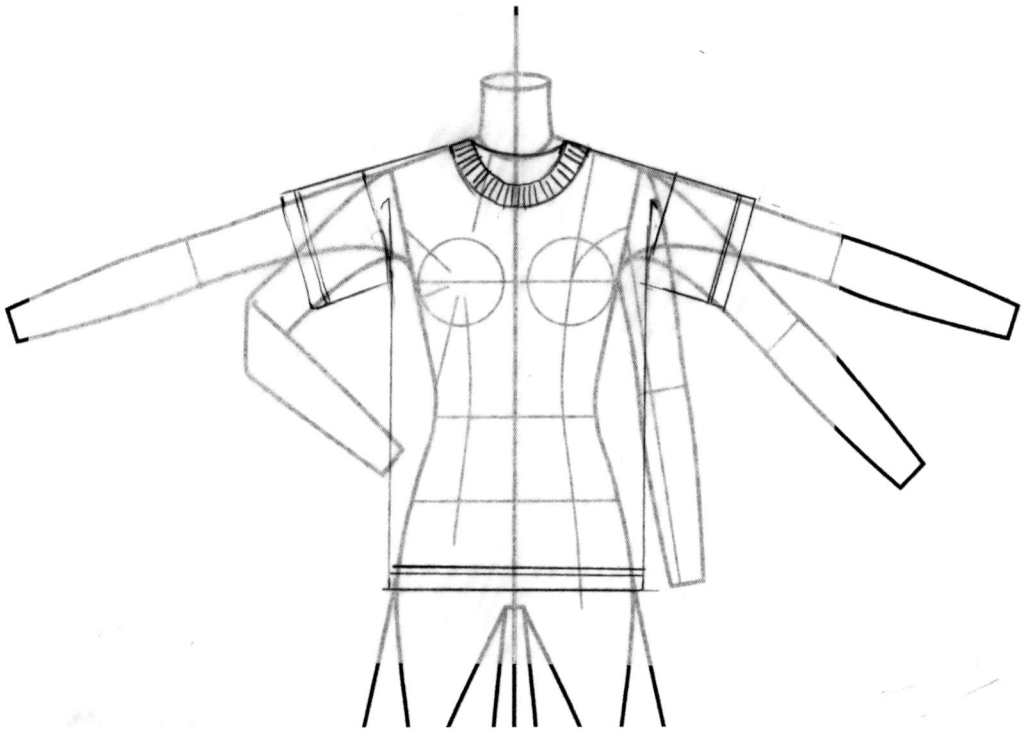

Sustainability in Product Development

We've already discussed sustainability in the design process in terms of materials and processes. These will carry through product development and production.

Something specific to product development is using 3-D modeling software like CLO3D to reduce the number of iterations needed in perfecting your sample. That saves a lot of time, effort, fabrics and trims, and if you're sampling overseas, a lot of air freight. One sample at a time, these things can start adding up.

When you model a design in software, you have the opportunity to turn the design over in the round and see it on a person. Sometimes a design gets ditched the second it's on a person. It just doesn't translate. Sometimes a design needs tweaking and it can really help to tweak at a 3-D level before sampling.

> *No coffin garments! Coffin garments are designs that focus interest only in the front and top area, what you would see of a person laying in a coffin.*

Sustainability in Business

Sustainability practices don't stop when you finish making a garment.

Offer tailoring services. When a garment fits better, the chances are people will wear the garment more and take care of the garment better instead of dumping it in the trash.

Relatedly, you can offer a repairs program or sell repair kits. You can post about repairs on your social media.

Offer a secondhand program. More and more companies are doing this. They accept carefully worn garments (of their brand) and sell them again in the secondhand section of their store or website. In turn, the donating customers get a discount on their next purchase at the same brand.

Start a recycling program. Companies accept donations of specific kinds of garments they know they can recycle and offer a discount to the donating customers for their store.

> *Recycled denim makes for good housing insulation. Look it up. Take that nugget and run with it.*

Customer education is an important component of sustainability. Have a dedicated portion of your website for information or a blog, include sustainability education in your social media, include digestible bits of info in regular newsletters, host online workshops, or all of the above.

Chiffon

Denim

Basic

Charmeuse

PVC

11

PORTFOLIOS

Planning Your Portfolio

FIGURE 11.1. LEFT
Illustrations are about
clarity of design details,
shapes, and textures. This
is the same dress rendered
in cotton poplin, PVC,
charmeuse, denim, and
chiffon.

This chapter is for people who want to make a beautiful portfolio in hopes of getting a job at a fashion design company.

You can of course use this book to help you apply to a fashion school. However, every school wants a different kind of portfolio. Always triple check the admissions requirements (and deadlines!) for each and every school.

A few things to consider when planning your portfolio:

◆ You'll want three to five projects for your portfolio. No one's going to look at all five. You want a variety of projects that you can show at different interviews depending on the kind of job you're interviewing for. Your portfolio will likely become more focused as you progress in your career and find your specialties.

◆ Not every project needs to be extremely elaborate. I will outline below which parts are necessary and which are optional.

◆ Not every project needs to feature complete outfits. There are many, many companies that design only one category of clothes, like outerwear or swimsuits.

- Think about what kinds of jobs you want to apply for and what skills you want to emphasize.

- Show you can design for different seasons, different price points, and different bodies.

At minimum for each project, you will need a mood board, a color and fabric board, a board with the illustrations of your outfits, and a board with front and back flats of each design.

> *I never wanted to design menswear until I had to do a project for school. I really changed my mind about menswear. You might want to try designing some categories you never considered before.*

A reality we don't always want to think about is the kinds of jobs you can realistically get in your area. I have had students who lived where the only design jobs available were for sporty, outdoorsy gear and they were not able to move. This category was not their favorite but it's what was available, so they made sure to include these kinds of clothes in their portfolio.

Putting together all those considerations, let's plan a few different portfolios.

Let's say you want to design womenswear, you love designing prints, and you're not really into designing eveningwear. You might want a portfolio that includes:

- Womenswear; designer price point; fall/winter; full collection; design own print and spin-off embellishments; include optional boards

- Collection of summer sundresses for plus size market; design own 2–3 prints; 6–8 bodies; 2–3 fabrics; minimum boards

- Womenswear; contemporary price point; seasonless separates; work clothes that aren't boring (appropriate for after work happy hour?); design own print; minimum boards + extra figures board to show day-to-night styling

- Womenswear vacation wardrobe for petites market; resort/cruise; include a couple of swimsuits, cut-and-sew knits, swimsuit coverups that don't overwhelm short bodies; design own print; minimum boards + close-up flats to show design details and construction

> *The term* petites *in the industry means short women, not necessarily thin women.*

What if you like to design for all genders, and you want to incorporate sustainable elements in the designs in different ways? How about a portfolio like this:

◆ Unisex dresses and tops utilizing zero waste cutting; minimum boards plus actual drapes and pattern of at least one dress showing the zero waste cutting process

◆ Menswear collection with complete outfits; spring/summer; upcycled suits; minimum boards

◆ Womenswear collection with complete outfits; fall/winter; using fabric manipulations as ways to use fabric scrap; minimum boards + many cool fabric manipulation samples

◆ Collection of dresses that can adjust from regular to maternity fit; seasonless; minimum boards + extra board to show pregnant figures wearing adjusted dresses

This is fun; let's do one more. You want to design superchic menswear for big guys. How about:

◆ Menswear collection of complete outfits for big guys; spring/summer; avant-garde, the design world is your oyster; include optional boards

◆ Develop two pairs of trousers for bottom-heavy guys: one pair of jeans, one pair of more formal slacks. Show through a series of flats and closeup drawings how you would alter the fit of most other pants to fit those guys

◆ Menswear collection of complete outfits for big and talls; fall/winter; classics made modern and flattering for the big guys; minimum boards

◆ Mens swim trunks that are in that nice sexy space in between banana hammocks and dad shorts; all sizes; design own print(s); minimum boards

Mood Boards

Mood boards are the first board people see, and should serve as a sneak preview to get people excited to turn the page. It should be like a great movie preview. They set the tone and the expectations for the project. Many people choose to do this last to summarize the project.

Mood boards should encapsulate quickly what your project is about, what the vibe is, and give a glimpse of the colors, textures, and shapes people can expect to see (**Figure 11.2a, next page**).

Too contained,
a little too elegant for what I wanted.
Missing the Rococo reference.

I hate the color story stripes and the font.
Both too graphic, clashes with the art.
And it's still too contained.

Need more room to sprawl,
but getting closer.

This was the final. In retrospect, I hate the font. I wish I left more room at the bottom
for the gold to flow. I would erase all the green background.

FIGURE 11.2A. LEFT
Variations and critique on
a mood board process

FIGURE 11.2B. RIGHT
A little boring, but clear
and straightforward.

ORGANIC TEXTURES

Mood board, inspiration board, theme board—they're all the same.

A good mood board should include your inspiration images artfully collaged, your project title, the season and year you're designing for, and perhaps a few words on what your project is about (**Figure 11.2b**). A few words, not a wall of text. No one's going to read all that. A few words, a couple of sentences. Get to the point. Recruiters have to look at a lot of projects and they have very short attention spans.

Your entire project can include some text but make it minimal. Let the images speak for themselves as much as possible. Very little text is essential (labeling fabrics, designating what season and year you're designing, some construction notes).

Don't make a mood board heavy on the red if you barely use red as a pop color. Don't emphasize a picture of corrugated cardboard if you're not going to reference it at all in your textures. Don't make your board moody and dark if your clothes are bright and playful.

How about people wearing clothes? Can you add them? If you want to include photos of your muse, that's great. That's actually really helpful in setting the tone. If you want to include a million photos of peacoats because you looked at them to design your own peacoats, no. Not necessary, not helpful. Present your original ideas and the vision you bring (**Figure 11.3, next page**).

Color and Fabric Board(s)

You need to include your color story, the fabrics you use, prints, whether sourced or designed yourself, and any fabric manipulations or embellishments used (**Figure 11.4**). They help people better imagine your collection, even if your illustration skills are relatively good. Nothing beats showing in real color and fabric the cool twisty folded fabric manipulation you developed during your design process. Use as many boards as you need to include this information. Format some beautiful boards (**Figure 11.5**).

Personally, I think the color, fabric, and manipulations board(s) are more important in expressing who you are as a designer than the mood board. Fabric knowledge is key for designers. Collaging mood boards isn't something you'll do very often over the course of your career.

FIGURE 11.3. ABOVE
I love the mindmap for my Syzygy project, so I included it (on the embroidered watercolor fabric I love so much) on the mood board for the project.

100% silk
charmeuse

Available in
pink,
white,
chartreuse,
black

100% silk
crepe

Available in
pink,
white,
chartreuse,
black

100% silk
organza

Available in
pink,
white,
black

100% linen

Available in
white,
black

100% cotton
twill

Available in
dark olive,
black

100% nylon
tulle

Available in
pink,
white,
black

Syzygy
Spring/Summer 2025

FIGURE 11.4. ABOVE Color and fabric board for my Syzygy project

FIGURE 11.5. RIGHT This is the fabric board from a project from 2006 with five eveningwear looks. All I have is this fuzzy cell phone pic, but it's still one of the best fabric boards I ever did. This project also won me enough money to pay off my student loans, which does make me love it that much more.

The biggest hurdle most students face is acquiring fabric swatches, especially in all the colors in your color story. One option is to buy some yardage in white, and use marker, watercolor, or fabric paint to color the fabric. Another option is to find photos of the fabrics you want and include them.

If you have a hard time sourcing fabrics, you can do your fabric manipulations in muslin, but any extra trims like beads should be as close to the real thing as possible. Even doing your fabric manipulations in white versions of all your real fabrics is better. Most do not expect many completed garments in the portfolio of someone still early in their career, but you can show you have an understanding of construction with these samples.

Illustrations

Illustration is like writing. If you share your ideas with good grammar and flowing syntax, if you write clearly and beautifully, people will be more inclined to pay attention. At the very least, they won't have to struggle to figure out what you're saying.

Consider your figure illustrations board your runway show. Try styling different outfits together, think about how the hair, makeup, and shoes can aid in selling your vision to your audience. Use figure poses that show off the designs the best. Use a pose with the legs apart to show off wide leg or flared pants. Use a pose with the arms away from the body to show off wide sleeves like a kimono sleeve or dolman. Use a back pose to showcase a deep scoop back or incredible embroidery along the back panel of a gown.

FIGURE 11.6. BELOW LEFT

The next time you hear me yammer on and on about #practicenotmagic and roll your eyes at me, remember this illustration and think about how far I've come.

FIGURE 11.7. BELOW

I really need someone to make me a pair of those knee-high boots, but as flatforms.

A growing trend in collection presentation is having models posing in tableaus instead of walking down runways. Think about a cool presentation or composition. I did this project (**Figure 11.6**) in college. I don't think the illustrations are that great, but I still love the composition. Check out those fold out *Vanity Fair* covers with multiple models/actresses for some composition inspiration.

Your designs don't necessarily need to be on people. You can illustrate them on dress forms, store mannequins, robots, hangers on a rack, whatever presentation suits the clothes the best.

When you're laying out the order of your figures, thing about how the colors and textures will flow across the page. Don't cluster all your peachy orange on one side and all your turquoise on the other.

I created a rough draft of this project (**Figure 11.7**) to drop in colors and label fabrics, cut it up and moved figures around so I could sprinkle the purple, chartreuse, and black evenly across the spread.

You can use whatever medium you are the best at, but I encourage using markers. They're fast, look great, and are very versatile (**Figure 11.8, next pages**).

Flats

Flats are the technical drawings of garments and require precision and clarity of design above all else. The proportions of the design elements are key here: the length of the sleeve compared to the bodice, the size of the collar compared to the bodice, the width of a placket compared to the rest of the shirt. Using a figure template will help. Where do you want the cuffs to end on the arm? How far down the back do you want the yoke to end?

Another key element is the placement of design elements. Where are the pockets and are they high up enough on the jacket to leave room for a proper pocket bag? Where on the chest is the appliqué? Which edges get the lace trim?

FIGURE 11.8. LEFT, RIGHT
Syzygy final illustrations

Flats at this stage, the final flats for your board, are really when the nitty gritty of the design gets nailed down. The details of what kind of closure, where to put the closure, where to put darts and seams and topstitching are a) part of transitioning design to product development and b) how you show recruiters that you know how a garment is supposed to come together.

Your flats should be drawn in Adobe Illustrator, but even hand-drawn are better than nothing. Flats on your board should be grouped and laid out in the same order as the outfits on your figure illustration (**Figure 11.9, next page**).

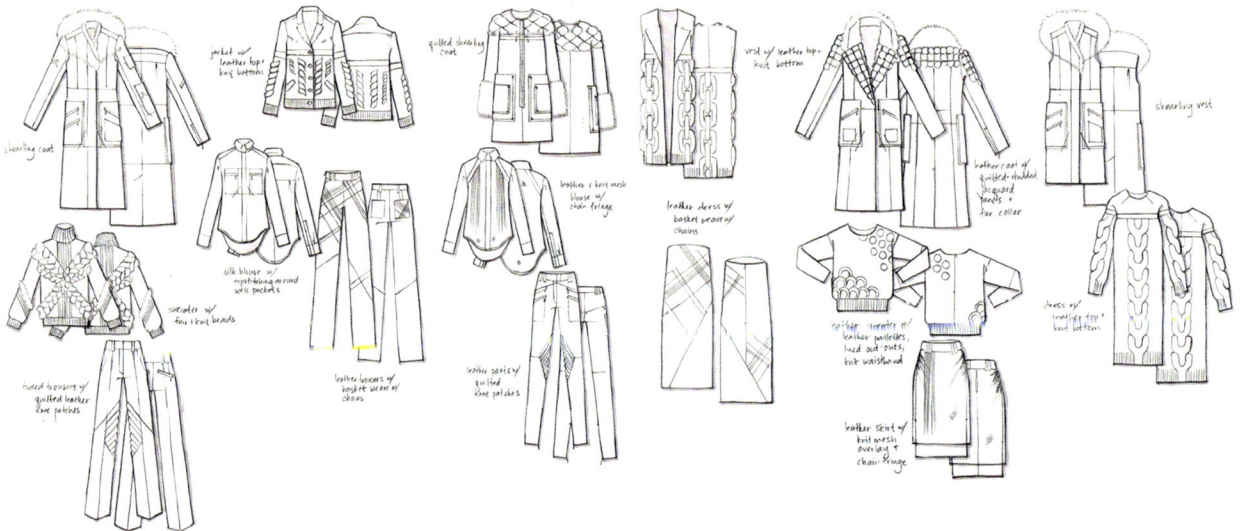

Optional Boards

The page with all your figure illustrations and the page with all your flats are not optional but you can add another section to be more thorough. You can create a page for each outfit that includes the figure illustration, all the flats for that outfit, swatches for each garment, and detail closeups (**Figure 11.10**). It shows that you are thoughtful about how to make the actual clothes. You don't have to re-illustrate everything. You can scan and copy and paste.

FIGURE 11.9. ABOVE
Layout of illustration with corresponding flats organized underneath.

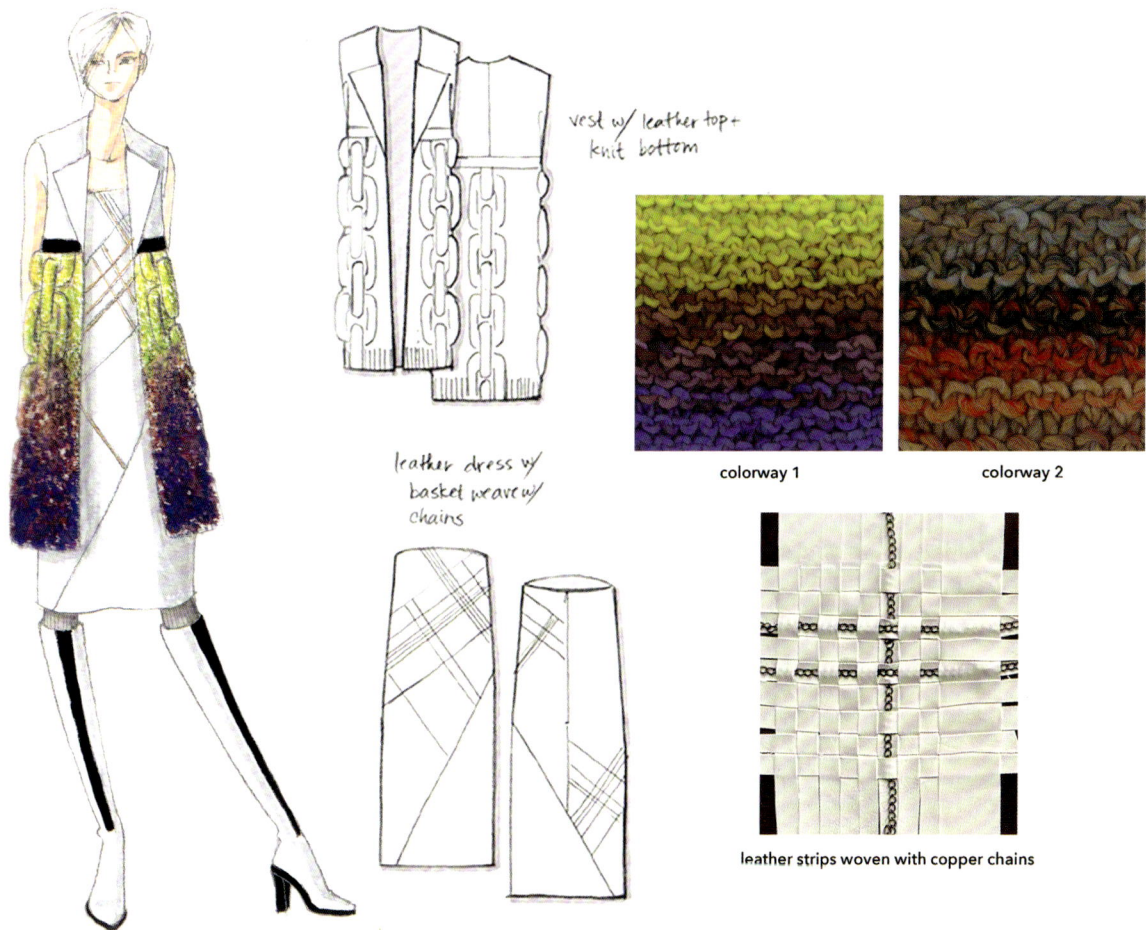

vest w/ leather top + knit bottom

colorway 1   colorway 2

leather dress w/ basket weave w/ chains

leather strips woven with copper chains

FIGURE 11.10. ABOVE
Layout of one outfit's illustration, flats, and swatches.

If you have a finished garment from your final illustrated designs, include photos. If you don't, it's not the end of the world. Your photos should be well-lit, clean, and professional. Include front, back, side, and detail shots. You can use your dress form as the model. If you use a human model, do not use distracting poses. Well, you can include a couple of editorial shots after you already have some clean front, back, and side shots.

Many wonder if works in progress are good to include. WIPs are only interesting if you have the finished product to show at the end. No one cares if you do a bunch of drapes on a dress form if you don't know how to turn that into a finished garment. But if you have some great photos of your finished gowns, some cool process shots would be excellent. If drapes are part of your design process and lead to final illustrated designs, you can include those drapes too.

If you have a lot of design sketches you have edited out (**Figure 11.11**), you can put together a croquis book. You can tell a lot about a designer by what they edit out. Design directors often like to flip through croquis books at interviews.

Croquis means quick sketch *in French.*

Tech packs are essential for anyone applying for a tech design job and optional for design jobs. You should include one if there are tech design job responsibilities included in the job listing. It's good to show you understand product development process and are thoughtful about how the garments will be made.

FIGURE 11.11. BELOW AND RIGHT Gah, I love sketching. I could have worked on this project forever, but I had to finish this book sometime.

Your Online Portfolio

Stop freaking out about someone stealing your work. Password protect it if you need to, but you want a website as your calling card.

The design of your website should match your general aesthetic as a designer and that of your projects. Your website should be well organized so anyone can find everything without guidance. If you are looking for both design and styling jobs, make sure you have separate sections for those portfolio projects. Make sure recruiters know what is supposed to be what.

Highlight the most exciting skills. I saw a portfolio that shoved their CLO3D skills into some miscellaneous section dead last. No. Companies are looking to hire people who have these coveted software skills. Bring that project forward. If you hate working with CLO3D and never want to work with 3-D modeling, don't bother including it at all.

Adding to Your Portfolio Over Time

Your portfolio should be updated periodically over the course of your career. Whenever you work somewhere, collect lookbooks you've helped with, designs you've worked on, linesheets you've put together, anything you've had your hands on. You need to include these materials in your future portfolio, with notes on your role in each project.

Portfolio projects showcasing work from a job don't need to look like the project I outline above. Just format your work professionally in your book.

If you're in between jobs, you should take the opportunity to update your portfolio with another project. Again, it doesn't need to be the biggest, most elaborate thing you've ever done, but you do need to show recruiters and design directors that you're keeping up with the trends or that your designs are current, even if they're not particularly trendy.

If you're looking to move into a new sector of the industry, it is especially important to include a new design project amongst your work experience to show people you are ready for the shift. It may be easier to find freelance gigs in the new sector you want to move to; include those projects and jobs in your portfolio and resume to help you move to a full-time job.

Rendering Tutorials

I teach fashion illustration as design communication. For a design portfolio, your illustrations should be all about clarity of design details, shapes, and textures. Artistic expression is important but a lesser priority for these kinds of illustrations.

Materials

Markers:
We're doing marker renderings because they're effective and fast. Get any brand of professional grade alcohol-based marker. Copic, Prismacolor, Blick, Winsor & Newton, Touch by ShinHan—I have all of them and like all of them. I pick markers to match the color of the fabric I'm rendering and if one brand doesn't have the color, I go to another brand. At art stores, I look like a frog hopping on lily pads, squatting in front of a marker display with a scrap of fabric, and hopping to the next display if I can't find the right match.

People love Copics and I get it, they're nice. But most brands are similar enough in quality that you can't blame a bad rendering on the marker. Insert pointed look here. I prefer buying Copics when I know I'm going to need refills in the future, like flesh tones and greys.

Marker Paper:

For marker renderings, I prefer using...wait for it...marker paper. It's called marker paper. All papers have a wrong side and a right side, even marker paper. Every brand is different. Test your paper! Bienfang, Copic, and Winsor&Newton make good marker paper. I'm sure there are others.

Some people don't like how flimsy marker paper is. I use a bit of cheap Bristol board as backing if I'm formatting a marker rendering for a portfolio or similar. Some render directly on Bristol but I hate it. Thick papers suck up too much ink, you don't have any blending time, and you don't get the same level of vibrance. There's the Rendr paper but I don't like the grey cast of the paper.

Colored Pencils:

I don't do full renderings in colored pencil because it's too slow. I use colored pencils to add textures and details. I have Caran d'Ache Luminance, Prismacolor, Faber Castell, Lyra, Derwent, and some other brands. I prefer the first two because they are the richest in color. Artists who use colored pencils as their main medium have different concerns, like blooming, but for small touches to marker renderings, many brands work well enough

Watercolor Pencils:

Watercolor pencils look like colored pencils but become like paint when you apply water. I love these pencils for rather particular applications, like fuzzy knit textures and tweed speckling, but I don't often use them as the main medium. Lucky for us, most watercolor pencils, like colored pencils, are sold in singles, so you can buy whatever individual colors you need. My favorites are Derwent Inktense and Faber-Castell Albrecht Dürer.

Pencil:

I sketch a lot, and nothing annoys me more than breaking a streak to sharpen my pencil (#firstworldproblems). I mostly use mechanical pencils for everything. Thin, harder lead pencils for underdrawings; thicker, softer leads for finishing touches. Because I am who I am, I will occasionally use a fat jumbo Faber-Castell regular graphite pencil because my hand needs to hold a different shape. I draw a lot. Not exactly necessary, but I like a .3mm mechanical drawing for very light underdrawings.

Adding White:

There will be different occasions to add a touch of white. For softer looks, I use a white colored pencil. My favorite whites are Prismacolor and Caran d'Ache Luminance. I hate gel pens. Sorry not sorry. They hate me too. They don't flow smoothly fast enough and I'm busy, I don't have time to wait for gel pens. I only use them when I need tiny, short strokes. Sometimes I use white paint pens. If you're doing tiny little sparkles, you don't have to worry about rippling marker paper too much.

The Mother Tutorial (FIGURE 11.12, NEXT PAGES)

Whatever you want to render, start here. This is The Mother Tutorial, from which all other ~~blessings~~ tutorials flow. I'm going to go over step-by-step the basics of how to render solid color fabrics with no extra texture. I'm talking about fabrics like cotton poplin, t-shirt materials, sweatshirt materials, and solid wool suitings like gabardine.

1. Start by lightly drawing the basics of your garment. Pay attention to the weight, thickness, and stiffness of the fabric and draw your garments accordingly. Silk jersey is heavy, thin, and slinky. Wool Melton is light, thick, and fairly stiff. Chiffon is light, very thin, floaty and limp. Organza is light, very thin, but far stiffer than chiffon. Leathers run the gamut. Don't draw in details like topstitching or textures. Draw the seams and any places where the color will change, like patches or color blocking. Use a light pencil to reduce smudging.

2. Fill in the garments with marker, matching the color of your fabric as closely as possible. Render in the direction of the garment so *if* your marker gets a big streaky, the streaks are at least going with the flow, so to speak.

   To prevent streaks, make sure your marker isn't too dry or apply a second coat of marker. I find chisel tips produce less streaking than brush tips. I usually color in the base with chisel tip markers and add shadows with brush tips.

   I also find it helpful to break up the markering at natural breaks in the garment. For example, color in the sleeve up to the seam and work with the marker ink for the short period of time it's still wet. You want sections to be wet at the same time and then dry at the same time. You'll get more streaking and patchiness if you're trying to color in a large area and you're randomly just trying color everything as fast as possible.

FIGURE 11.12. BELOW

The Mother

3. Now we add shadows to make your figure look three-dimensional. First, pick a shadow color (or two). I prefer to shade with a darker version of the fabric color. The shadow color can be a little duller than the fabric color, but I usually don't use greys to shadow (unless the fabric is grey or close to grey). Using grey gives a dull overall effect but shading with darker versions of the fabric color keeps the vibrancy of the color while adding depth.

You might choose greys if you want a duller, more muted effect overall. I might choose to shade colors like khaki or soft blues with grey, but I wouldn't do that to bright yellow.

shaded w/ colors

shaded w/ greys

4. Pick a light source. If your light is coming from the right, the left side
    of each arm, each leg, the neck, the torso will be shadowed. Include
    the left side of the skirt, including the left side of any folds/gathers/
    pleats/whatever drapes you have going on.

    Render in the direction of the garment: along the sleeve, along the pant
    leg. Follow the shapes of the garments, follow the crinkles of pants
    around the knees and render your shadows into zigzags. Follow the
    curves of breasts with curving shadows.

5. Next add the shadows under the light. Shade the bottom half of
    breasts, as they curve under and away from the light. Same with bot-
    toms. Same with any similarly round shapes in clothes.

FIGURE 11.12. LEFT, RIGHT
The Mother

6. Next add drop shadows or cast shadows. When a person holds a parasol up in the sun, the parasol casts a shadow on the person. If a person wears a full skirt, the skirt will cast a shadow on the rest of the legs. The fuller the skirt, the bigger the shadow. Chins cast shadows on necks, torsos cast shadows on arms on the dark side of the light. Armpits are generally dark because of these cast shadows.

Pay attention to the width of my shadows. When you shade a cylinder to create depth, you don't add a skinny little shadow along one side. You shade a full quarter to a third of the width, a hair from the edge. As our bodies are a series of cylinders, I want you to render your figure shadows similarly.

The last bit are separation shadows. They are skinny little shadows to separate parts of garments. These are things like collars on shirts or jackets. I render a skinny little shadow on the outside of the collar to separate the collar from the bodice/chest. These shadows are not for seams. Seams don't cause shadows. I will drop a little separate shadow along blazers closed over a button-up shirt and the front edge of blazer buttoned up over the other side.

7. This step isn't necessary, but I find it adds depth and richness. I like to add a second, darker shadow color. I drop them on the inside quarter/third of my bigger shadows to give renderings dimension.

8. Last, add details like topstitching, the lines of rib knits, seams, and outlines of pockets. You can use a darker graphite pencil or a dark colored pencil. On darker clothes, I like to use a white colored pencil or even a pale grey for a slightly more subtle look.

FIGURE 11.13. RIGHT
50 Shades of White

Rendering Details for Various Colors, Textures, and Prints

WHITE FABRICS (FIGURE 11.13)

1. Pick a grey tone for shadows as carefully as you would pick any other color marker. Think about what other clothes you're rendering. Blue jeans pair well with white tees rendered with cool grey shadows. Olive drab, khaki, green suitings, and tweeds pair well with white button-up shirts with greenish French grey shadows. There are even greys with pinky purply undertones.

2. I definitely add the second, darker shadow to create more dimension. To me, white clothing renderings look a little unfinished without them.

3. I also make sure to beautifully render the skin, hair, and other garments.

4. Sometimes I add a drop shadow behind the whole figure for dramatic effect, but you have to decide if that look works with your designs and illustration style.

natural
grey
1,2,3
(copic)

warm grey
1,2,3
(copic)

cool grey
1,2,3
(copic)

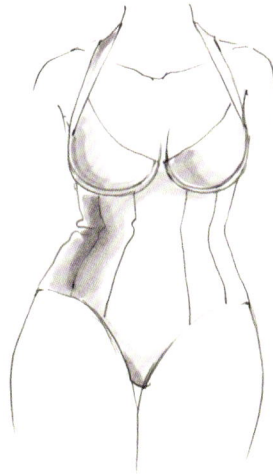

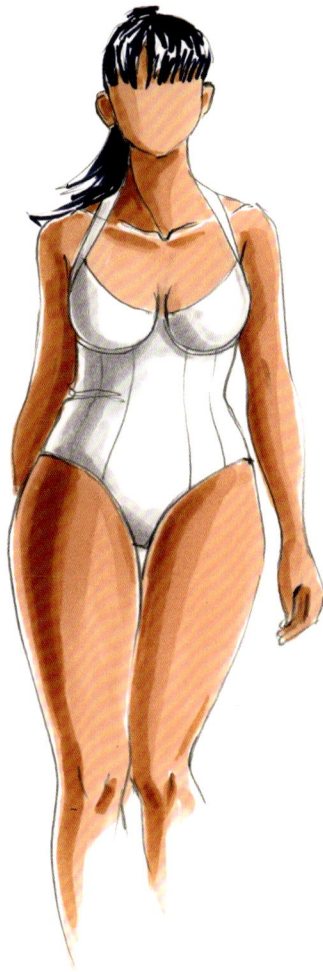

BLACK FABRICS (FIGURE 11.14)

1. There are such things as light blacks and dark blacks. Marker brands have all kinds of blacks, like black, jet black, and special black. When push comes to shove, you can use the darkest grey color available as your base tone and add black shadows on top.

2. There are also different colors of black. Some are literally called "green black" or "blue black" and they are very, very dark but usually not really black. Test anything that would remotely work.

3. Focus on your fabric. Some black fabrics are actually quite light, such as black denim.

4. Add details with a white colored pencil or pale grey colored pencil. If the fabric is very shiny, like PVC, white gel pen would look better.

FIGURE 11.14. BELOW
I deliberately lightened these swatches and illustration so you can see the variations of undertones clearly.

Black (Prismacolor)

Jet Black (Copic)

Cool Gray 10 (Copic)

Cool Grey 90% (Blick)

Warm Black (Blick)

Black (Copic)

Warm Gray 10 (Copic)

Warm Grey 90% (Blick) (I would use this for blk denim)

Black Special Black (Copic)

Warm Grey 90% (Prismacolor) (or this one)

layered
Blick Warm Black
Blick Black
Chartpak Super Black (fine tip)

FIGURE 11.15. BELOW

Remember: you're adding texture, not stripes.

DENIM (FIGURE 11.15)

Denim is a cotton fabric with indigo yarns going along the grain, and white or undyed yarns woven in the cross grain, in a twill weave. This twill weave is what creates the subtle diagonal texture on the surface of denim. The different color yarns are why the inside of your jeans are often so much lighter than the outside.

1. Start with The Mother Tutorial, matching your base color with your denim swatch.

2. Add the twill texture. On dark denim, use a very sharp white colored pencil to draw a series of parallel diagonal lines. On light denim, use a skinny graphite pencil. Sharpen your pencil often; you want light, thin, subtle diagonals. Sketch patches of twill texture where the light hits your figure, like the tops of thighs.

3. Do not draw long diagonals across the whole garment. This will flatten out your figure.

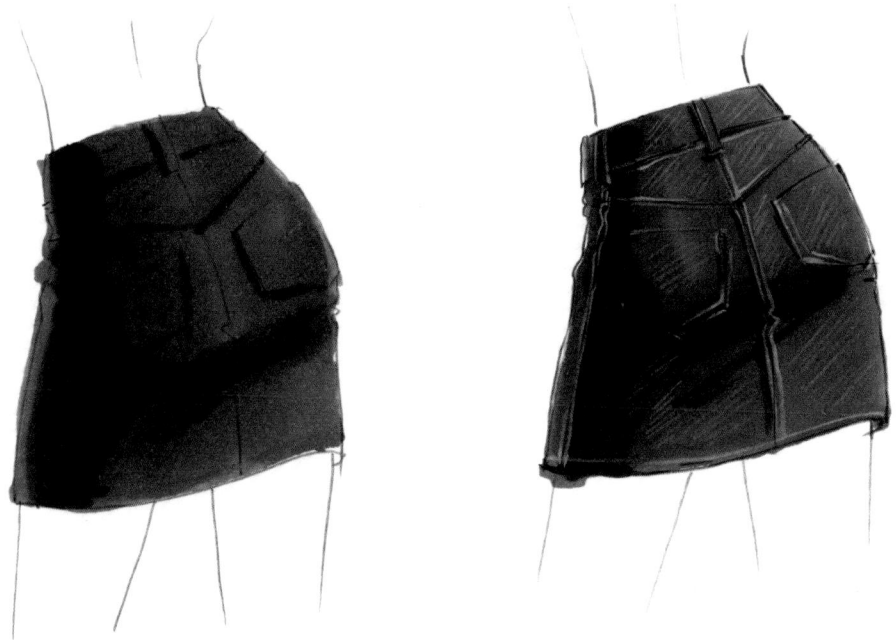

FISHNET (FIGURE 11.16)

1. Do not draw big straight grids across your garment. Round your mesh grids around bodies. Follow the direction of drapes with your mesh lines.

2. Break up your line quality. Solid lines of the same width flatten out the figure.

3. Lighten up the mesh rendering in highlighted, tight spots like mesh tights over the tops of thighs.

FIGURE 11.16. BELOW
These are wider fishnets, where you can count the yarns. Finer meshes belong in the sheer fabrics rendering category.

FIGURE 11.17. BELOW

In my university classes, I
called this speckled tweed
to differentiate it from
others. Petition across
the industry to make this
official.

TWEED (FIGURE 11.17)

Tweeds are wool fabrics, or wool blends, that can be woven thinner for
blazers and thicker for coats. Tweeds are a bit loosely woven, so the surface
texture is on the coarser side, but the overall fabric is soft, not stiff. Tweeds
have more than one color, which can show up as a herringbone pattern, or
what looks like, from a distance, grains of sand mixed together. Later, I will
show you how to render some patterns like herringbone but first I want
to show you how to render a solid tweed with a sprinkling of different colored speckles.

1.   Start with The Mother Tutorial, matching your base color with the back-
     ground color of your tweed swatch.

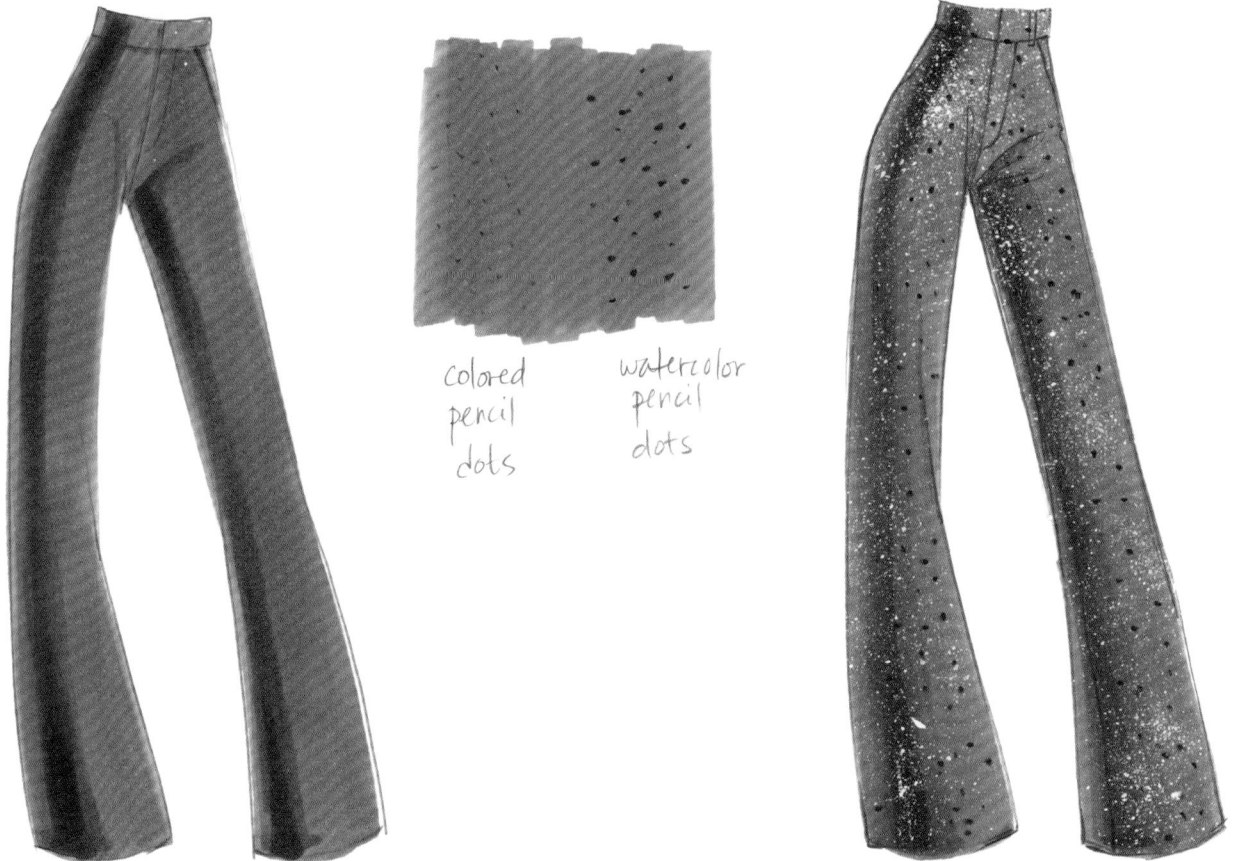

colored
pencil
dots

watercolor
pencil
dots

2. There are several ways to make speckles. You can use a colored pencil and popopopopopopop stab your paper a million times. It's the most ~~nonexistent~~ subtle look, and generally the most annoying for your arm and any neighboring people. Do not try this in a library. However, you can get better (and quieter) results if you use a barely wet watercolor pencil. Dip your sharpened watercolor pencil in a bit of water and give it a second to soak. Tap off excess water and test some speckles on some scrap paper.

3. Another method is to use some paint and a very stiff brush. I use opaque gouache and a toothbrush. Gently dip your brush in your paint and position your brush over your paper. Slowly run your thumb over the brush, spraying paint speckles across your illustration

   Test test test first! You may have to figure out the right water-to-paint ratio that works best for you, depending on what paint you're using.

   Keep your brush close the paper. If you're too high above the paper, you'll spray paint everywhere. Cover all the not-tweed parts of your paper with scrap paper so you're not spraying everywhere. I keep my speckles on the non-shadow areas of my garments. This keeps from my illustration looking flat. Once the paint is dry, sometimes I'll go in with a wet watercolor pencil to make a few bigger speckles or different colored speckles, depending on the fabric I'm rendering. (You're using such tiny specks of paint that it should not buckle your marker paper. If it does, you may have gone a bit overboard.)

Shiny Fabrics

I separate shiny fabrics into two categories: soft shine and hard shine. Soft shine fabrics are like leather, satin, and velvet. The shine on these fabrics is more subtle and, well, soft. PVC is a prime example of hard shine. The highlights are sharp, crisp, and glaringly white.

FIGURE 11.18. BELOW Focus
on the specific color of
your fabric's highlights.
Some soft shine fabrics
have a different color
reflect.

SOFT SHINE (FIGURE 11.18)

1. Start with The Mother Tutorial, matching your base color with your fabric swatch.

2. Use the side of a colored pencil to softly color in highlights. Pick the color that closest resembles your fabric highlights. Think about placing highlights opposite of your shadows: top of chest, arm facing the light, tops of shoulders.

    Build up the white intensity as you get to the centers of your highlights. You can use a white charcoal pencil if you're looking for a more intense, but still soft, textured look. Do not try to layer charcoal pencil on colored pencil. Their base mediums will fight each other. With charcoal pencil, you can smudge it a little with your finger or a smudge stick for a softer effect. Play around on a scrap, see if you like the effect.

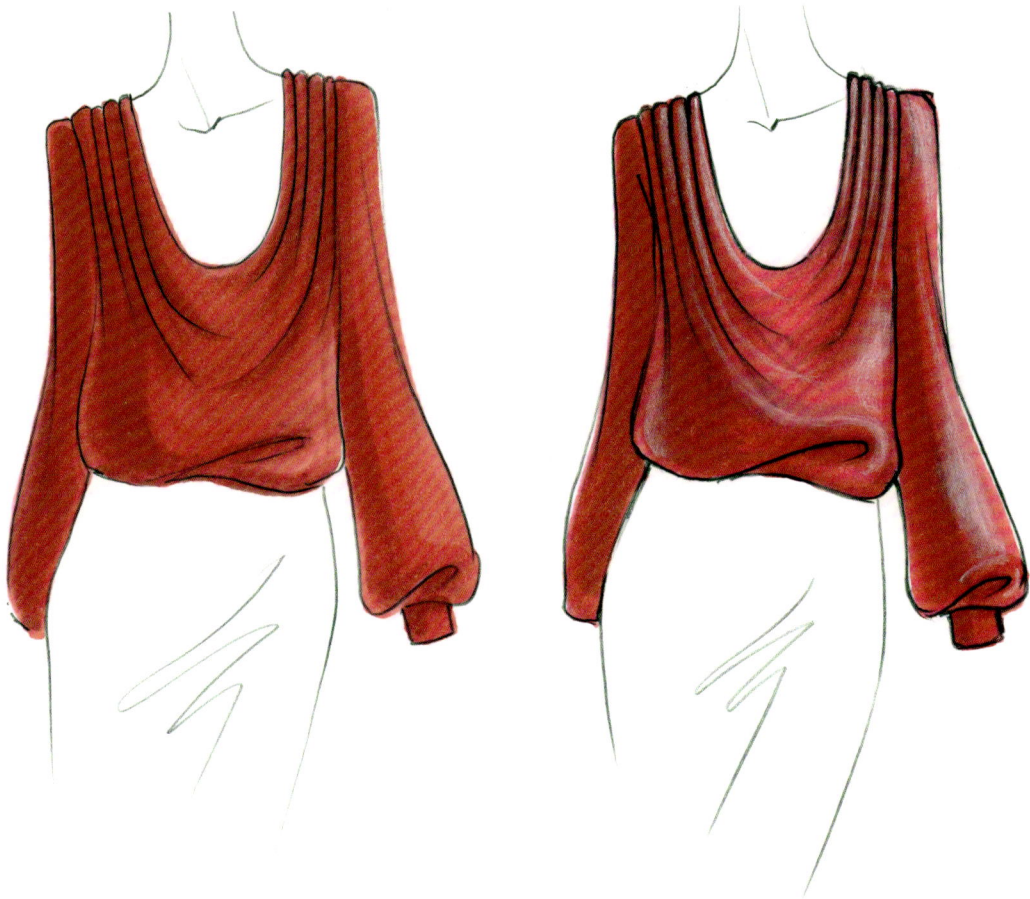

HARD SHINE (FIGURE 11.19)

1. You'll need three or four markers for this rendering. The first marker is your fabric color. Then, choose one or two shadow colors. Last, you'll need a marker that is a very light tint of your fabric color. I call this the halo color, because it will halo your highlights.

2. Isolate the highlight areas, which are the opposites of your shadow areas, like the top of your chest, the part of your leg facing the light, and the tops of folds and wrinkles. Use your halo color to circle your highlights.

3. Follow The Mother Tutorial, while leaving the highlight and halo areas alone. Add some tiny/skinny highlights with a white gel pen or paint pen as needed.

    Some people find it easier to drop the shadows first, and then isolate the highlights in the areas opposite the shadows.

FIGURE 11.19. BELOW You can also render metal this way, like suits of armor. The only difference is to pick the right marker colors.

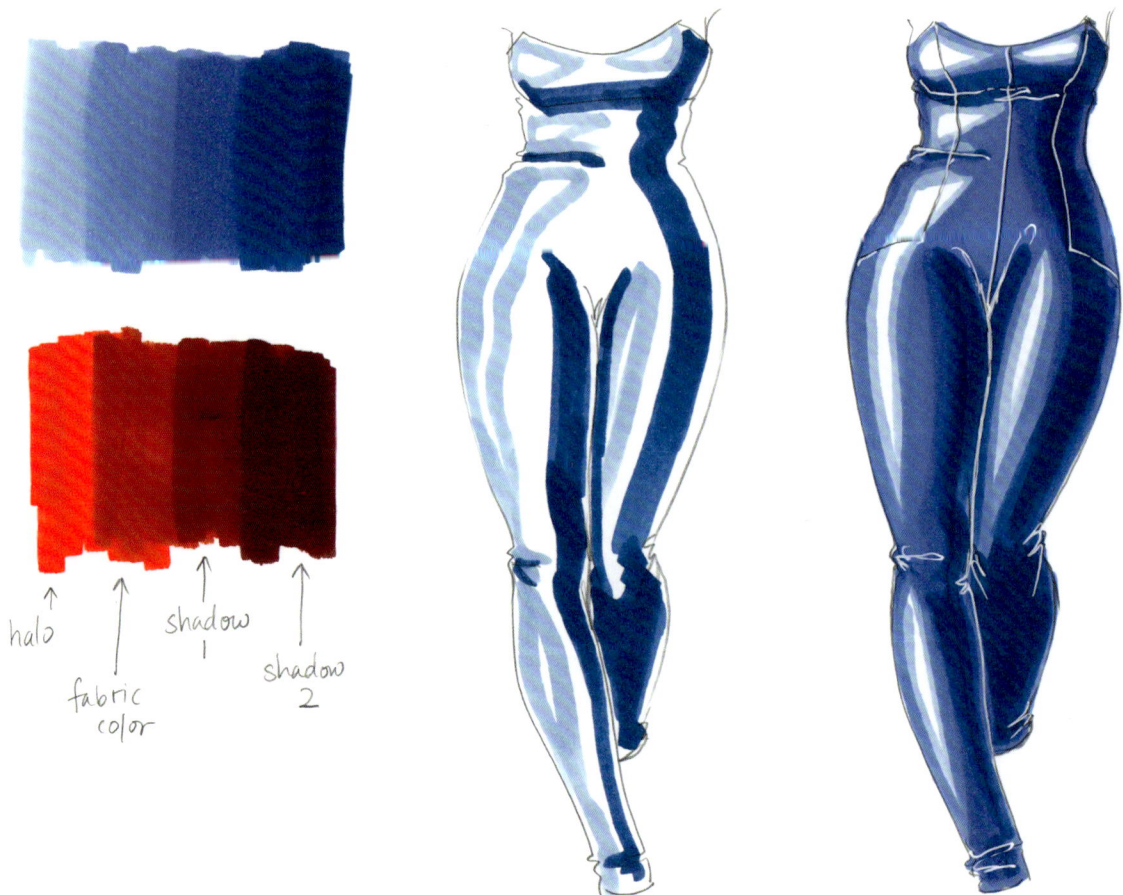

halo

fabric color

shadow 1

shadow 2

SEQUINED FABRICS (FIGURE 11.20)

1. Sequined fabrics are in the hard shine category. Draw and illustrate your base fabric, highlights, and shadows per the hard shine tutorial.

2. Get your markers together. You'll need markers for your fabric, shadow, and halo colors. Also get markers that are one shade darker than your fabric, shadow, and halo colors. Some of these colors can be multipurpose. You can use dark red for red shadows and red sequins.

3. Use the marker one shade darker than your fabric color, which will likely be your shadow color, to dot on a bunch of sequins over your base fabric color.

4. Choose a marker one shade darker than your shadow color and dot on a bunch of sequins in the shadow areas. Choose a marker one shade darker than your halo color and dot on some sequins in the halo areas. You are aiming for about 70% coverage.

5. Add sparkle crosses. Think about how the light will hit a random sequin just right and sparkle. You can add sparkle crosses or sparkle Xs. I like to draw them in dark pencil in the light areas and in white gel pen in darker areas so the sparkles show up sharply.

   Start from the center of the cross and flick out in four directions so you get the sharp points at the ends.

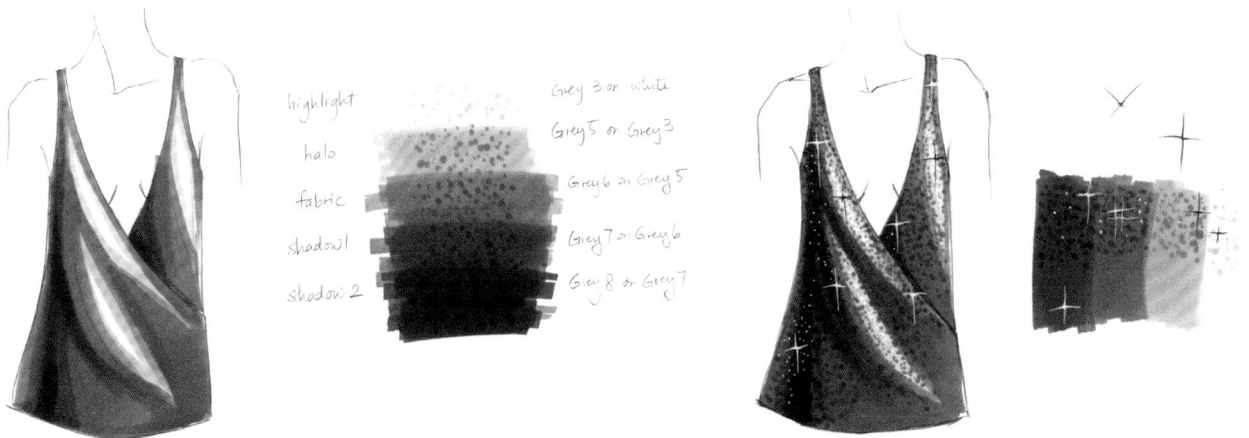

PAILLETTES (FIGURE 11.21)

Paillettes are basically large sequins usually sewn on the garment at the top so they dangle and shimmy with the wearer's movements. Sequins are small, so no matter how they're sewn, they stay affixed and close to the body.

1. Draw and illustrate your base fabric, highlights, and shadows per the hard shine tutorial.

2. Using a color a shade darker than your shadow color, illustrate your paillettes all over your garment. Aim for about 70–80% coverage. Add some paillettes right on the edges of the garment silhouette, just how they would appear in real life.

3. Now you're going to highlight individual paillettes. Using a white paint pen, illustrate the centers of your paillettes, leaving the darker color from step 2 as a shadow/border around the white. Aim to paint about 70% of your paillettes with these white highlights. Focus these high-lighted paillettes to the highlighted areas of the garment/body, but do scatter a few in the shadows. Add sparkle crosses or Xs as explained in the sequins tutorial.

FIGURE 11.21. BELOW
It's pronounced "pie-yets."
Mmm...pie.

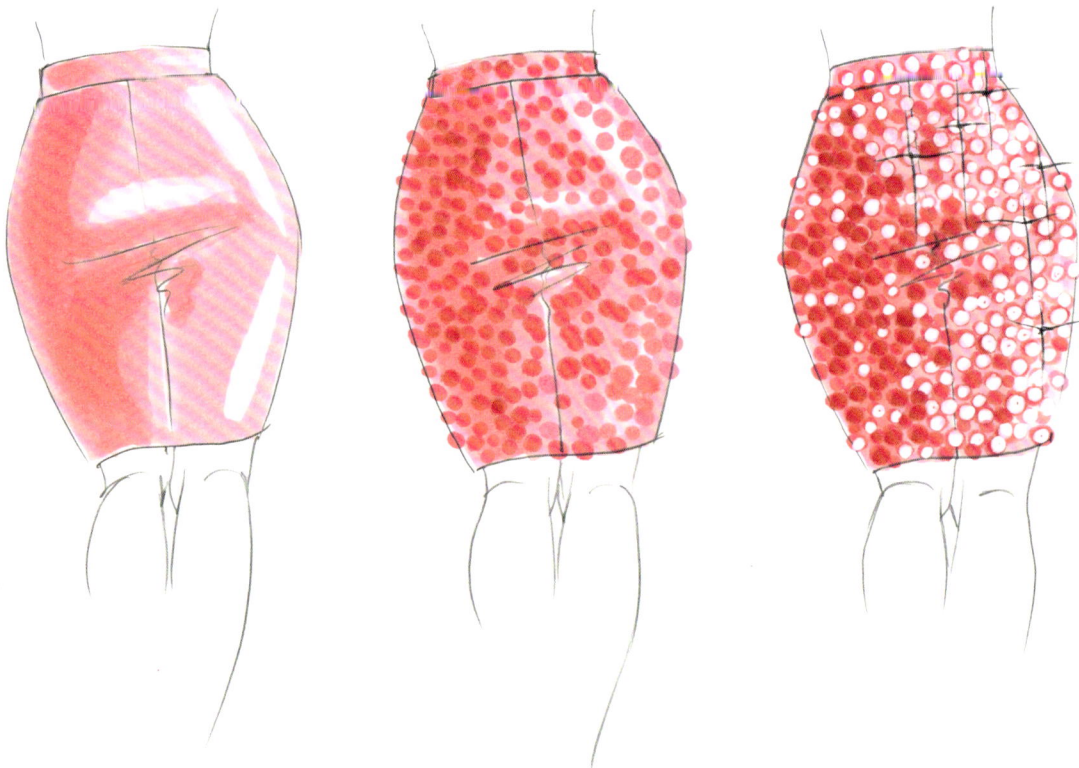

FIGURE 11.22. BELOW
Silver/grey pearls are
rendered the same way,
but using different colors.

PEARLS (FIGURE 11.22)

Pearls are soft shine materials, but round.

1. Pearls are rarely pure white, so choose some dark cream/eggshell markers for shading. Drop in shadows that wrap around the sphere to emphasize the round shape. Keep your shadows a hair away from the pencil edge. This space designates light bouncing off the neighboring pearl. Drop a dot of white paint pen for highlights.

2. When redrawing the garment outlines, I like to draw a bit darker in the shaded area to emphasize the shadow. This is especially true for pearls.

Prints and Patterns

THE PATTERNED FABRICS TUTORIAL (FIGURE 11.23)

Listen. Going from solid fabrics to prints and patterns is a leap. My university students always found it a bit of a rude awakening. Don't freak out I have a step-by-step guide to render any patterned fabric. I've had plenty of students whose first pattern renderings were muddy messes but who turned in beautiful final projects with enough practice.

1. Pick colors. Figure out which areas get marker and which details/textures require colored pencils. If sections of the pattern design are big enough to require marker, also get a shadow color for that color.

    If you're rendering a blue fabric with very skinny white stripes, you'll need blue and dark blue markers and the white pen or pencil that works best for you. If you're rendering green fabric with big yellow flowers, I would get green, dark green, yellow, and dark yellow markers.

    If you're rendering green leaves on a pale pink background, I would color the whole thing pink and then color in the leaves. In cases like this, I would test the markers layered on top of each other, as the colors may change a lot.

2. Draw your garments. Map out and draw your pattern very lightly. There are multiple parts to this.

3. First, pin/tape your fabric to a wall and step back about 8 feet (about 2.5 meters). Take note of how much detail you can see at that distance. Sometimes we obsess a little too much on every detail and get muddy results. Render what is visible from that distance. Sometimes I get questions about how to render slightly textured fabrics like linen. From 8 feet, you can barely discern enough texture to render. Let it go.

4. Next, you have to scale down the pattern. Put the fabric on the palm of your hand (or vice versa) and notice the size difference and scale. Draw a bit of the pattern next to your figure's hand to assess the scale before drawing the pattern on your final garment.

5. Study the grainlines of your garments so you're laying the pattern down correctly. Is your dress cut on the bias? Put your pattern on a 45-degree diagonal. Let's say your pattern is rows of flowers along the grain (parallel to the selvedge). These rows should run up and down your front, back, sleeves, and pant legs. These rows should run across shoulder yokes on shirts and dresses.

6. Render your fabric base per The Mother Tutorial. If you're rendering big pastel flowers on a dark background, I would leave blanks for the flowers.

7. Render your pattern. Remember to add shadows to substantial elements like large flowers. If your pattern is something like a small polka dot, I would use a darker color to render the dots that are in the shaded areas. Finish up the rest of the rendering as usual, adding some details and textures with your pens and pencils.

8. Do you have to render every single dot, every single leaf, every single flower? No, not really. You can, if you want. Aim for at least 75% coverage. Focus your details on unshaded areas, closer to your figure's face. (People naturally look at someone's face first.) We see less detail in shaded areas in real life. Try to fade out or taper off your patterns, instead of abruptly stopping the rendering harshly.

9. On the other hand, you will need to express the pattern all the way to the edge in some places. Creating this odd halo of solid color fabric with all the stripes/plaid/flowers only in the middle will flatten out the figure and just look, well, weird.

NB: I cannot stress enough how much I encourage you to do a practice run on a scrap piece of paper. All practice runs should be done on the same kind of paper as your final version, as paper can dramatically alter rendering results, including marker color.

STRIPES AND PLAIDS (FIGURE 11.24A-E, NEXT PAGES)

I'm including any sort of grid pattern in the stripes and plaids section, purely for rendering considerations. These include gingham, madras, windowpane check, tattersall check, and tartans. (What's the difference between a plaid and a tartan? A tartan is a type of plaid where the horizontal stripe formation is identical to the vertical stripe formation.) All these fabrics have different levels of thickness and crispness, so draw your garments accordingly.

You render these following the patterned fabrics tutorial, with some special tips to prevent your figure from looking like a chess board.

Pick colors and media. You will likely need an assortment of colored pencils, gel pens, fine tip markers, and/or paint pens. Draw your garments. Do a small practice rendering on scrap paper to sort out your scale. Render your fabric background per The Mother Tutorial.

1. Refer back to the chapter on drawing clothes on bodies and wrapping horizontal ellipses around our cylindrical body parts. I have provided some basic diagrams that show how garment patterns are shaped to give you an idea of how vertical stripes should be drawn. Combining that knowledge, lightly draw in your grids or stripes, scaled down per the patterned fabrics tutorial.

2. Pay attention to the drapes of your garment and let your stripes follow those drapes. Your stripes should roll and flow with your fabric. Again, if you want to only fill about 75% of the garment with the pattern, don't cut things off abruptly but, rather, taper the stripes off.

3. Many people ask about stripe matching. Stripe matching can only happen when you have straight edges joining like the center front, center back, and side seams on a boxy shirt. Shoulder yokes are cut on the cross, so those stripes won't match unless you have a classic tartan. You can also match stripes on curves if the curves are mirror images of each other. I wouldn't stress about it too much. My recommendation is to look at photos of garments similar to what you're rendering and pay attention to how the stripes meet at seams and closures.

4. On a design note, take a minute to design using grainlines. You can cut pockets, yokes, and cuffs on the bias to add a twist to shirts.

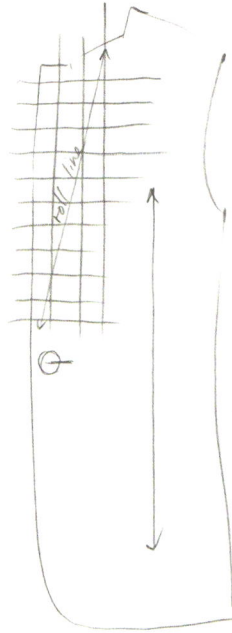

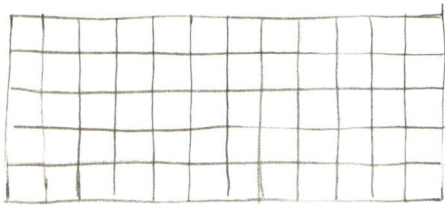

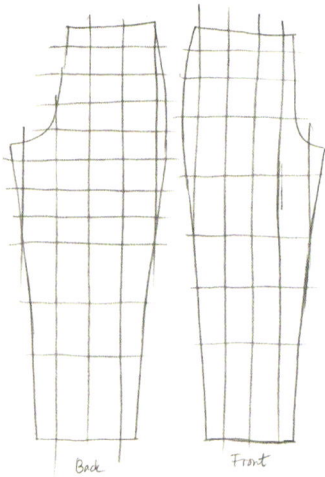

Back   Front

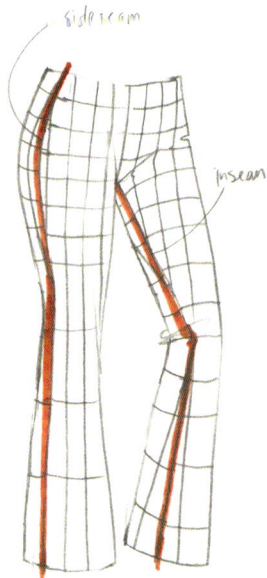

side seam

inseam

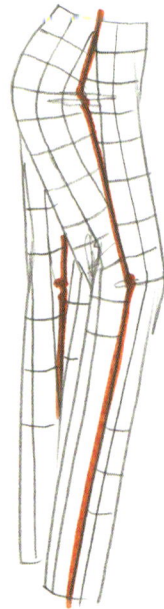

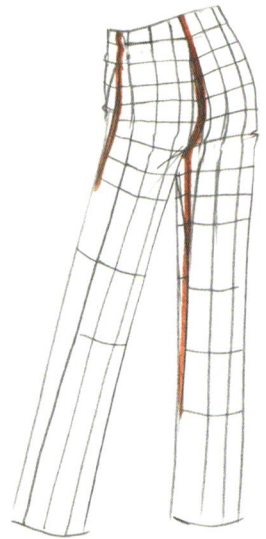

FIGURE 11.24A-E. LEFT AND

RIGHT You can always
Google "XYZ dress pattern"
for guidance.

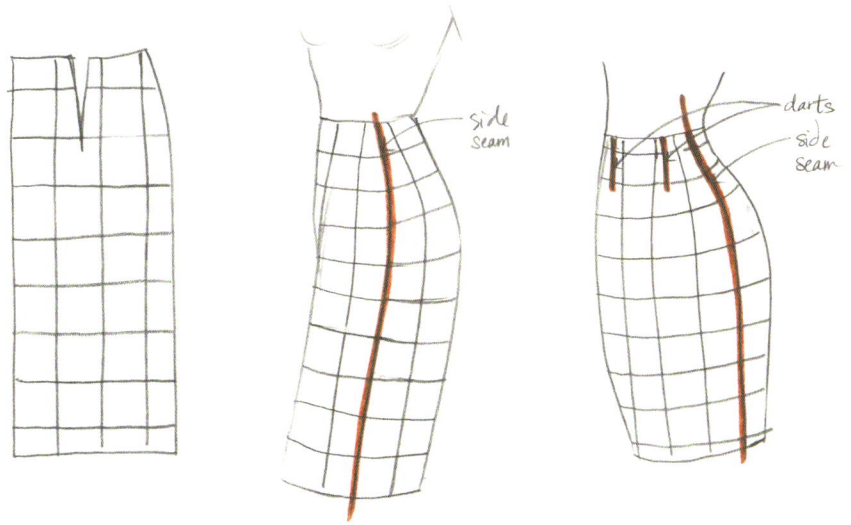

side
seam

darts
side
seam

darts

POLKA DOTS (FIGURE 11.25)

Follow the steps for the patterned fabrics tutorial. When rendering small dots, you can use a marker to render dots in the correct size and color as your fabric. If your dots are lighter than the background color, you can use a paint pen to paint in your dots. Painting in these tiny bits should not ripple the paper too much. If you don't have an exact color match, try marker over your fully dried paint pen dots. If your dots are in a grid formation, refer the stripes and plaids tutorial for help on layout.

FIGURE 11.25. BELOW Notice how the dots get closer together at gathers, like above the cuff and above the skirt.

FIGURE 11.26. BELOW

CORDUROY (FIGURE 11.26)

Corduroy is not that difficult to render, but I used to teach it quite late in the semester because it's a mashup of multiple previous tutorials. Refer to the patterned fabrics tutorial to scale down the wales correctly. Use the stripe diagrams from the stripes tutorial for corduroy wale direction.

1.   Follow The Mother Tutorial to render the base of the garment. With a colored pencil that is one shade off from your marker color, draw in stripes along your garments. Play around with different marker and colored pencil color combos to get the effect that matches your fabric best.

2.   Use a darker colored pencil to add stripes in the shaded areas. Sometimes corduroy can have a soft sheen to it like velvet. Drop some skinny highlights with a white colored pencil. Refer back to the section on shiny fabrics for highlight placement.

HERRINGBONE (FIGURE 11.27)

My guess is herringbone is called as such because the patterns look like fishbones protruding from its spine. Herringbone can be a pattern woven in the wool as a type of tweed or it can be a print applied to other fabrics. To render herringbone, follow the patterned fabrics tutorial with specific considerations.

1. Herringbone is comprised of two colors making tiny diagonal stripes. The colors are about 50/50 so pick one to be your background color. It's usually easier to go with the lighter color. Render the base fabric per The Mother Tutorial.

2. I would describe herringbone as a striped fabric in which each stripe is made up of a lot of skinny diagonal stripes. You can see that, right? Lightly draw in the main stripes. Refer back to the patterned fabrics tutorial and the stripes and plaids tutorial for guidance on scale and stripe direction.

3. With a frequently sharpened colored pencil, lightly hash in your small diagonal stripes within the stripes. When we rendered denim, we broke up the twill texture into patches to avoid flattening out the garment. Do the same with the herringbone. Follow the drapes of the fabric and avoid over rendering in the shaded areas.

4. Sometimes, herringbone is scattered with tiny colored speckles. Use the tweed tutorial to spray these speckles across your herringbone.

FIGURE 11.27. BELOW
Eventually, with practice, you'll be able to render herringbone without drawing the stripes first.

FIGURE 11.28. BELOW

I recommend practicing houndstooth on the grid before rendering it on a garment.

HOUNDSTOOTH (FIGURE 11.28)

1. Draw your garment per your fabric's weight and drape. Houndstooth fabrics are typically two colors. Choose the lighter color as your base and render per The Mother Tutorial. Lightly draw in a grid per our stripes and plaids tutorial.

2. Using your darker color marker, color in every other box, leaving every other row blank.

3. Now we're going focus on the lighter color boxes below each dark color box. Split them into quarters, diagonally.

4. Using the darker marker, color in the little triangles in the upper left corner of each dark box. Then color in the long sections coming out of each upper-right corner and lower-left corner.

   I know this is called houndstooth because the shapes look like sharp dog teeth, but to me, they look like a front view of a dog with pointy ears. I had my classes chant quietly "little dog ears, little dog legs" while rendering houndstooth and I swear it helped.

DITSY PRINTS (FIGURE 11.29)

Ditsy prints are any print where the elements are very, very small and scattered across the fabric to appear more random than following a distinct repeat. Ditsy prints are usually flower prints.

I would render ditsy prints like I render tweed, except the base fabrics are usually much lighter, like cotton poplins instead of thick woolens. I would draw the drapes to reflect this fabric weight. You will likely need more tiny flowers than tweed speckles.

Cover the rest of the illustration with scraps of paper. You may need to "spray" the paint a few more times. Always wait for each layer to dry before adding another spray, or the paint layers will start running into each other. Wait for everything to dry again before adding extra dots with a wet watercolor pencil.

FIGURE 11.29. BELOW Ditsy prints and ditzy prints are the same.

FIGURE 11.30. BELOW

Also check out my Syzygy project illustration for more sheer illustrations. I used a lot of organza.

Sheers

SHEER FABRICS (FIGURE 11.30, NEXT PAGE)

The difference between the most common sheers, like chiffon, organza, tulle, and mesh, is the weight and stiffness, so draw your garments accordingly. The key factors in rendering sheers is 1) picking the right colors and 2) figuring out your layers.

1. Lay your sheer on top of white paper. Find the marker that looks like that color. Don't think of it as "sheer magenta" or "sheer brown"—truly look at the color on white as if it was opaque and match your marker to that color.

2. Lay your sheer folded into a double layer. That's what two layers of sheer will look like. You can achieve that look with a double layer of marker or another marker. Repeat with three layers of sheer.

3. Draw your garment and lightly draw your body under your sheer garment. Render your figure per The Mother Tutorial. If your figure is wearing something opaque underneath the sheer garment, like a tank top under a blouse, render that too. I like to render these leaving a little bit of space between the marker and the pencil line, to give a more faded illusion. I also like to use only one shadow color, with less contrast than usual. I like to leave some white of the paper in places I know there will be gathered/folded-over fabric on the garment.

4. Let all that marker dry. Yes, marker can stay wet on marker paper for a few minutes. Color in your sheer garment with your one-layer-color marker.

5. Identify all the spots where you would see two layers of sheer. This can be folds, this can be the back of billowy sleeve, or a collar laying on the chest of a shirt. Color these areas with your two-layer-color marker.

6. Do the same with areas that are three or more layers of sheer.

FIGURE 11.30. BELOW
Also check out my Syzygy project illustration for more sheer illustrations. I used a lot of organza.

FIGURE 11.31. BELOW Tulle
is soft. There's also this
net stuff called "crinoline"
which is used to make...you
guessed it, crinolines. It's
very stiff. Draw and render
accordingly.

TUTUS AND TIGHTLY GATHERED SHEERS (FIGURE 11.31)

The principles of sheers still apply here, except the increasing folds and layers are concentrated at the gathers.

1. When you draw your garment, make sure you draw the hem very, very lightly; a heavy pencil line for the hem will ruin the soft, delicate nature of a single layer of tulle. If you have two layers of tulle, draw very light intertwining pencil lines.

2. When markering, try starting from the gathers and flicking out/down, so that your marks taper and fade toward the hem. You can also try a blender marker to soften your edges.

3. Keep layering until you get the effect you want. Let marker dry between layers.

LACE (FIGURE 11.32)

Almost all laces are a combination of a bunch of flowers held together by some sort of fine mesh or net/webbing. Without the flowers, your fabric is just mesh or net. Without the mesh or net, your flowers fall apart and are just patches. Sometimes the lace designs include some other element, like fruit. Sometimes there are filler shapes like other flowers or leaves or geometric shapes like circles. But mostly, it's a lot of flowers held together with some mesh or net.

1. Draw your garment, choose your colors, render whatever's under your sheer garment and let dry. If your lace is on a mesh background, or the webbing is very fine and close together, render the garment per the sheer fabrics tutorial. Remember, you are rendering how your fabric appears from 8 feet away. If your webbing is thick and far apart, like many guipure laces, leave it blank for now.

2. Using what you've learned from the patterned fabrics tutorial, lightly draw in the flowers of your lace. Color in your lace using the medium that expresses your lace best.

3. Now for the background mesh or net. With guipure lace, you'll want to draw the individual lines of the webbing all over the lace. With something fine like Chantilly lace, you can either stop here because you've already rendered the sheer backdrop, or you can very lightly drop in some very fine hashmarks.

4. Heavy laces like guipure often look 3-D. Drop in some shadows on some very thickly tatted flower petals as needed. If you end with some white lace on white paper, like you would with the sides of a poofy sleeve, lightly trace some of the flower shapes to define them better.

FIGURE 11.32. BELOW
Guipure lace on the left, Chantilly on the right

FIGURE 11.33. BELOW

Technology is currently
being developed to make
faux fur without the use of
plastics! Very exciting.

Animals, Great and Small, Real and Faux

FUR (FIGURE 11.33)

1. Very lightly draw out your fur garment shapes. Draw over those lines
    with a new, slightly darker, broken line that resembles the hairs of the
    fur swatch you're rendering. If you have a short, dense fur, draw short
    lines close to each other. If you have a shaggy, long-haired fur, use your
    lines to express that.

2. Draw big fluffy shapes as applicable. You want a luxurious big fur
    collar? Exaggerate that a little. Skinny collars and stoles look cheap
    and anemic.

3. Color in your fur. Use your marker strokes like your pencil strokes to
    express your fur hairs. Render in the direction of the fur. Fur pieces in a
    garment are always cut so the hairs go the same direction. Hairs point
    down the sleeve, down the front, down the back. Do not render every
    which way.

4. Again, render your shadows mimicking your fur hairs, whether they are
    short and tight or long and shaggy.

5. Use a colored pencil to render in some texture. You can draw some
    pencil strokes to resemble hair. For very short hair, you can try doing
    a rub-off with the side of a colored pencil over a bumpy surface like
    watercolor paper. Add some soft white pencil highlights if you have a
    particularly glossy fur.

LEOPARD (FIGURE 11.34)

Leopard print is done in a multitude of textures and colors. I've seen everything from golden brown to purple and neon pink. You can render leopard print per the patterned fabrics tutorial. Here I want to discuss leopard print in different textures.

1. With traditional leopard print, you have a camel/light brown background. You have these dark brown squiggly splotches partially outlined with thick curved lines. They look like uneven parentheses. If your leopard print is shiny like satin, wait for your marker to dry and add some white highlights per the shiny fabrics tutorial. If you want hard shine, like leopard print PVC, use a white paint pen. Honestly, trying to get halo effects with all the leopard spots sounds exhausting and too busy looking.

2. With leopard print fur, render your background fur per the fur tutorial. When rendering the spots, use those marker brush strokes to make the spots look a little jaggedy/shaggy. Add fur textures on the background and black areas for an extra fuzzy look.

FIGURE 11.34. BELOW If you need examples of leopard print for reference, look up any Roberto Cavalli collection ever. RIP to the man who used leopard like it was a neutral.

ZEBRA, COW, AND GIRAFFE (FIGURE 11.35)

1. Draw your garment and render your background color per The Mother Tutorial.

2. Cows have black or brown splotches of random sizes and shapes. I've seen cow prints that look like a Rorschach test. I've seen cow prints that look like a crime scene in a black-and-white movie. I've seen cow prints that look like the unfortunate results of a Tinder date. Pick a style and knock yourself out. If your splotches are brown, don't forget to drop some darker brown shadows to those areas.

3. Zebra is simple but not always easy. You want organic lines, not straight stripes. You want crooked waves, not curves. You want thick and thin lines that taper to a point.

4. Giraffe patterns are more orderly. They are golden brown with a darker brown pattern of what looks like unorganized cobblestones.

5. The running theme with these three is organic shapes not in perfect grid formations. When manufactured, the single tile is so big that you don't see the pattern repeating unless you make something with several yards of material.

ALLIGATOR AND CROCODILE (FIGURE 11.36)

What's the difference between alligator and crocodile? When it comes to rendering, nothing.

1. Draw and render your garment per The Mother Tutorial.

2. Your typical alligator skin has two different sections of texture. The middle section has larger scales/tiles, square-ish in shape, in rather neat rows. On either side of this section of tiles, there are smaller scales that are rounder and look more like bubbles randomly squished together. The further they get from the square tiles, the smaller and rounder they get. Use a colored pencil to draw in these tiles and bubbles. Refer to your swatch to pick the correct color for these lines. Is this part that difficult? No. Is it tedious? Yes.

3. Using a shadow tone marker, color in the scales in the shadow areas individually to maintain a pebbly texture.

4. Crocodile is typically shiny, so drop in some highlights with a white gel pen.

FIGURE 11.36. BELOW It's almost meditative, to plop marker onto individual scales for shadows. Plop. Plop. Plop. Brush tips work best here.

FIGURE 11.37. BELOW

The university gave me a
little money to buy things
for my rendering class,
so I ordered a roadkill
snakeskin off some dude
with a five-star rating on
Etsy. The internet is a wild,
wild place, my friends.

SNAKESKIN (FIGURE 11.37)

1. Draw your garment. Almost all snake leather is a patterned texture embossed onto cow, goat, or lambskin. Snake pattern is also often used on all manner of fabrics as a print. Follow the stiffness/drape of your snake fabric. Color in the base color and shadows per The Mother Tutorial.

2. Using a colored pencil, draw in columns of organic, crooked diamonds, using lines that vary in thickness. In between each diamond, draw in one or two crooked circles. The organic layout of snake scales creates this crooked zigzag effect. Scale down your specific snake pattern per the patterned fabrics tutorial.

3. Using the same colored pencil, lightly crosshatch inside the diamonds in a column. Leave the next column of diamonds blank. Crosshatch alternating columns of diamonds. I like to punch up the contrast of the diamond shapes with a black fineliner. If your snake is on a shiny material, add some highlights with a white colored pencil.

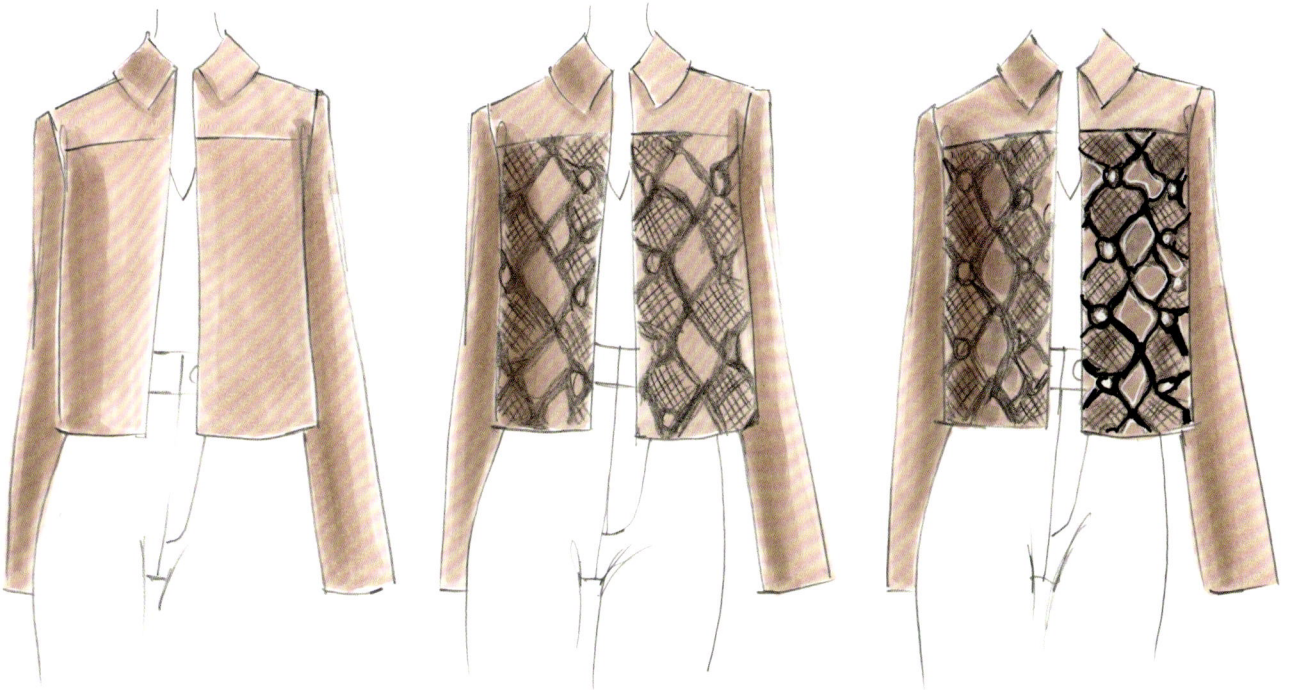

Pattern Meets Texture

QUILTED FABRICS (FIGURE 11.38)

1. Very lightly draw out the silhouette of your quilted garment. Lightly draw in your quilted shapes. Pay careful attention to the silhouette. You want to see the rounded poufs of the quilting in the silhouette of your garment. If you have a fat, overstuffed parka, you want those sections very round. If you have a lightly padded vest, your curves will be far more subtle.

2. Marker in your base fabric color. Next, we drop in some shadows. With quilted fabrics, you shadow each quilted shape individually. You follow the rules of shading from The Mother Tutorial (dark side away from light, under the light, etc.) for every separate piece.

3. Remember how fat your quilting is. That overstuffed parka should get very round shadows. The lightly padded vest will be largely flat in the middle and curve down only at the edges. Some quilted sections will be entirely in shadow because they are in such a dark spot of the garment. On sections directly facing the light, I would make the shadows a bit smaller and/or lighter.

4. Add texture as needed. Quilted parkas are often made of shiny nylon. Leather quilted handbags are quite common. I've seen some quilted vests in suedes and corduroys.

fat + juicy poofy

soft + subtle

FIGURE 11.39. BELOW

Velma may have been my muse here. Solve crime, but make it fashion.

CHUNKY KNITS (FIGURE 11.39, NEXT PAGE)

1. Draw your garment lightly. Draw big. You can exaggerate a little bit to really sell the cozy appeal of a chunky knit sweater. Draw a little over-sized, draw a little extra cozy, draw some floopy, floppy folds and cowls, draw some luscious rolls of soft, thick, knit fabric. We're not talking about t-shirt fabrics. You can use The Mother Tutorial for most cotton jerseys.

2. Lightly draw in any 3-D elements like cables or fat ribs. Any stitch pattern that is so chunky, you'll need to shadow them individually. If you have fat cables sticking out of the sides of your sleeves, you need to draw those 3-D cables in the silhouette of the sleeve. Follow the principles you learned in the pattern fabrics tutorial about how to scale down the pattern.

3. Color in your base fabric color. Shadow your garment per The Mother Tutorial. Shadow your fat cables and ribs. I like to use a second or even third shadow color to add event more depth.

4. Choose a colored pencil one shade darker than your base marker color. We're going to add a soft fuzzy layer all over the knit surface with the colored pencil. When using a light paper like marker paper, I like to slide a sheet of roughly textured paper beneath it, like cold press watercolor paper, and do a rubbing.

5. Choose a colored pencil one shade darker than your shadow marker color and add that fuzzy pencil layer to the shadows as well. Chances are your knit fabric is fuzzy around the edges. If so, bring some of that bumpy/curly/fuzzy quality to the edges of your garment with your colored pencils.

6. Take a dark pencil to punch out the details, like individual ribs and cables. If your knit is so big you can see individual stitches from 8 feet away, drop in some patches of stitches, like denim twill and corduroy wales. Focus your detail work in the areas where the light is hitting your garment.

FIGURE 11.39. BELOW
Velma may have been my muse here. Solve crime, but make it fashion.

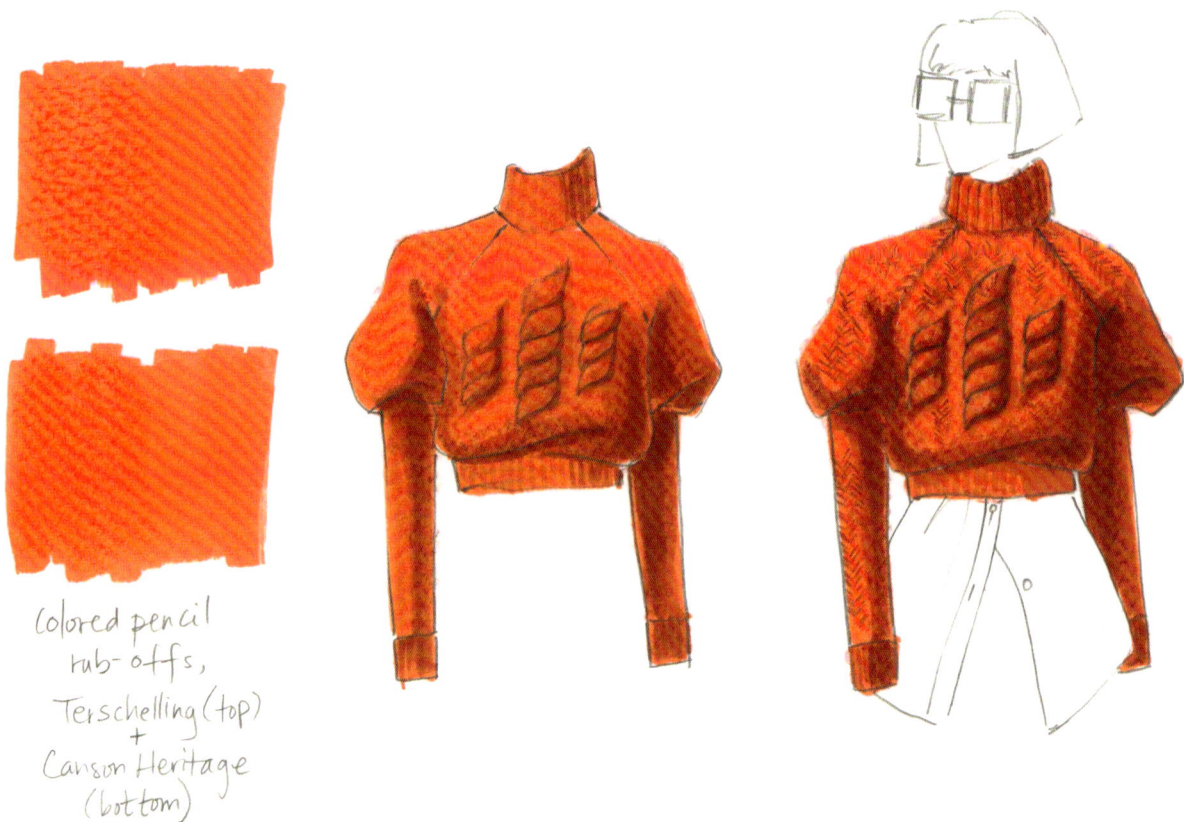

Colored pencil rub-offs, Terschelling (top) + Canson Heritage (bottom)

BIBLIOGRAPHY OF FABRIC BOOKS

Baugh, Gail. *The Fashion Designer's Textile Directory*. Barron's Educational Series, 2011.

Gullingsrud, Annie. *Fashion Fibers: Designing for Sustainability*. Fairchild Books, 2017.

Hallett, Clive, and Amanda Johnston. *Fabric for Fashion: A Comprehensive Guide, Second Edition*. Laurence King Publishing, 2022.

Hallett, Clive, and Amanda Johnston. *Fabric for Fashion: The Swatch Book, Revised Second Edition*. Laurence King Publishing, 2021.

Shaeffer, Claire. *Claire Shaeffer's Fabric Sewing Guide*. Chilton Book Company, 1989.

FASHION SCHOOL IN A BOOK

DESIGN JOURNAL

THE **PRACTICAL WORKBOOK** FOR COLLECTION DEVELOPMENT

Design your fashion collection and create a work-in-progress portfolio with the artistic direction in this design journal!

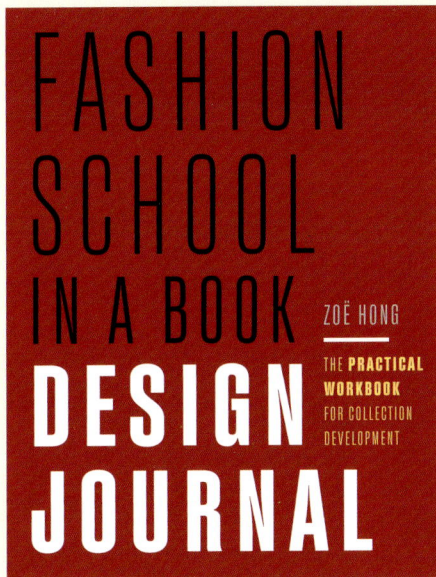

Zoë Hong's *Fashion School in a Book* outlines the creation of a fashion collection from early inspiration to final product. The text offers lessons on how to develop a cohesive (environmentally sustainable!) collection based on shapes, silhouettes, colors, patterns, and fabrics. As you make your way through the exercises in the book, this *Fashion School in a Book Design Journal* becomes a record of your work in progress. By the end of the course, you'll have created a record of your design process in these pages.

Full of practical exercises and artistic direction, use this companion journal to get the most out of *Fashion School in a Book*!

ACKNOWLEDGMENTS

I'm not great at writing emotional sentiments, but I do want to thank the people who have been key in the creation of this book:

- My YouTube subscribers, especially the ones who have been following me since the very beginning

- My university students, who fostered my love of teaching and grew with me

- My Patreon students, who help me create a true classroom community vibe online

- My family and friends, who helped me survive 2023, the worst year of my life, especially James, Sue, Efrat, Kenny, Nahla, Jennif, and Beth

- My sister, Chris Hong, who was the person who told me to start a YouTube channel

- My ride-or-die from fashion school, Susie Yang, who read my first draft and sent over helpful notes

- My friend Patricia Wooster, who taught me so much about the publishing world

- My editor, Maggie Yates, who patiently held my hand through my first book writing, editing, and publishing process

- My publisher, who told me upfront that I should write in my voice, with all my sass and ridiculousness

Last but not least, I would like to thank you, dear reader, who bought and read this book, apparently to the very end. I hope it inspires you to stretch your creativity to its limits, create something new and exciting, and work toward your wildest fashion dreams.

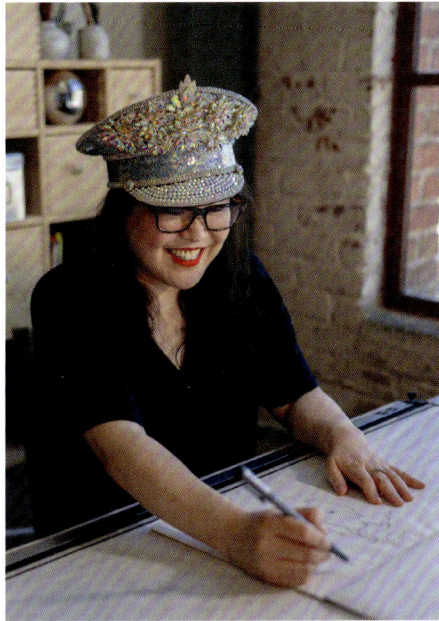

Photo © Jerm Cohen

ABOUT THE AUTHOR

Drawing upon her years as a fashion designer, illustrator, and instructor at one of the world's most prestigious fashion universities, Zoe Hong has built one of the largest fashion education platforms online.

Zoe's design career, from intern to creative director, highlighted with competition wins and TV appearances, has taught her industry best practices that she, in turn, teaches to her students. Zoe helps aspiring designers build their knowledge and cultivate their creativity to enter and thrive in the workforce as designers, makers, and entrepreneurs.

Sustainability has always been at the fore of Zoe's approach to design and business. "Future Heirlooms," the motto of Zoe's first label, reflected her dedication to balancing design, ethical fashion practices, and sustainability. Zoe continues to lead by example, teaching to prioritize environmental health alongside creativity and ethical responsibility.